# The Forgotten Sky

## *A Guide to Astrology in English Literature*

J. C. EADE

Clarendon Press · Oxford
1984

*Oxford University Press, Walton Street, Oxford OX2 6DP*

*London New York Toronto*
*Delhi Bombay Calcutta Madras Karachi*
*Kuala Lumpur Singapore Hong Kong Tokyo*
*Nairobi Dar es Salaam Cape Town*
*Melbourne Auckland*

*and associated companies in*
*Beirut Berlin Ibadan Mexico City Nicosia*

*Oxford is a trade mark of Oxford University Press*

*Published in the United States*
*by Oxford University Press, New York*

*British Library Cataloguing in Publication Data*
*Eade, J.C.*
    *The forgotten sky.*
    *1. Astrology in literature    2. English*
    *literature—History and criticism*
    *I. Title*
    *820.9'37    PR149.A79/*
    *ISBN 0-19-812813-4*

*Library of Congress Cataloging in Publication Data*
*Eade, J. C. (John Christopher)*
    *The forgotten sky.*
    *Includes index.*
    *1. English literature—History and criticism.*
*2. Astrology in literature.   3. Astrology.   I. Title.*
*PR149.A798E24 1948    820'.9'356    84-1830*
*ISBN 0-19-812813-4*

*Typeset by Joshua Associates, Oxford*
*and printed in Great Britain*
*at the University Press, Oxford*

*Necessarium est quod sic exponatur littera,*
*vel nihil erit dictum quod dicit auctor*

Robertus Anglicus,
Commentary on Sacrobosco

The sun the moon the stars will speak to non-
astronomers in spite of their ignorance of
science. In fact it's high time that this
happened

Saul Bellow, *Humboldt's Gift*

# Contents

# List of Illustrations

# References

Ball, Richard, *An Astrologo-Physical Compendium*, London, 1697.

Blagrave, Joseph, *An Introduction to Astrology*, London, 1682.

Bonatus, Guido, *Liber astronomicon*, Augsburg, 1491.

Bouché-Leclerc, Auguste, *L'Astrologie grecque* (1899), Brussels, 1963.

Eisner, Sigmund (ed.), *The Kalendarium of Nicholas of Lynn*, London, 1980.

Goldstine, H. H., *New and Full Moons 1001 BC to AD 1651*, Philadelphia, 1973.

Haly (Albohazen Hali filius Abenragel), *Liber completus in iudicijs stellae*, Venice, 1485 (also known as *De iudiciis astrorum*).

Lilly, William, *Christian Astrology*, London, 1647.

Middleton, John, *Practical Astrology*, London, 1697.

Nicholas of Lynn: see Eisner.

North, J. D., 'Kalenderes enlumyned ben they: Some Astronomical Themes in Chaucer', *Review of English Studies*, n.s. XX (1969), 129-54, 257-83, 418-44.

Oppolzer, Theodore von, tr. Owen Gingerich, *Canon of Eclipses*, New York, 1962.

Partridge, John, ΜΙΚΡΟΠΑΝΑΣΤΡΩΝ; *Or An Astrological Vade Mecum*, London, 1697.

Searle, John, *An Ephemeris for Nine Yeeres, Inclusive, from . . . 1609 to the yeere 1617*, London, 1609.

Stahlman, William, and Gingerich, Owen, *Solar and Planetary Longitudes for Years -2500 to +2000 by 10-Day Intervals*, Madison, 1963.

Tuckerman, Bryant, *Planetary, Lunar and Solar Positions, A.D. 2-1649*, Philadelphia, 1964.

# Part I: Astronomy

## INTRODUCTION

There are some systems that are complex in their totality but simple in their constituent parts. The subject of this handbook—the astronomy and the astrology employed by English writers, chiefly between Chaucer and Dryden—is one such. Its language, its jargon, may appear to the layman as abstruse as the terminology of Galenic medicine or of alchemy; but a more proper comparison would be with the language of the law. Astrology may sometimes be jargon-bound, a 'mystery'; but it also has a precision of reference, a narrowness of application, that makes it amenable to those who understand its basic grammar.

But few of us these days do understand the subject, and we are therefore all too likely to suppose in an author an intention to mystify or to dupe when his allusions are astrological—particularly since quack astrologers are so often figures of fun or the butts of satire. As, of course, they frequently deserve to be. Even so, the most complex and extended astrological outburst in the literature known to me, that in Act IV, sc. ii of John Fletcher's *The Bloody Brother* (first published in 1639), which has hitherto been treated as though it was a pyrotechnic display or as so learned as to have been ghost-written by Ben Jonson—when this passage is examined on its own terms, it proves to be, astrologically speaking, entirely respectable and 'rational'. One may wish to conclude (at least on first acquaintance) that the expertise that went into its composition was misplaced, that no audience could conceivably have kept pace with it; but even then one must not be content to assume that the scene is irrational nonsense.

There are three primary considerations which the reader is

invited to keep in mind in using this handbook: (1) that the basic tenets of astrology are entirely arbitrary and wholly irrational, but that the system built upon them is often elegant and rich in suggestion; (2) that its constituent elements interlock with each other, often providing a complex of checks and balances that leads to reasonable certainty in one's findings; and that (3) the system is schematic, so that unorthodoxy or an insecure grasp of the subject can often be readily detected.

To give each of these points brief illustration: first, that the system is arbitrary but elegant. Among the many ways in which the twelve signs of the zodiac are classified there is one which assigns them a gender. Since male conventionally precedes female and since Aries the Ram is traditionally first in the order, the second sign, Taurus the Bull, is obliged to be a feminine sign: nonsense. On the other hand, at the beginning of *The Kingis Quair* James IV tells us that the moon has moved into Aquarius the Water Carrier from Capricorn the Goat. In Aquarius she 'rynsid hir tressis like the goldin wyre', whereas in Capricorn she had 'heved hir hornis bright'— 'hornis' being a hair style: elegant.

Second, that the elements in a given astrological scheme must interlock. In *The Duchess of Malfi*, III. ii, a fragmentary horoscope is discovered in which it is stated that between 12 and 1 a.m. on 19 December the Duchess was delivered of a child. It is claimed, simultaneously, that the 'Lord of the first' in the horoscope is 'combust in the ascendent'. Now, since 'combustion' involves a planet in being less than 8½° from the sun, and since the first house equals the ascendant, the eastern horizon, it will follow that the sun must itself be close to rising—which of course it cannot be when the time is between 12 and 1 at night near the middle of winter. The passage, then, cannot simultaneously satisfy all the constraints of the situation it purports to depict: its interconnectedness fails.

Third, the schematic nature of the subject. In his Fable, 'How the Tod maid Confessioun to Freir Wolf Waitskaith', Henryson has a fox emerge and peer into the heavens to observe where the planets are. He notes the position of all seven, each one in a different sign of the zodiac. The configuration the fox observes, however, not only did not take place in Henryson's lifetime, but had not occurred since at least AD 0. In fact the fox observes the planets by descending Ptolemaic order and (with the exception of Venus and the moon) places each one in its 'proper mansion'. Venus has wandered into the Crab (the moon's mansion) and the moon into Aquarius (one of Saturn's mansions). The basic elements of the pattern are there, however—enough for us to be certain that we are here dealing with a disruption (probably a conscious disruption) of a schematic arrangement.

Previous studies of the place of pre-Newtonian astrology in society have dealt almost exclusively with attitudes towards the subject. None of these studies would equip the layman to approach a particular reference with the confidence that he could assess its complexities or (indeed) its plain sense. It is the purpose of the following pages to remedy this deficiency.

The Ptolemaic universe was governed, at least at one level of thinking, by orderly, harmonious, circular motion; its model consisted of a concentric nest of spheres with the earth at the centre of all. In philosophical and religious terms this conception had, of course, profound implications. But even at the level of conceptualisation, when the 'fixed' stars were plotted on a celestial globe equally distant from the earth at its centre, this was no mere necessity imposed by the physical limitations of the object but a reflection of the imagined structure of the heavens itself.

But then the habit of geocentric thinking stays with us—we still make the sun 'rise' and 'set' and the stars still appear to revolve around us. We are therefore not required to make much in the way of imaginative adjustment in order to enter the universe as it was visualized before Copernicus. What we require, instead, is a firm sense of our bearings, a sense that will allow us to feel our way round the heavens that encircle us.

It is therefore with the various systems of co-ordinates which allow us to plot position in the heavens that we should begin.

ORIENTATION

## I. 1 Ecliptic and Equatorial Circles; the Zodiac

By means of inference based on continued observation man came to know many centuries ago where the sun lay in relation to the invisible backdrop of the fixed stars. In the process he discovered that the heavens may be inscribed with two 'great circles' (circles dividing a sphere into equal halves). One defines the path along which the sun appears to travel, the *ecliptic*; and the other lies at the midpoint between the two still points of the heaven, the celestial equator. The *zodiac* is a band of sky whose north and south confines lie parallel to the ecliptic, each at a remove of 6 degrees. Values vary, but a total breadth of 12 degrees is a very widely accepted figure.

Each sign of the zodiac may therefore be regarded as a rectangle, 30° from side to side and 12° from top to bottom, with the ecliptic bisecting it horizontally. The constellations bearing the same names as the zodical signs, however, do not fit neatly into these frames. (See sec. I. 15.)

## I. 2 Obliquity of the Ecliptic

Further observation showed that these two circles intersect each other at an angle of roughly 23½°. The angle defines the obliquity of the ecliptic. It came to be realized that over the centuries this angle was gradually decreasing (though astronomers considered that this decrease must be part of a cycle). The methods and instruments of naked-eye observation, however, were too crude to have any real precision in the short term or to detect the real current value.

Those that are significant for our purposes are followed here by the actual value as determined by Oppolzer (see I. 22):

| | | |
|---|---|---|
| Ptolemy, AD 138 | 23° 51′ 20″ | 23° 40′ 37″ |
| Toledo Tables, c.1080 | 23° 33′ 30″ | 23° 33′ 25″ |
| Regiomontanus, 1490 | 23° 30′ | 23° 30′ 07″ |
| Copernicus, 1500 | 23° 28′ 30″ | 23° 30′ 07″ |
| Tycho Brahe, 1592 | 23° 31′ | 23° 29′ 34″ |

## I. 3 Co-ordinates

The position of a body in the heavens has generally been referred either to the ecliptic or to the celestial equator. Throughout the period with which we will be dealing reference to the ecliptic was preferred. The point of origin for both systems is known as *the first point of Aries*, the intersection between the two circles which marks the vernal (spring) equinox as opposed to the autumnal equinox (the language, of course, is oriented to the northern hemisphere).

## I. 4 Celestial Longitude/Latitude

Distance along the ecliptic is measured in degrees of *celestial longitude*, and was traditionally counted by signs, each of 30°. Thus, the longitude of a body would not be expressed as 40°, but as Taurus 10, Taurus being the second of the signs.

Distance in a north-south sense was measured at right angles to the ecliptic in degrees of *celestial latitude*. The sun has, by definition, a zero latitude, but that of the planets varies, north and south. (See I. 20. 3.)

## I. 5 Right Ascension/Declination

Measurement by reference to the celestial equator, on the other hand, is counted in degrees of *right ascension* along the celestial equator and in degrees of *declination* at right angles to the equator. Right ascension is often expressed in hours and minutes, 1 hour being equal to 15°.

## I. 6 The Tropic Circles

Since the sun travels along the ecliptic, not the celestial equator, its latitude will always be zero, but its declination will vary according to how far distant it is from the equinoctial points (Aries and Libra). When it is passing from Aries to Libra in the northern summer, the limit of its travel towards the north, 23½°, is reached when it arrives at the sign of *Cancer*. Similarly its southern travel in the northern winter is limited by its arrival in *Capricorn*. 'Tropic' derives from the Greek verb for 'turn round', and the Latin-derived equivalent, 'solstice', pictures the sun as standing still, i.e. ceasing to move further north/south before starting to return towards the equator.

## I. 7  Right and Oblique Ascension

The term *right ascension* is also used in reference to the degree of the celestial equator that comes to the *meridian* with a given degree of the ecliptic, the meridian being that great circle which runs from north to south, passing through one's zenith.

The relation of right ascension to celestial longitude does not vary with the latitude of observation, and so can be tabulated once for all when a value has been assigned to the obliquity of the ecliptic.

See Mathematical Formulas 1 for the conversion of longitude to right ascension.

The term *oblique ascension*, on the other hand, is used in reference to the degree of the celestial equator that comes to the *horizon* with a given degree of the ecliptic. This varies with the latitude of the observer.

See Mathematical Formulas 5 for determining the oblique ascension of the horizon.

## I. 8  Arctic and Antarctic Circles

Since the planes of the ecliptic and of the celestial equator are inclined to each other at 23½°, it will follow that the poles of these circles are also 23½° distant from each other. The Arctic and Antarctic circles are centred on the equatorial poles and pass through the ecliptic poles. The longitude of the north ecliptic pole is 270° (Capricorn) and the longitude of the south ecliptic pole is 90° (Cancer).

## I. 9  The Colures

The great circle which joins the ecliptic poles, the equatorial poles, and also passes through the first points of Cancer and Capricorn, is known as the solstitial colure, since it joins the points of solstice; while the great circle that joins Aries and Libra (the equinoxes) and passes through the equatorial poles is known as the equinoctial colure.

The 'equinoctial' (sc. circle), on the other hand, is a common alternative name for the celestial equator.

## I. 10 Local Co-ordinates: Altitude and Azimuth

The position of a body in the heavens may also be plotted by reference to the actual terrestrial location from which it is being observed. The grid employed here is defined by the horizon of the observer and by the meridian, or rather by the visible semicircle of it which runs from due north to due south through the zenith (the point directly overhead). On this system a body's position is defined, on one axis, by parallels of *altitude* above the horizon, a scale terminating in 90° at the zenith. (These circles of altitude are sometimes called 'almucantars'.) Circles of *azimuth*, on the other axis, define a body's angular distance, measured at right angles to the horizon, from some fixed point. Nowadays they are read in a circle from north through east.

## I. 11 Elevation of the Pole

Terrestrial latitude may be expressed by the *elevation of the pole*, its height above the local horizon. It will be obvious that for someone at the earth's equator the celestial equatorial poles will be on the horizon, and for someone at either terrestrial pole, the appropriate celestial pole will be directly overhead. It follows, then, that for every degree travelled away from the terrestrial equator, the appropriate celestial pole must rise one degree above the horizon. The height of the pole will accordingly define one's terrestrial latitude.

## I. 12 The Celestial Equator

Given (a) the height of the pole and (b) the direction of true north-south, the point of intersection between the celestial equator and the meridian may be found. It will, by definition, be at a point along the meridian 90° distant from the pole. An arc which joins due east to due west and passes through this point of intersection will define the visible part of the celestial equator.

It follows from this that the altitude of the celestial equator where it crosses the meridian will be the complement of one's latitude. Thus: London's latitude is 52°N; the equator therefore intersects with the meridian at a point (90 − 52 =) 38° above the south horizon.

## 1 *Meridian Altitude*

The height of the celestial equator being thus known, the maximum and minimum *meridian altitude of the sun*—its height at noon—may be found (Fig. 1). Since the sun's

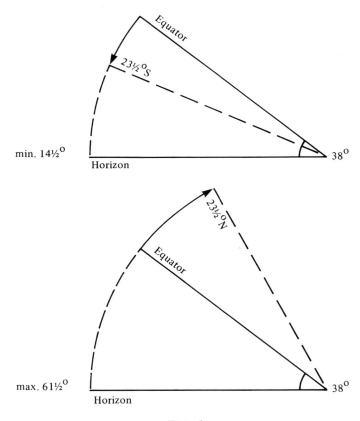

FIG. 1

maximum declination is 23½°, its minimum altitude at the latitude of London (52°N) will be (38 − 23½ =) 14½°, and its maximum altitude will be (38 + 23½ =) 61½°. All values intermediate between these extremes will occur twice every year, once as the sun moves towards the particular solstice, and again, as it returns towards the equator. If, then, a writer gives the sun's altitude as a means of dating, it is necessary to know, further, which leg of its northern or of its southern course the sun is on. This is usually discoverable by reference to which sign of the zodiac it is in.

## 2 Sun's Declination

Given (a) the sun's meridian altitude and (b) the co-latitude of the place of observation, the sun's declination may be found directly. To take an example: suppose the place to be London (52°N) and the sun's meridian altitude to be taken twice, but at some interval. Suppose, further, that the altitude

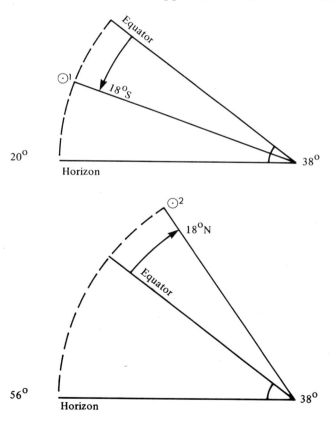

FIG. 2

is found to be 20° on the first occasion and 56° on the second (Fig. 2). Now: 20 − 38 = −18° and 56 − 38 = +18°. On the first occasion the altitude is *less* than the co-latitude, and the sun is therefore south of the equator; on the second occasion the altitude is *greater* than the co-latitude, and the sun is therefore north of the equator.

As with altitude, declination will not, by itself, define time of year directly: one needs to know which leg of its course the sun is on.

To find declination from longitude and obliquity, see Mathematical Formulas 2 (in Appendix).

## SEASONAL DATING

### I. 13   Dating by Zodiacal Sign

One of the commonest ways in which the writers of our period define the time of year is by reference to the zodiacal signs. These twelve sections of the zodiac are named after the constellations that at one time lay within their boundaries. They are (reading across):

| | | | |
|---|---|---|---|
| Aries | Taurus | Gemini | (Spring quarter) |
| Cancer | Leo | Virgo | (Summer quarter) |
| Libra | Scorpio | Sagittarius | (Autumn quarter) |
| Capricorn | Aquarius | Pisces | (Winter quarter) |

The 'cardinal' signs (Aries, Cancer, etc.) are the ones most commonly employed, for the obvious reason that they mark the start of the seasons. For instance, in the phrase 'Sol entering into Aries' the implication that Spring is just beginning tends to be more strongly present than the concomitant that it is somewhere near the middle of March by the calendar.

### I. 14   The Shift in the Vernal Equinox

A slight inaccuracy in the Julian Calendar (I. 24) had the effect of making the calendrical date at which the sun entered the sign of Aries (the Vernal Equinox) slowly fall earlier and earlier. We now associate this event with 21 March. In Chaucer's lifetime, however, it fell on or about 12 March. Interpolation in Tuckerman's planetary tables (I. 21. 2) gives, for instance, the following figures:

at 4 p.m. GMT on 12 March the sun was at
360° 18′ in 1340
360° 04′ in 1341
359° 50′ in 1342
359° 36′ in 1343
360° 20′ in 1344 (Leap Year)

In general terms (and with the possibility of small fluctuations in mind) we can tabulate the change in the date of the Vernal Equinox as follows:

|  | March |
|---|---|
| 1579–1706 | 10 |
| 1451–1578 | 11 |
| 1324–1450 | 12 |
| 1197–1323 | 13 |
| 1068–1196 | 14 |
| 940–1067 | 15 |
| 812–939 | 16 |
| 684–811 | 17 |
| 556–683 | 18 |
| 428–555 | 19 |
| 300–427 | 20 |
| –299 | 21. |

Note: it is not uncommon to find editions of literary texts asserting that if Mercury, for instance, is in Taurus, the date lies between mid-April and mid-May. But it could, of course, only be from the *sun*'s lying in Taurus that such a conclusion would follow.

As we shall see (I. 20. 4), Mercury does stay within a certain distance of the sun, such that if it were indeed somewhere in Taurus, the sun would be lying within the segment bounded by Aries 10 and Gemini 20; but without more information we could not place the date implied by Mercury's position any more firmly than to say it lay between the end of March and the beginning of June.

## 1 *Variation in Seasons*

The length of the sun's stay in a given sign was known to vary in the course of the year, as did the length of the seasons. Chaucer was therefore not right to affirm (in the *Treatise on the Astrolabe*, I. 10) that 'the sonne dwellith therfore nevere the more ne lasse in oon signe than in another'.

Thomas Buckminster's *Almanacke and Prognostication* for 1598 gives the following information about the seasons:

| | | | |
|---|---|---|---|
| Aries | 10 March | 31 days | |
| Taurus | 10 April | 31 days | Spring: 93 days |
| Gemini | 11 May | 31 days | |
| Cancer | 11 June | 32 days | |
| Leo | 13 July | 31 days | Summer: 94 days |
| Virgo | 13 August | 31 days | |
| Libra | 13 September | 30 days | |
| Scorpio | 13 October | 30 days | Autumn: 89 days |
| Sagittarius | 12 November | 29 days | |
| Capricorn | 11 December | 30 days | |
| Aquarius | 9 January | 29 days | Winter: 89 days |
| Pisces | 8 February | 30 days | |

The only dates where this commonplace pamphlet fails to agree with Tuckerman's tables are for Aquarius (properly 10 Jan.) and for Pisces (properly 9 Feb.).

Robert Recorde (*Castle of Knowledge*, 1556, p. 31), on the other hand, gives the dates of the seasons (in general terms, rather than for a specific year) as follows:

| | | |
|---|---|---|
| Aries | Spring | 11 March |
| Cancer | Summer | 11 June |
| Libra | Autumn | 14 September (called 'Harvest') |
| Capricorn | Winter | 12 December. |

## I. 15 Precession of the Equinoxes

The earth has what may be described as a wobble on its axis which has the function of making the equatorial poles describe a circle round the ecliptic poles once every 25,800 years. One of the effects of this slow movement (1° in 72 years) is to cause an apparent shift of the stars towards the east, such that their celestial longitude is constantly, if slowly, increasing.

As a result of precession, therefore, the constellations which at one time occupied the signs to which they gave their names have shifted into the adjacent sign to the east: the sign Aries, for instance, is now occupied by the constellation Pisces, while the constellation Aries now lies in the sign Taurus.

## 1 Sign or Constellation?

References to 'Mars in Aries' or to 'Sol in Leo' may seem to be potentially ambiguous, in that the author could be referring either to the given constellation within the zodiac or to the sign that bears the same name. This is not a besetting problem, however. In an astrological context, or where a planetary dating is in question, we will almost always find that it is the sign, not the constellation, that is intended.

## 2 Prima Arietis

The extent of precession was, of course, a matter of keen interest, the most common method of recording it being to take the position at a given epoch of 'the first star in Aries' (*prima Arietis*).

This star should not be confused with *alpha Arietis*, the first star in the constellation as listed in Bayer's catalogue of 1603, whose identifications are still in common use. *Prima Arietis* was the first star of the constellation in Ptolemy's listing, but *gamma* (the third) in Bayer's.

Various longitudes for *prima Arietis* are recorded in Renaissance handbooks, and they indicate that no highly accurate value for annual precession had been arrived at. Tycho Brahe, however, settled on a value of 51″ per annum for epoch 1600, and this value gradually gained acceptance.

Two values given by English Renaissance writers for the then current distance between the first point of Aries and the first star of Aries were 27° 53′ (Thomas Hood, 1590) and 27° 42′ (Thomas Blundeville, 1594). They may be compared with the much more accurate value given by Tycho, for epoch 1600, of 27° 37′. We may be sure that Hood and Blundeville would have seized upon Tycho's figure had it been then available—the spread of information was extremely rapid, and the 'correct' value of no little importance, since it provided the constant figure that had to be added to the celestial longitudes in a star catalogue in order to bring it up to date.

## THE STARS

### I. 16  The Fixed Stars

The stars of the pre-Newtonian universe were 'fixed' in a number of senses. First, their number—those, at least, to which any attention was paid—was distinctly finite (I. 17. 4); second, their positional relation to each other was considered not to vary by comparison with the planets (the Greek *planein* means 'to wander'); third, they were all imagined to lie on the surface of a sphere and so were fixed in relation to their distance from the earth, brightness being a function of size.

Here I express the common view. I do not wish to imply there were no exceptions to it.

### I. 17  Ptolemy's Sky

The prominent stars (those readily visible to the naked eye) were grouped in two ways: first, and more importantly, into imaginary figures, the constellations; and, second, according to their common magnitude.

The codification provided by Claudius Ptolemaeus (Ptolemy) in a catalogue compiled in AD 138, but which in fact gave values valid for epoch AD 60 (*Almagest*, Books VII and VIII), lasted with only minor revisions and with updating for precession (I. 15) as an authoritative document until the sixteenth century. Ptolemy divided the heavens into three areas: the northern constellations (21 in number), the zodiacal (12 in number), and the southern (15 in number), totalling 48.

His list begins with Ursa minor (the Little Bear) in the far north, and works round in a descending spiral from west to east. Because of the northern latitude of the observations, few stars were recognized in the region of the south pole. This part of the sky was not mapped effectively until the

European voyages of trade and exploration in the late sixteenth century.

The preservation of the Ptolemaic system can be seen in many places, particularly in the famous pair of planispheres for which Dürer drew the constellation figures in 1515. The numbers on these charts relate directly to the Ptolemy catalogue, and the attitude of the figures reflects the verbal descriptions he gives. The second star in Hercules, for instance, is the one 'on the right shoulder alongside the armpit'. The specificity of the descriptions assisted in conventionalizing the way in which the figures were drawn.

## 1 The Northern Constellations

In this section I give the number of stars in each constellation according to Ptolemy and Hyginus. (Ptolemy's totals, *Almagest*, Bks. VII and VIII, are followed by the number of ungrouped stars associated with the given constellation.)

The values I present for Hyginus derive from *Poeticon Astronomicon* Book III (in *Fabularum Liber*, Basel, 1535). This edition, the tenth after the *editio princeps*, contains drawings of the constellations which are clearly intended to answer to the text's descriptions of where the stars are located. In a number of cases, however, the enumeration ('three in the head, one in each shoulder, . . .') is not matched by the total given. In these instances I have preferred the total the enumeration implies; but I have also given, in round brackets, the total to be found in Bunte's Teubner edition (*Hygini Astronomica*, 1875).

|  | Ptolemy | Hyginus |  |
|---|---|---|---|
| Ursa minor | 27 + 8 | 21 | Little Bear |
| Ursa major | 7 + 1 | 7 | Great Bear |
| Draco | 31 | 15 | Dragon |
| Cepheus | 11 + 2 | 19 |  |
| Boötes | 22 + 1 | 14 |  |
| Corona borealis | 8 | 9 | Northern Crown |
| Hercules | 28 + 1 | 19 |  |
| Lyra | 10 | 9 | Lyre |
| Cygnus | 17 + 2 | 13 | Swan |
| Cassiopeia | 13 | 12 (13) |  |
| Perseus | 26 + 3 | 18 (19) |  |
| Auriga | 14 | 7 | Charioteer |

|              | Ptolemy | Hyginus  |               |
|--------------|---------|----------|---------------|
| Ophiuchus    | 24 + 5  | 17       | Snake Holder  |
| Serpens      | 18      | 22       | Snake         |
| Sagitta      | 5       | 4        | Arrow         |
| Aquila       | 9 + 6   | 4        | Eagle         |
| Delphinus    | 10      | 10       | Dolphin       |
| Equuleus     | 4       | (omits)  | Little Horse  |
| Pegasus      | 20      | 18       |               |
| Andromeda    | 23      | 20       |               |
| Triangulum   | 4       | 3        | Triangle      |
| subtotal:    | 360     | 261 (263)|               |

## 2 The Zodiac

|             | Ptolemy  | Hyginus   |               |
|-------------|----------|-----------|---------------|
| Aries       | 13 + 5   | 18 (17)   | Ram           |
| Taurus      | 32 + 11  | 14 + 6    | Bull          |
| Gemini      | 18 + 7   | 18        | Twins         |
| Cancer      | 9 + 4    | 18 (17)   | Crab          |
| Leo         | 30 + 5   | 19        | Lion          |
| Virgo       | 26 + 6   | 18 (19)   | Virgin        |
| Libra       | 8 + 9    | 4         | Scales        |
| Scorpio     | 21 + 3   | 15        | Scorpion      |
| Sagittarius | 31       | 15        | Archer        |
| Capricorn   | 28       | 22 (24)   | Goat          |
| Aquarius    | 42 + 3   | 14 + 30   | Water Carrier |
| Pisces      | 34 + 4   | 41        | Fishes        |
| subtotal:   | 349      | 252 (253) |               |

## 3 The Southern Constellations

|             | Ptolemy | Hyginus  |            |
|-------------|---------|----------|------------|
| Cetus       | 22      | 13       | Whale      |
| Orion       | 38      | 17       |            |
| Eridanus    | 34      | 13       | River      |
| Lepus       | 12      | 6        | Hare       |
| Canis major | 18 + 11 | 19 (20)  | Great Dog  |
| Canis minor | 2       | 3        | Little Dog |
| Argo        | 45      | 23 (26)  | Ship       |
| Centaurus   | 37      | 24       | Centaur    |
| Lupus       | 19      | 11 (10)  | Wolf       |
| Hydra       | 25 + 2  | 26 (27)  | Snake      |
| Crater      | 7       | 7        | Bowl       |

| Corvus | 7 | 8 (10) | Crow |
|---|---|---|---|
| Ara | 7 | 4 | Altar |
| Corona australis | 13 | (omits) | Southern Crown |
| Piscis notius | 11 + 6 | 12 | Southern Fish |
| subtotal: | 316 | 186 (192) | |
| total: | 1,025 | 699 (708) | |

## 4 Ptolemy's 1,025 Stars

Ptolemy enumerates 1,025 stars, three of them being in common between Boötes/Hercules, Auriga/Taurus, and Piscis notius/Aquarius. Each is assigned a magnitude (except for those placed in the three categories 'cloudy, obscure, and unformed'). The magnitudes run from one to six:

| 1st | 2nd | 3rd | 4th | 5th | 6th | other |
|---|---|---|---|---|---|---|
| 15 | 45 | 208 | 474 | 217 | 49 | 14 |

The stars of first magnitude were so few in number and so prominently placed that some of them came to take on identities as well known as those of the constellations. The stars are:

> Arcturus (in Boötes)
> Vega (in Lyra)
> Capella (in Auriga)
> Aldebaran (in Taurus)
> Regulus (in Leo)
> Denebola (in Leo)
> Spica (in Virgo)
> Rigel (in Orion)
> Betelgeuse (in Orion)
> Achernar (in Eridanus)
> Sirius (in Canis major)
> Procyon (in Canis minor)
> Canopus (in Argo)
> Rigil Kent (in Argo)
> Fomalhaut (in Piscis notius/Aquarius)

The names of the stars predominantly reflect the influence of the Arabs on astronomy in the Middle Ages. 'Algol' (a bright star in Perseus), for instance, means 'the Ghoul', since the snaky head of Medusa was mistaken for, or converted into, the head of that evil spirit.

Many of the stars were given further identity by being invested with the nature of a particular planet, and could themselves play a part in the detailed working out of a horoscope.

### I. 18 Later Additions

Voyages of exploration in the sixteenth century and, in addition, the increasing use of the telescope in the seventeenth and eighteenth centuries generated a large number of new constellations. They had little influence on creative literature, however, and need not concern us here. By far the most adequate account of the developments in celestial cartography is to be found in D. J. Warner's *The Sky Explored* (New York and Amsterdam, 1979).

### I. 19 Rising and Setting (Cosmical, Chronical, Heliacal)

One function of the sun's travel through the sky in the course of the year is that the stars, naturally, have periods of visibility and invisibility. Appearance and disappearance at dawn or dusk were particularly likely to be noted by essentially agricultural communities.

Among these seasonal appearances the association of the sun with the 'Dog Star' (Sirius in Canis major) is perhaps the most widely remarked upon. In the latitudes of Europe and Britain when Sirius rises at dawn (cosmically) the sun is in or near the middle of Leo. In many places the weather is then at its hottest, and the pestilence commonly associated with that heat is sometimes described (as for instance by Spenser) as the Dog's noxious breath.

To master the system of what were called *poetical* risings and settings, one needs to recognize, first, that the term 'cosmical' applies to sunrise, and 'chronical' applies to sunset. Over a short period a star that rises with the sun (cosmically) will set with the sun (chronically), and a star that sets as the sun rises (cosmically) will rise as the sun sets (chronically).

This, of course, will be true only for a limited period in the year, since the sun will gradually move on round the zodiac. The third kind of poetical rising and setting, the 'heliacal', takes account of this.

It will be useful to plot the successive fortunes of a sample star in order to see the progression. I choose Regulus (in Leo) giving times of visibility for the latitude of London in round figures and without taking the effects of dawn and dusk into account. We may begin the cycle with the time of maximum visibility.

*Visibility of Regulus*:

| sun in: | sunset: | | Regulus sets: |
|---------|---------|---|---------------|
| Pisces | 5.00 p.m. | – | 6.40 a.m. |
| Aries | 6.00 p.m. | – | 5.20 a.m. |
| Taurus | 7.00 p.m. | – | 3.20 a.m. |
| Gemini | 8.00 p.m. | – | 1.20 a.m. |
| Cancer | 8.20 p.m. | – | 11.00 p.m. |
| Leo | 8.00 p.m. | – | 9.00 p.m. |
| Leo 10 | 7.40 p.m. | – | 8.30 p.m. |
| Leo 20 | | invisible | |

| | Regulus rises: | | sunrise: |
|---------|----------------|---|----------|
| Virgo | 4.40 a.m. | – | 5.00 a.m. |
| Libra | 2.40 a.m. | – | 6.00 a.m. |
| Scorpio | 12.40 a.m. | – | 7.00 a.m. |
| Sagittarius | 10.40 p.m. | – | 7.30 a.m. |
| Capricorn | 8.30 p.m. | – | 8.00 a.m. |
| Aquarius | 6.20 p.m. | – | 7.40 a.m. |

We can see the pattern in this: initially (with the sun in Pisces), since the star is located in the last third of Leo, it rises at sunset and sets at dawn—obviously the condition under which it will be visible for longest. Then, however, the sun begins to approach the sign in which the star lies, encroaching on the time in the evening when it will be first visible, and causing the star to set earlier in the morning. Eventually the sun catches it up and obscures it. Soon after, however, it begins to rise in the early morning, gradually extending the period of the night in which it will be visible. Simultaneously, the winter nights are becoming longer and sunrise falls later and later, extending the period of visibility at the other end.

Obviously the profiles of the stars will vary considerably, depending not only on what their longitude is, but also on whether they lie within that disc of the sky whose radius equals the latitude of the place of observation. Stars within this disc will never set, just as stars within the equivalent disc centred on the opposite pole will never rise. This class of stars, since they do not go below the horizon, will not have cosmical or chronical, only heliacal, risings and settings.

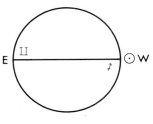

Chronical setting of ♐
(Sacrobosco)

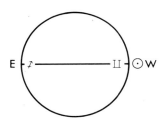

Chronical rising of ♐
(Robertus)

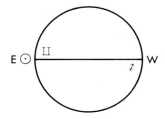

Cosmical setting of ♐
(Lucan)

FIG. 3

References to these phenomena can be confusing when taken out of context. Sacrobosco, the author of an important medieval treatise on the sphere, quotes a passage from Lucan's *Pharsalia* (IV. 528): 'Tunc nox Thessalicas urgebat parva sagittas.' The words 'Thessalian arrows' allude to Sagittarius, whom the 'short night' was pressing to do something. What? According to Sacrobosco to set chronically (at sunset). (See Fig. 3.) This provoked his commentator Robertus Anglicus to comment that Lucan 'does not speak of setting at sunset, but rather of rising . . . Lucan speaks of a time when the sun was towards the end of Gemini, and then, when the sun moved towards setting in this sign, Sagittarius rose chronically . . .' (my translation; for the Latin see Lynn Thorndike (ed.), *The Sphere of Sacrobosco*, Chicago, 1949, p. 174).

Despite Robert's comment, however, it is clear in the context that Lucan was talking neither about chronical setting (Sacrobosco), nor about chronical rising (Robert), but about cosmical setting, since the people watching the skies are waiting for the dawn—as, after all, the phrase 'the short night urged . . .' would itself suggest.

## THE PLANETS

### I. 20 Literary Reference

Literary reference to the planets and to their motions greatly simplifies the celestial mechanics of the Ptolemaic universe, and we have no need here to become embroiled in epicycles and deferents. Even the fact that the planets vary in latitude seldom, if ever, impinges on the poet. Instead, he confines his attention to their motion along the zodiac and to their positions relative to each other. But to understand what is involved, we need to know something about their behaviour in gross terms, as viewed by the naked eye from the earth.

### 1 Ptolemy's Seven

The seven 'planets', in order of ascent were

moon
Mercury

> Venus
> sun
> Mars
> Jupiter
> Saturn.

Some authors distinguish the sun and the moon from the others by referring to them as the 'luminaries'. For the most part, however, all seven are referred to as 'planets' indiscriminately.

## 2 Revolution Periods; Mean Daily Motion

It was, of course, essential to record how long it took these seven erratic bodies to return again to a given point—to determine their *revolution periods*. These came to be tabulated in round figures as follows:

| | |
|---|---|
| Saturn | 30 years |
| Jupiter | 12 years |
| Mars | 2 years |
| the sun | 365¼ days |
| Venus | 348 days |
| Mercury | 339 days |
| the moon | 29 days. |

For the purposes of short-term calculation the *mean daily motions* of the planets were also required:

| | |
|---|---|
| Saturn | 0° 2′ 01″ |
| Jupiter | 0° 4′ 59″ |
| Mars | 0° 31′ 27″ |
| the sun | 0° 59′ 08″ |
| Venus | 0° 59′ 08″ (1° 22′ max.) |
| Mercury | 0° 59′ 08″ (1° 40′ max.) |
| the moon | 13° 10′ 36″ (15° 02′ max.) |

## 3 Latitude

The other main peculiarity of the planets was that, unlike the sun, they did not stay precisely on the centre-line of the zodiac but moved north and south of it to varying degrees.

> The extent of the movement is a function of the angle at which the plane of the planet's orbit round the sun is inclined to that of the earth's orbit around the sun.

The maximum values assigned to movement in latitude (with some variation, naturally enough, between authorities) were:

|         | northern | southern |
|---------|----------|----------|
| Saturn  | 2° 48′   | 2° 49′   |
| Jupiter | 1° 38′   | 1° 40′   |
| Mars    | 4° 31′   | 6° 47′   |
| the sun |          | zero     |
| Venus   | 9° 02′   | 9° 02′   |
| Mercury | 3° 33′   | 3° 35′   |
| the moon| 5° 17′   | 5° 12′.  |

These are common Renaissance values, in the sense that they are shared by William Lilly, the English astrologer (*Christian Astrology*, 1647, pp. 57 ff.) and by Vincenzo Coronelli, the Italian cosmographer and geographer (*Epitome Cosmographica*, 1693, Book III, ch. v). The values offered by Martianus Capella, the 4th/5th-century encyclopaedist, look rough and ready by comparison (see *Martianus Capella and the Seven Liberal Arts*, ed. W. H. Stahl *et al.*, Columbia University Press, 1971, I. 198-9; Stahl gives similar values from Theon, Cleomedes, and Pliny):

|           | total north–south travel |
|-----------|---------------------------|
| Saturn    | 3°                        |
| Jupiter   | 5°                        |
| Mars      | 5°                        |
| the sun   | 1° (in Libra)             |
| Venus     | 12°                       |
| Mercury   | 8°                        |
| the moon  | 12°.                      |

From Capella's figures we can see why the zodiac was conventionally 12° broad, since this figure embraced the maximum latitudes, those of Venus and the moon. It is a big leap from Capella to the Renaissance, however. By Chaucer's day the values had a greater air of precision: the tables compiled by Simon de Bredon (Bodleian Library, MS Digby 178) for 1343 include north and south latitudes for the planets which are essentially the same as those of the *Alphonsine Tables* (1250s). Bredon's maxima are:

|         |        |
|---------|--------|
| Saturn  | 3° 05′ |
| Jupiter | 2° 04′ |

| Mars     | 7° 07'   |
|----------|----------|
| Venus    | 7° 22'   |
| Mercury  | 4° 13'   |
| the moon | 5° 00'.  |

*4 Motion of the Inferior Planets*

For the purposes of naked-eye observation and within the terms that concern us here, it makes no essential difference whether we say the sun moves round the earth or the earth moves round the sun. On either system there are three 'superior' planets and two 'inferior':

| *heliocentric system* | *geocentric system* |
|-----------------------|---------------------|
| Saturn Jupiter Mars   | Saturn Jupiter Mars |
| earth                 | sun                 |
| Venus Mercury         | Venus Mercury       |
| sun                   | earth               |

For the inferior planets there is a sequence of events in their orbits such that from appearing to be in line with the sun as seen from the earth, they pass to a position 'ahead' of the sun, then fall back to come into line with it again, then pass to a position 'behind' the sun, and finally return to catch it up (cf. Fig. 4).

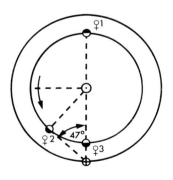

♀1 — superior conjunction

♀2 — maximum elongation

♀3 — inferior conjunction

FIG. 4

In this context 'behind' is of course ambiguous, since it could imply 'at the back of . . .' and so 'hidden by . . .'. The term, or its ambiguous equivalents, is so common in the literature, however, that we should retain it. Here 'ahead' will mean 'having a lesser longitude than . . .' and 'behind' will mean 'having a greater longitude than . . .'. Similarly 'in line with' will mean 'having the same (geocentric) longitude as . . .'.

The greatest distance which Venus puts between herself and the sun is called her *maximum elongation*. In our period it was in general considered to be 47°; while Mercury's maximum elongation was taken to be 22°.

## 5 Venus as Rogue

It is remarkable how often in literary reference Venus is represented as behaving in an impossible way. Sometimes she is presented as being at an impossibly large remove from the sun; sometimes she appears, in the same period of twenty-four hours, both ahead of the sun (as Lucifer, the morning star) and as behind the sun (as Hesperus, the evening star); sometimes she is even represented as coming up in the west.

Notoriously, Henryson begins *The Testament of Cresseid* with Venus rising as the sun sets—the two bodies are supposedly something like 180° apart. For reasons that have never been convincingly explained, Henryson presents an impossible situation—one that it is reasonable to suppose both he and his audience recognized as impossible. The best that can be said is that the scene may be intended to convey a violent disjunction, one similar to that Spenser (*Faerie Queene*, V, Proem 8) culls from Herodotus, where the sun twice rose in the west and twice set in the east.

To take another instance: in Part II, ch. xv, of *Anna Karenina*, Levin is out shooting and it begins to get dark. He sees Venus low in the west and decides to remain where he is until Venus appears *above* the branch of a nearby tree.

Here great caution is required. The verb 'appear' (and its close synonyms) may be used, in application to Venus, in any of at least three ways: it may mean Venus rises above the eastern horizon—as she can do in the period before dawn; it may mean that she becomes visible—as she does, in the west, as the light begins to fade; or she may 'rise' over the longer term, that is become visible for progressively longer periods at sunset, as she moves away from the sun. On any given day however, her visible motion after sunset can only be downwards towards the western horizon. It is not that Tolstoy's slip is of any great consequence in itself; rather it is a demonstration of how easily anomalies and inconsistencies can occur when the constraints are not kept in mind.

## I. 21 Tabulation

When a poet decided upon an astronomical flourish to begin his topic, it is difficult to imagine that he ran outside to see how in fact the heavens lay. Either he knew in broad terms based on experience, or else he consulted whichever kind of astronomical tables lay to hand.

### 1 Astronomical Tables

In descending order of scale, and vastly increasing order of volume in publication, the documents that tabulated astronomical position were Astronomical Tables, Ephemerides, and Almanacs.

The three most important sets of Astronomical Tables in our period were the *Toledo Tables* (constructed *c.*1080), the *Alphonsine Tables* (constructed *c.*1270) and the *Rudolphine Tables* (first published in 1627). Compilations of this type are 'perpetual', in the sense that they present sets of values (one table for mean motion by century, another for mean motion by intervening years, and so on) from which the position of a planet can be calculated for any given instant. The tables are extremely cumbersome to use, even when the complex principles of computation have been mastered.

> It takes up to twenty minutes (and at least one page of A4) to obtain a single value for any planet except the sun.

It is therefore not in the least surprising that consolidated tables for a given stretch of years were also published—even though their life expectancy was obviously limited. These Ephemerides typically give planetary longitudes (for noon at a specific place) from day to day, and planetary latitudes at 10-day intervals. For astrological rather than astronomical purposes they also give the aspects (angular relations) the planets have to each other and (in other columns) the aspects that the moon has with them.

This is no mean addition: in the course of a year the moon will take on over 500 separate aspects with the other six. In many ephemerides the hour at which each aspect occurs is also specified.

The information presented in the typical almanac was at first simpler. In the sixteenth century compilers contented themselves, on the whole, with giving the sun's entry into the zodiacal signs and occasionally the positions of the moon and of the planets. By the late seventeenth century, however, there was an enormous variation in the information the competing almanacs contained, some being scarcely less complex than an ephemeris. There was a massive sale by this time— one estimate is that the annual printing came to 400,000 copies.

See Cyprian Blagden, *Studies in Bibliography*, XI (1958), 107-16.

I have compared together fourteen different almanacs for the year 1696, asking them the question, 'when did New Moon fall in March?' (this for the purposes of checking their astronomical accuracy). Five give the answer 6.00 p.m. on the 15th (perhaps a rounded figure); and while only two of the other nine agree as to the precise minute (offering 5.41 p.m.), the range is a mere 23 minutes (5.28 p.m. to 5.51 p.m.).

## 2 Modern Aids

In order to check upon the validity of an astronomical dating in a play or a poem one needs either a set of contemporary tables (preferably an Ephemeris), or else a set of modern tables, together with the knowledge that they will not give one a falsely precise value.

In my experience of checking several hundred medieval and Renaissance values against modern computer-generated tables, I am satisfied that within the margins acceptable to a literary scholar or an historian (as opposed to an astronomer, whose criteria are much more stringent) the agreement is very high. This, though, should be no surprise. It will be seldom that, for literary purposes, one needs to know to within less than a degree where such and such a planet was—indeed, one will be lucky if the literary evidence gives one a margin of less than 30° ('Mars in Sagittarius'). On the contrary, there is something rather insulting in the notion that our forbears did not know to within a tolerably narrow margin where the planets were located. This being the case, modern tables will in general do duty where contemporary ones are lacking.

We have been well served in recent times with information about the state of the heavens in the past. The entire period dealt with here is covered in various ways. The standard books of reference are:

> Bryant Tuckerman, *Planetary, Lunar, and Solar Positions, 601 BC-AD 1* (Vol. I) and *AD 2-1649* (Vol. II), Philadelphia, 1962, 1964.
> W. D. Stahlman and O. Gingerich, *Solar and Planetary Longitudes for Years -2500 to +2000*, Madison, 1963.
> H. H. Goldstine, *New and Full Moons 1001 B.C. to A.D. 1651*, Philadelphia, 1973.

This means that from 1200 to 1800 it is possible in a few minutes to find the longitudinal position of any one of the seven planets at any instant of time, with the exception of the moon over the last 150 years of the period.

## 3 Validity

Tuckerman in particular makes it easy to check a given item of information. The difficulty, instead, is to know (as I have hinted) whether the answers provided are misleadingly precise. As a test example, I have compared the figures given in an almanac for 1551 produced by Simon Heuringius. In addition to the sun's positions, this almanac gives daily positions for the moon—in a manner, moreover, that requires one to know that this is what they are: the buyer, it seems, was assumed to know.

Heuringius's values are valid for noon on the given day. Tuckerman's values, on the other hand, are valid for 4 p.m. when referred to Greenwich; we should therefore adjust them, to bring them into line with Heuringius. Now, the moon moves, on average, 13° a day (I. 20. 2), which may be converted into ½° an hour; the time difference of 4 hours will therefore require a reduction in Tuckerman's values of an even 2 degrees.

Again I stress that approximation of this kind is acceptable for our purposes.

We will bear in mind, too, that a discrepancy of 1 degree in relation to the moon's motion would represent an error in time of only two hours; in the case of the sun, on the other hand, a discrepancy of 1 degree would represent an entire day.

|  | Tuckerman | Heuringius |
|---|---|---|
| 5 Jan. 1551 | 8 Capricorn | 8 Taurus |
| 10 | 9 Pisces | 9 Pisces |
| 15 | 9 Taurus | 10 Taurus |
| 20 | 15 Cancer | 16 Cancer |
| 25 | 28 Virgo | 27 Virgo |
| 30 | 8 Sagittarius | 8 Sagittarius. |

The only glaring discrepancy is in the case of 5 January— and this may be laid at the printer's charge. In the almanac itself Sagittarius precedes and Aquarius follows, making it clear that 'Capricorn' is the correct sign here.

Heuringius's time for the New Moon in January 1551 is 11.27 p.m. on the 5th. Goldstine gives 10.24 p.m.—only half a degree of difference.

Heuringius also gives some values for Mercury, Venus, and Mars: all eleven values for Venus are correct to within a degree or so, as are the five values for Mars, with the exception of that for January, where Mars is said to enter Gemini on the 8th, though it was not to do so until the 20th. The five values for Mercury, on the other hand, are much less satisfactory:

|  | Tuckerman | Heuringius |
|---|---|---|
| 7 Feb. | 1 Pisces | 1 Pisces |
| 4 June | 6 Cancer | 1 Cancer |
| 21 June | 3 Leo | 1 Leo |
| 15 Sep. | 7 Libra | 1 Libra |
| 3 Oct. | 5 Scorpio | 1 Scorpio |

Even here, though, where Mercury's purported position lags behind his actual position by several days, we can say that within the broad terms that creative writers use (tending as they do to place a planet merely in a given sign) these discrepancies are not unduly serious.

Finally, Heuringius also gives times for two eclipses: a solar eclipse beginning at 1.05 p.m. on 31 August, and a lunar eclipse beginning at 8.30 p.m. and ending 'aboute xi the clock' on 20 February. Oppolzer (I. 22) has figures that place the start of the solar eclipse at 12.58 p.m., and which yield 5.54 p.m. for the start of the lunar eclipse, its maximum being at 7.39 p.m. and its end at 9.42 p.m.

In the case of the solar eclipse the discrepancy is a mere seven minutes. With the lunar eclipse, on the other hand, it is considerably more, but even so there is more than an hour's worth of overlap.

## 4 Checking a Date

Where the positions of several planets are given in a single configuration, the task of searching for a date to match them is simplified by the fact that one may begin to look first at the outermost (slowest) planet. If Saturn is said, say, to be in Leo, Mars to be in Aquarius, and the sun in Cancer, and the period concerned is any time in the first half of the fifteenth century, then one may quickly scan the period to find those years when Saturn's longitude is between 120° and 149°. The field is thus quickly narrowed to between August 1416 and July 1418 and between June 1446 and August 1448. During this time the longitude of Mars was within the required limits (vague as these are) between 8 November and 15 December 1416 and between 27 November 1447 and 4 January 1448. But as the sun was in Cancer between 13 June and 13 July at this epoch, it is obvious that the constraints of our random example cannot be satisfied as they stand. The next step would therefore be to attempt an explanation in more symbolic terms: the sun in Cancer, for instance, implies a midsummer date, whereas the claimed positions for Saturn and Mars might, upon inquiry, prove to have an astrological, rather than an astronomical, significance.

## 5 Interpolation

A set of tables has to reach a compromise between excessive length (as would result from giving daily positions) and unacceptable approximation (as would result from having too great an interval between dates). Tuckerman's tables adopt ten-day intervals for the slow-moving outer planets (Saturn, Jupiter, Mars) and five-day intervals for the faster inner planets (Venus, Mercury, the moon). In order to arrive at a time in between those tabulated one needs to use simple interpolation. This is a system of averaging the interval: if a planet moves 5° in 10 days, its average motion over the period will be half a degree a day, and it can be said to move 2° in four days—and so on. Exactly the same principle operates (for our purposes) in more complex instances. If the moon's 4 p.m. position was 27° 42′ on 4 January and 100° 12′ on 9 January 1495, when did it reach 90° (enter Cancer)?

The distance travelled in five days was 72° 30′. The difference between 27° 42′ and 90° 00′, however, is 62° 18′. We therefore set up the following ratio:

$$72° \ 30′ : 5 \text{ days}$$
$$62° \ 18′ : x \text{ days} = 4.296 \text{ days} = 4\text{d } 7\text{h } 6\text{m}.$$

This result, then, must be added to 4 p.m., 4 January, to give 11.06 p.m., 8 January.

## I. 22 Tables of Eclipse

One other extremely useful aid upon occasion is the tables of solar and lunar eclipse (hand-computed!) by Theodore von Oppolzer. His *Canon der Finsternisse* (Vienna, 1887) has been reissued by Owen Gingerich, as *Canon of Eclipses* (New York, 1962).

The book contains useful charts plotting the paths of solar eclipses, and formulas for determining the visibility of lunar eclipses (Gingerich, p. xxxiv).

## I. 23 Retrogradation

Among the various forms of erratic behaviour in the planets, the only one that need concern us here is retrogradation. In one sense the phenomenon is merely an optical effect deriving from our point of observation; but in another it shares with comets and eclipses an element of the freak, the disordered, that threatens the basic sense of stability and harmonious motion that underpins the universe with which we have to deal.

Just as the term 'opposition' has a merely geometric and positional sense, as well as a threatening metaphoric one, so retrogradation has a merely geometric, as well as a metaphoric one. When it is said, darkly, that a planet is 'retrograde', what does this mean? We may note, first, that the phenomenon is an optical one, referred to the backdrop of the fixed stars. The appearance of movement 'backwards', in other words, is merely a function of the earth's much faster motion. We can grasp the principle, without distortion, by analogy. If you are in a car and someone else on foot is walking past a line of arches, when you first see them they may be framed in a particular arch. As you speed past and look back, however, you may see them again framed in an arch—but one further back than the original arch. In this sense, and in relation to the arches, the person will have moved 'backwards'.

This is where the straight-line analogy ceases to work, but it will do as a start. We can now transfer to the planet itself: as the earth approaches, the planet will appear for a while to be still, then to move backward as the earth sweeps past. As the earth bends further on its course the planet will appear to be still again, before resuming its normal motion.

These phases were, of course, of keen interest as having a material effect on the prediction of the planet's position. Lilly (pp. 57 ff.), for instance, gives the following values:

|  | 1st station days | retrograde days | 2nd station days |
|---|---|---|---|
| Saturn | 5 | 140 | 5 |
| Jupiter | 5 | 120 | 4 |
| Mars | 2–3 | 80 | 1 |
| Venus | 2 | 42 | 2 |
| Mercury | 1 | 24 | 1 |

## CALENDRICAL COMPUTATION

### I. 24  Old Style and New Style

For most purposes we are content to say that the year is 365¼ days long, the quarter day being accumulated as 29 February each leap year. This convention, however, requires some periodic adjustment, since the 'tropical' year (the period of the sun's return to the same point in the heavens) is in fact some 11 mins and 14 secs shorter than 365 days and 6 hours. In other words, without some adjustment the calendar would begin to fall back, and an event which we wished to have fall at exactly the same time each year would gradually fall earlier and earlier—at the rate of one day in every 128 years. When Julius Caesar reformed the Roman Calendar in 44 BC, this fine adjustment was not made, so that the date of the Spring Equinox gradually regressed, at the rate of one day in every 128 years or so. In 1582, therefore, Pope Gregory XIII again reformed the calendar and introduced *New Style* dating. The reform required the omission of ten days from the calendar in the first instance, in order to bring the Spring Equinox back to 21 March, and the fine adjustment needed in the longer term was gained by saying that the century years 2000, 2400, 2800, . . ., would be leap years, but intervening century years would not.

## I. 25 The English Reform

Protestant England was unwilling to follow the Catholic Church in this change, so that the *Old Style* calendar continued in use there until 1752. Between 1582 and 1700 the Julian (Old Style) calendar was ten days behind the Gregorian (New Style) calendar. But in the New Style the year 1700 was not a leap year, so that when England finally came to change, the gap had increased to 11 days. The English jumped from 2 September to 14 September in 1752 (by Act of Parliament, 24 Geo. II, c. 23).

> One hears it said that those who shouted 'give us back our eleven days' were uncomprehending—but I have thought that if they were small merchants or landlords, the loss of revenue in a quarter thus truncated could have been serious.

## I. 26 Conversion of Dates

The difference between the two calendars was further complicated by the fact that in the Old Style calendar, for some purposes, it was the practice to begin a new year on 25 March, Lady Day.

Astronomy was not one of them, however: astronomical tables and almanacs begin their year on 1 January. Moreover, given the very common civil use of the almanac, many people must have been accustomed to regarding 1 January as the start of the year.

The difference between the two styles is sometimes indicated by an oblique: 2 February 1712/13, for instance, identifies the year as N.S. 1713. Usage was by no means consistent, however. Letters written by Alexander Pope, all within seven weeks, are dated 'Jan. 9. 1713', 'Feb. 25th 1714', and 'February the last day, 1713'.

If only one year is given, it ought to be one year too low by N.S. reckoning: 'Jan. 1715' should normally mean 'Jan. 1715/16'. But even at the time people found themselves confused (or at least created confusion). Lady Mary Wortley Montagu dated a letter 'Jan. 16, O.S. 1717'; but from other evidence we know that the letter was written not on 27 January 1718, but on 27 January 1717. In other words, 'O.S.' here applies only to the day, not to the year.

### 1  An Example

The need for caution in this area is obviously considerable. Pope provides us with another case in point. Addison's *Cato* was first acted on 14 April 1713, and Pope wrote a Prologue for it: Rowe's play *Jane Shore*, on the other hand, was first produced on 2 February 1713/14—ten months after *Cato*. For this Pope wrote an Epilogue which contained references to *Cato*. The sequence of events is straightforward, when once it has been established to which year '2 February 1713' belongs. Pope's Twickenham editors, however, took the date in the wrong direction, making it 2 February 1712/13 and placing *Jane Shore* before *Cato*. They were then constrained to explain how it was that the Epilogue to *Jane Shore* contained references to *Cato*—which, by their reckoning, had not yet appeared.

### I. 27  Using Day of the Week

With doubtful dates it is sometimes possible to clear an ambiguity by reference to the day of the week. Had Pope's letter of '9 Jan. 1713' been (correctly) dated 'Monday', it would have been written in 1713/14.

Either a perpetual calendar or a check on the Julian Day number will give an answer.

## I. 28  The Julian Day

This system was so named by Joseph Justus Scaliger in honour of his father Julius Caesar Scaliger. It takes its origin in 1 January 4713 BC and an entire cycle takes 7980 years to complete. It will be clear, then, that it is extremely useful for reckoning intervals over a long period. And it is no less useful for computing what day of the week any given date fell on. The Julian Cycle is itself a multiple of three other cycles: the 28-year solar cycle, the 19-year lunar cycle, and the 15-year Indiction cycle.

The point of origin was determined as follows: the Indiction cycle began in AD 313 and repeats after 15 years; but 313 falls two short of being evenly divisible by 15. The Solar cycle, on the other hand (which brings the date back into line with the days of the week) repeats after 28 years, and Scaliger wanted to find a leap year which was simultaneously the first in a solar cycle and in which January 1st was a Monday. This was satisfied by the year 1560, but 1560 falls 8 short of being evenly divisible by 28. Finally, the Easter cycle introduced by Dionysius Exiguus has AD 532 as a year 1, and this was simultaneously the year in which his reckoning of the Christian Era began. Furthermore, 532 is evenly divisible by 19. Scaliger knew (at last) in which year his system should commence. Its number had to have the following properties: it had to be an even multiple of 19 (Lunar Cycle), such that when 8 was subtracted it would be evenly divisible by 28 (Solar), and when 2 was subtracted it would be evenly divisible by 15 (Indiction). Now,

$$-4712 \ / \ 19 = 248$$
$$-4712 + 8 \ / \ 28 = 168$$
$$-4712 + 2 \ / \ 15 = 314$$

and $-4712$ is the first number, reckoning backwards, that will meet these constraints. The year $-4712$ is the year 4713 BC.

Let us return to Pope's date. Let us assume that it was New Style. What day of the week was 9 January 1713? Our cycle begins at 4713 BC, so we have 4713 × 365.25 days to bring us to AD 0, and 1712 years complete from AD 0. This gives us (4713 + 1712) × 365.25 days = 2,346,731.25 days.

We now have to perform three other operations: the first is to discard decimals of a day; the second is to take into account the gap between New Style and Old Style (I. 24). (We recall that after 1700 the interval was 11 days.) The third is to add the days of the year current—in this case 9 January days. Now, 2,346,731 minus 11 plus 9 is 2,346,729. This figure must now be divided by 7, and we enter with the remainder into the following table:

0 Monday
1 Tuesday
2 Wednesday
3 Thursday
4 Friday
5 Saturday
6 Sunday

Our total, when divided by 7, gives no remainder; so the day was a Monday.

### I. 29 *Anno Mundi*

The 'Year of the World' was often used in tabulations that were involved with more than one calendar. It is the supposedly elapsed time since Creation. Archbishop Ussher, for instance, in his *Annals of the World* (1658) uses three time schemes. At one point (p. 2) he gives the date of the 'translation' of Enoch into heaven:

| The year of the world | the Julian Period | the year before Christ |
|---|---|---|
| 987 | 1697 | 3017. |

Ussher (sig. A4$^V$) makes AD 1 equal Julian Year 4714. Therefore 1 BC equals Julian Year (4714 minus 1 =) 4713; so that 3017 BC equals Julian Year (4714 minus 3017 =) 1697, as required.

### I. 30 The Astronomical Day

The astronomical day was considered to begin at noon on the calendar day. Thus, the calendar day 1 April 1602 began at midnight, and the astronomical day 1 April 1602 began at 12.00 hrs. on that calendar day. When entering a set of astronomical tables to calculate the place of a planet at

10 p.m. on 1 April 1602, one would therefore proceed as follows:

> 1600 complete
> 1 year complete
> 3 months complete
> 9 hours complete.

In most instances further adjustment would be necessary to take account of the difference in longitude between the place of observation and the place for which the tables were drawn up. And yet another adjustment is required for the difference between True Sun and Mean Sun (known as the Equation of Time).

The (fictional) Mean Sun travels at an even rate every day—as it must be supposed to do if the astronomical tables are not to be hopelessly complicated. The True Sun may be up to a quarter of an hour fast or slow on the Mean Sun in the course of a year.

## I. 31 Semidiurnal Arcs (Sunrise and Sunset)

Instead of tabulating the times of sunrise and sunset throughout the year, many handbooks give the 'semidiurnal arc' for a given day. From this figure several 'conclusions' (as Chaucer would have called them) can be derived. To take an example: Searle (p. 15), whose pole is elevated 52°, gives the semidiurnal arc as 7 hrs. 28 mins. when the sun is at Taurus 15.

See Mathematical Formulas 3 for a way of calculating this quantity. Now, if the time between sunrise and midday is 7 hrs. 28 mins., it follows that:

(1) sunrise will be at (12.00 − 7.28 =) 4.32 a.m.
(2) sunset will be at 7.28 p.m.
(3) There will be 14 hrs. 56 mins. of daylight and 9 hrs. 4 mins. of darkness (excluding dawn and dusk)
(4) each 'unequal' hour of day will contain (14.56 / 12 =) 1 hr. 14 mins. 40 secs., and each unequal hour of night will contain 45 mins. 20 secs.

While times of dawn and dusk are not tabulated, they are conventionally reckoned as lasting while the sun is less than 18° below the horizon.

See Mathematical Formulas 4 for the calculation. An easier way to determine dawn and dusk is to use an astrolabe, since the sun's nadir may easily be laid on 18° of altitude, thereby placing the sun itself 18° below the horizon. The appropriate times may then be read directly.

It has, of course, not been my intention to give a comprehensive account of astronomy—merely to explain those components which are essential if one is to come to an understanding of medieval and Renaissance astrology. To this topic we may now pass.

# Part II: Astrology

## INTRODUCTION

Astrology has, traditionally, two main branches: the natal and the judicial. The first kind casts a 'nativity' for the moment of birth; the second erects a 'figure' to answer the particular questions (in adult life) of the 'querent'—'should I go to war?', 'is my wife faithful?'.

Having erected the nativity or the figure (he might equally call either a 'scheme'), the astrologer interprets it as best suits the needs of the particular inquiry; if the scheme is for a birth, he will talk of fair complexion or brown, of small stature or large, of long life or short; if the question concerns a theft, he will talk of chambermaids or ostlers, of upstairs or downstairs, of near distance or far. The whole is, of course, a hoax; but the apparatus and the complexities of the subject have a decided fascination.

The possibilities of permutation, the supposed effect of the seven planets in any of the twelve signs and in any of the twelve houses—already one thousand and eight possibilities each with its dire or benign potential—make the astrologer's trade at once a flexible and a complex one. Guido Bonatus, for instance (*Liber Astronomicon*, 1491, sig. k5$^v$ ff.) lists 146 items for consideration in analysing a horoscope. Mercifully, though, we will not be obliged to explore all the avenues on each occasion. We will be concerned with understanding the basic procedures.

Any astrological reference one encounters, if it is at all complex, will have two distinguishable components: one will consist of the 'positional' elements in the given scheme; and the other will consist of the 'doctrinal' elements, inferred by a system of conventions from the positional data.

For example, the horoscope in Samuel Beckett's novel

*Murphy* finds that 'Herschel in Aquarius stops the water'. The 'water', in this context, is Murphy's urine—'Aqua(rius)' and 'water' having an obvious connection. But in addition to recognizing the plausibility of this association, we may properly ask whether the statement is astrologically sound. To answer at this level, we must inquire (1) whether the planet Uranus (Herschel being its discoverer) was indeed in Aquarius at the time of Murphy's birth; and (2) whether the doctrinal implications of its being there are indeed those the novel's astrologer, Suk, claims.

I do not presume, here, that Beckett's use of astrology should have been sound—which I would take to be unwarrantably pedantic—but I do wish to know whether it was—which I take to be of legitimate critical interest.

'Herschel in Aquarius stops the water'. Anyone with the competence to analyse this statement would be likely to conclude two things about it: one (the doctrinal point) would be that, anomalously, Aquarius is not one of the 'watery' signs at all, but one of the 'airy' ones (II. 15); and the second point would be that it was in fact more than half a century since Uranus had been in the position Suk requires of it.

The precise time of Murphy's coming into the world is not clear, but the margin is so great that this is of no consequence.

The point is not that we have smartly caught Beckett out; it is rather that we may now see that he is employing the jargon of astrology to his advantage without troubling to be correct. To realize this is of some consequence in one's assessment of the novel. Much of the wealth of its temporal detail can be verified in Whitaker's *Almanac* for 1935. The astrological detail, however, does not (as one might have presumed, in ignorance) work at this same level. Our requirement is to be protected from just such reasonable assumptions as this, and to be able to establish for ourselves the level at which an author pitches his pronouncements.

To this end we shall be much more interested in the 'positional' elements than in the 'doctrinal'. We shall wish to know, for example, whether a scheme can be constructed from the data available; whether, if it can, the scheme makes sense; whether, if it cannot, this is because the data are insufficient, or because the treatment is confused and self-conflicting. The primary doctrines of astrology very largely remained stable from the time of Ptolemy onwards—as indeed they were bound to do. Until the discovery of Neptune, Uranus, and Pluto, for instance, there was no motivation (and no warrant) for distributing the planets differently among the signs of the zodiac.

The Arab astrologers did make additions and refinements, many of them of a highly technical variety. One can find Messahala, Alkindus, Haly, and Alchabitius cited by such as Bonatus as equal authorities with Ptolemy; but as regards the positional elements outlined here—the basic grammar of the subject—there is little change.

> I make exception only for the conventions relating to 'orbs' and to platic aspects—II. 18. 3 and 4; and for the difference in the methods used to define the boundaries of the astrological houses.

Much of our topic, then, remains stable. For this reason I have concluded that it is unnecessary, and would be unduly cumbersome, to document in detail each source for the doctrines expounded here. One may look equally to Haly (a medieval Arab authority) or to William Lilly (a major English renaissance authority), or to a hundred authors in between, to justify (for instance) the assertion that the exaltation of the sun lies at Aries 19 (II. 14).

## ESTABLISHING THE HOUSES

### II. 1 Signs and Houses; Cusps

The astronomical model outlined in Part I contained two great circles of prime importance: the celestial equator and the ecliptic. In the framework now to be considered two great circles are again of prime importance: one is again the ecliptic, divided into its component parts, the zodiacal *signs*; and the second is a circle divided according to a variety of methods, each of them producing the twelve astrological *houses*. The initial boundary of each house (they being read in anticlockwise order) is called its *cusp*.

Much confusion will be avoided if we bear in mind the comment of Bonatus when speaking of the houses: 'each one of these divisions is called a house (*domus*), or a cusp, or a tower (*turris*), and not a sign, simply' (sig. d4v; my translation). *Sign* or *mansion* should be reserved for use in connection with the zodiac, and *house* in connection with the celestial equator.

## II. 2 The Four Quadrants

In order to explain how the division into houses operated we need to imagine a particular sky in a particular place.

Wherever you are on the earth's surface, one half of the heavens will be visible to you (or potentially so) and your local meridian will be a due north–south line, dividing that visible half into an eastern and a western quadrant. This line, known in astrological terms as the midheaven, or 'medium coeli', or M.C., marks the start of the *10th house* in most systems. Its cusp is the meridian and it extends towards the east. That part of your local horizon that runs through east, on the other hand, defines the beginning of the *1st house*, so that it lies below the horizon. The part that runs through west defines the cusp of the *7th house*, which lies above the horizon. Finally, the semicircle that divides the invisible half of the heavens in two defines the cusp of the *4th house*, which lies diametrically opposite the 10th.

This much is relatively simple; the division of the main houses, the *angles*, or *cardins*, in astrological parlance is easily relatable to one's surroundings. What, though, of the intermediate houses? Their definition is far more abstract, and there are five competing systems that we must consider.

## II. 3 The Astrological House Systems

### 1 The Equal House Division ('Ptolemy')

This is the simplest method, the one that many modern handbooks prefer and which they commonly ascribe to Ptolemy, though he does not in fact detail a system. It operates in one of two ways: (1) determine the degree of the ecliptic that lies on the meridian, make that the 10th house, and add successive even signs (30°) to define the remaining houses; (2) define the degree of the ecliptic that lies in the ascendant (this will vary with the latitude of the observer), make that the 1st house, and add successive even signs to define the remaining houses.

The first method will displace the 1st house from the ascendant; the second method will displace the 10th house from the meridian. Both are unsatisfactory on this account.

A brief example may be of assistance here. Suppose that it is discovered that Taurus 10 lies on the meridian. The 11th house will be defined by Gemini 10, the 12th by Cancer 10, and the first by Leo 10. But under the second system, at latitude 52° north, Leo 23 would lie in the ascendant if Taurus 10 lay on the meridian. On this system, then, the 10th house would be defined by Taurus 23, the 11th by Gemini 23, the 12th by Cancer 23, and the 1st by Leo 23.

Note: in most tabulations one will find the houses are given in the order 10, 11, 12, 1, 2, 3. The remaining houses are not given, since they lie diametrically opposite. If the 10th house is Taurus 23, then the 4th house will be Scorpio 23; if the 11th house is Gemini 23, the 5th house will be Sagittarius 23; and so on.

## 2 The Arithmetic System (Porphyry)

This method works by simple arithmetic, but it does take account of the importance of the meridian and the ascendant, and it locates the 10th house on the meridian and the 1st house on the eastern horizon. Its way of determining the intermediate houses is simply to subtract the longitude of the 1st from the longitude of the 10th, divide by three, and add the result successively to the longitude of the 10th.

To continue with our previous example: there we had Taurus 10 on the meridian and Leo 23 in the ascendant. The difference in longitude is $(143° - 40° =)$ $103°$. Rounding to the nearest degree determines that $(40° + 34° = 74°)$ Gemini 14 lies in the 11th house and $(74° + 34° = 108°)$ Cancer 18 lies in the 12th. Adding a further $34°$ brings us to $142°$, while accumulating the discarded fractions of a degree (we now have three thirds) returns us to $143° =$ Leo 23, as required.

If there are $103°$ in the first quadrant, as here, there will be $(180° - 103° =)$ $77°$ in the second quadrant. A similar operation will therefore quickly lead to the longitude of houses 2 and 3.

## 3   *The Right Ascension System (Alchabitius)*

This is the first of the technically more complex systems. It had a wide currency in the middle ages. It is implicit, for instance, in the *Alphonsine Tables* (compiled in the 1270s) and in the tables compiled for 1386 by Nicholas of Lynn (ed. Eisner, pp. 146 ff.). It is also implicit in the outline Chaucer gives in his *Treatise on the Astrolabe* (I. 36, 37).

One is obliged to say 'implicit' here, since none of the sources actually describes the procedure. The values they give, however, can only be reproduced by following the 'Alchabitius' method. A word of warning: some descriptions of the method (for instance the one James Wilson silently takes from William Leybourne's *Cursus Mathematicus* (1690) in his *Complete Dictionary of Astrology* (1819), s.v. 'Figure') are logically possible, but in no way reflect how Alphonso, Chaucer, and others operated the method.

The procedure is as follows: take the distance along the celestial equator between the *right* ascension (not the oblique ascension) of the ascendant and the right ascension of the meridian. Divide this interval by three and successively add the result to the right ascension of the meridian. Conversion of these new right ascensions to longitudes will define the intervening houses.

Continuing our example: the right ascension of Taurus 10 is 37° 34′; the right ascension of Leo 23 is 145° 22′. A third of the difference is 35° 56′. The longitude answering to (37° 34′ + 35° 56′ =) RA 73° 30′ is 74° 48′ = Gemini 14 for the 12th; the longitude answering to (73° 30′ + 35° 56′ =) RA 109° 26′ is 107° 56′ = Cancer 17 for the 12th. Finally (as a check), 109° 26′ + 35° 56′ = RA 145° 22′, whose answering longitude is Leo 23, as required.

For the other houses, the right ascension of the 11th plus 120° gives the right ascension of the 3rd, and the right ascension of the 12th plus 60° gives the right ascension of the 2nd.

Since this is the method that Chaucer reflects in his *Treatise*, in my view it is incumbent on those scholars fond of erecting horoscopes for the Wife of Bath, and other of his characters, to follow it. The alternative methods, after all, give different results, and so can well distort the interpretation subsequently placed on the figure.

## 4 *The Vertical Circle System (Campanus)*

It will be plain, by now, that the systems differ chiefly in the method they take to divide the distance between the 10th house and the 1st into thirds. The 'prime vertical' is that great circle which starts on the east point of the horizon, passes through the zenith, through the west point of the horizon, and back to east. Points 30° and 60° above the horizon may be found on this circle, and other great circles drawn, which will pass through these points and through north and south. The places at which these latter circles meet the ecliptic will define the intermediate houses.

Continuing with the figures we have been using, with Taurus 10 on the meridian this system will place Gemini 8 in the 11th, Cancer 15 in the 12th, returning to Leo 23 in the ascendant.

## 5 *The Equatorial System (Regiomontanus)*

This is the system the Renaissance called the 'rational' system and it is the one that has greatest currency in English renaissance handbooks. It varies from the Campanus system solely by making its one-third division along the 90 degrees of the celestial equator that lie, at any instant, between the 10th house and the 1st house.

I indicate in Mathematical Formulas 6 how the procedure works, since there will be those who will find it useful to know how to operate the system in detail.

For the sake of comparison, I here give the values that the Equatorial System would generate for our given example. This time the 11th house will be defined by Gemini 24, and the 12th by Cancer 29—in other words, in this instance the effect of using the equator, not the prime vertical, is to push the boundaries of the houses on further to the east.

Since not only the signs but—as we shall see (II. 16)— even the degrees of the zodiac were invested with particular properties, it will be obvious that the consequences of employing one system rather than another could be very material. We would do well, then, to be on the alert for whatever slight indications there are to determine which particular system was in use in a given instance. Moreover, if there is no clear

indication of which system was in fact employed, we should
be prepared to test the alternatives to find the best match
we can.

## II. 4  Comments

### 1  Comparison of Results

The consequences of using one system of house division rather
than another are best seen synoptically. I here present an
example with Aries 10 in the ascendant, at latitude 52°N.

| *Equal House 1* | *Equal House 2* | *Arithmetic* |
|---|---|---|
| mc = 10th | mc Cap. 4 | mc = 10th |
| 10 Cap. 4 | 10 Cap. 10 | 10 Cap. 4 |
| 11 Aqu. 4 | 11 Aqu. 10 | 11 Aqu. 6 |
| 12 Pisc. 4 | 12 Pisc. 10 | 12 Pisc. 8 |
| 1 Aries 4 | 1 Aries 10 | 1 Aries 10 |
| asc. Aries 10 | asc. = 1st | asc. = 1st |
| 2 Taur. 4 | 2 Taur. 10 | 2 Taur. 8 |
| 3 Gem. 4 | 3 Gem. 10 | 3 Gem. 6 |
| *Right Ascension* | *Vertical Circle* | *Equatorial* |
| mc = 10th | mc = 10th | mc = 10th |
| 10 Cap. 4 | 10 Cap. 4 | 10 Cap. 4 |
| 11 Aqu. 4 | 11 Cap. 11 | 11 Cap. 18 |
| 12 Pisc. 6 | 12 Cap. 29 | 12 Aqu. 12 |
| 1 Aries 10 | 1 Aries 10 | 1 Aries 10 |
| asc. = 1st | asc. = 1st | asc. = 1st |
| 2 Taur. 10 | 2 Gem. 11 | 2 Gem. 0 |
| 3 Gem. 8 | 3 Gem. 26 | 3 Gem. 21 |

From this table we can see that if a medieval author was
using the Alchabitius system and a modern critic subjected
the text to an analysis based on the Regiomontanus system,
degrees from the wrong sign would lie on two of the cusps in
the first quadrant and on one of them in the second.

### 2  Note on Demarcation

In the standard astrological diagram the beginning of the 1st
house is conceived of as coinciding with the eastern horizon
of the observer. By a convention of astrology, however, a
celestial body lying within 5° of the cusp of its anticlockwise

neighbour is regarded as being effectively in that next house. For instance, if the 3rd house began with Gemini 10, a planet located in the 2nd house, but at Gemini 6, would be taken as belonging in the 3rd house. It is for this reason that we find Chaucer saying (*Treatise on the Astrolabe*, II. 4): 'what celestial body that is 5 degrees above thilke degre that ascendith, or withinne that nombre . . . yit rikne they thilke planete in the ascendent. And what planete that is under thilke degre that ascendith the space of 25 degres, yit seyn thei that thilke planete is "like to him that is [in] the hous of the ascendent".' (ed. Robinson, p. 551.) This is confused in its conclusion, in that the planet 25° below the horizon is inevitably in the ascendant house. It is the planet 5° *above* the horizon that is 'like to him' that is actually in the ascendant. The *OED* defines the house of the ascendant (s.v. 'Ascendant') as including '5 degrees of the zodiac above this point [sc. the horoscopic point] and 25 below it'. It is misleading, however, to put the matter this way (and presumably a reflection of a misreading of Chaucer). It is not the house that is displaced by trying to poke its head above the horizon; it is the planet whose longitude is within 5° of the ascendant that is 'like' to one that is actually below the horizon and actually in the first house.

## II. 5  Tables of Houses

To calculate from scratch what degrees define what houses is a cumbersome business—sufficiently so to warrant the publication of tables (drawn up for a specific latitude) which allow one to determine the cusps of the houses by inspection, when once a simple initial calculation had been made.

### 1  Layout; 'Time from Noon'

The tables (see illustration) have twelve sections, one for the sun in each of the signs. In the first column one finds 'Hours and Minutes', running from 0.0 hrs. for the sun in Aries 0 through to 24.00 hrs. for the sun in Pisces 30 (which is the same place, of course, completing the circle). This column is headed, confusingly, '*Time from Noon*'. What it contains is the *right ascension of the meridian*, converted to an expression of time.

In medieval tables this column tends to specify the right ascension of the meridian, plus 90°.

Looking at Lilly's tables (illustration) we see that with the sun in Cancer 0 (longitude 90°) the degree of the celestial equator also on the meridian is 90°, which converts to 6.00 hrs. If, on the other hand, the sun is in Taurus 0 (longitude 30°), the right ascension of the meridian will be 28°, not 30°, as would be the case if the two circles kept an even pace. Thus, against Taurus 0 one finds '1.52 hrs.', not '2 hrs.'.

Let us now take an example and see in more detail how the tables are operated. Let our time and place be London (52°N) at 4 p.m. on 15 March 1450. Here we have four ingredients: place/latitude, time, date, year. The tables have an annual basis, so year does not affect us. Latitude, however, does, so that tables for Edinburgh or Paris will not do for London.

The critical factor here is that if the elevation of the pole changes, then the degree of the ecliptic that comes to the ascendant (and so defines the 1st house) will vary. Astrologers, anxious to broaden the basis of their market where they could, were capable of claiming that tables for London would serve 'without any Error considerable' for the whole of England (thus Partridge, sig. 2*ʳ). But there are variations between Plymouth and York, for instance, which such as Partridge would take notice of in the presence of a client. One of the common arguments against astrology was that twins were observed not to suffer identical fates. Answer: one had to be born first. What then of two individuals born at identical times? Answer: they were not born in the same place.

From an ephemeris, an almanac, or some other source we determine the position of the sun in the zodiac for our given day: 15 March at this epoch puts the sun at Aries 4. We now trace the answering value in the Time from Noon column, to obtain 00.15 hrs. This is the right ascension of the meridian at noon on our chosen day. To this we must now add the correction for our desired time: 4.00 p.m. We return to the table, then, looking for 4.15 hrs. The chances are that we shall need to proceed by proportion (known in our period as 'the rule of three'). To take, for example, the values relating to the 3rd house in Lilly's table. Lilly gives positions answering to

## A Table of Houses for the Latitude of 52. degrees.

| ☉ in ♈ Time from Noon | | 10 House | 11 House | 12 House | 1 House | 2 House | 3 House |
|---|---|---|---|---|---|---|---|
| **Ho** | **Min** | **♈** deg. min. | **♉** deg. min. | **II** deg. min. | **♋** deg. min. | **♌** deg. min. | **♍** deg. min. |
| 0 | 0 | 0 0 | 12 51 | 28 55 | 27 2 | 16 7 | 4 31 |
| 0 | 4 | 1 0 | 14 1 | 29 46 | 27 42 | 16 47 | 5 17 |
| 0 | 7 | 2 0 | 15 11 | 0 ♋ 36 | 28 28 | 17 28 | 6 3 |
| 0 | 11 | 3 0 | 16 21 | 1 26 | 29 1 | 18 8 | 6 50 |
| 0 | 15 | 4 0 | 17 29 | 2 15 | 29 41 | 18 48 | 7 36 |
| 0 | 18 | 5 0 | 18 37 | 3 4 | 0 ♌ 21 | 19 28 | 8 23 |
| 0 | 22 | 6 0 | 19 44 | 3 53 | 1 0 | 20 8 | 9 9 |
| 0 | 26 | 7 0 | 20 51 | 4 42 | 1 39 | 20 48 | 9 56 |
| 0 | 29 | 8 0 | 21 59 | 5 29 | 2 18 | 21 27 | 10 42 |
| 0 | 33 | 9 0 | 23 6 | 6 18 | 2 58 | 22 8 | 11 30 |
| 0 | 37 | 10 0 | 24 12 | 7 6 | 3 38 | 22 48 | 12 17 |
| 0 | 40 | 11 0 | 25 16 | 7 53 | 4 17 | 23 27 | 13 3 |
| 0 | 44 | 12 0 | 26 22 | 8 40 | 4 56 | 24 8 | 13 51 |
| 0 | 48 | 13 0 | 27 26 | 9 27 | 5 35 | 24 48 | 14 37 |
| 0 | 52 | 14 0 | 28 30 | 10 12 | 6 14 | 25 28 | 15 24 |
| 0 | 55 | 15 0 | 29 34 | 10 59 | 6 54 | 26 9 | 16 11 |
| 0 | 59 | 16 0 | 0 ♊ 37 | 11 45 | 7 22 | 26 50 | 16 59 |
| 1 | 3 | 17 0 | 1 38 | 12 30 | 8 12 | 27 30 | 17 46 |
| 1 | 6 | 18 0 | 2 41 | 13 16 | 8 52 | 28 11 | 18 33 |
| 1 | 10 | 19 0 | 3 43 | 14 1 | 9 31 | 28 52 | 19 21 |
| 1 | 14 | 20 0 | 4 45 | 14 47 | 10 10 | 29 33 | 20 9 |
| 1 | 18 | 21 0 | 5 45 | 15 32 | 10 49 | 0 ♍ 14 | 20 57 |
| 1 | 21 | 22 0 | 6 46 | 16 17 | 11 29 | 0 55 | 21 45 |
| 1 | 25 | 23 0 | 7 46 | 17 2 | 12 8 | 1 36 | 22 32 |
| 1 | 29 | 24 0 | 8 46 | 17 46 | 12 47 | 2 17 | 23 20 |
| 1 | 33 | 25 0 | 9 46 | 18 31 | 13 27 | 2 58 | 24 9 |
| 1 | 36 | 26 0 | 10 46 | 19 16 | 14 7 | 3 40 | 24 58 |
| 1 | 40 | 27 0 | 11 45 | 20 1 | 14 46 | 4 22 | 25 46 |
| 1 | 44 | 28 0 | 12 45 | 20 45 | 15 25 | 5 2 | 26 35 |
| 1 | 48 | 29 0 | 13 44 | 21 29 | 16 5 | 5 45 | 27 23 |
| 1 | 52 | 30 0 | 14 41 | 22 12 | 16 45 | 6 26 | 28 12 |

Table of Houses from William Lilly, *Christian Astrology*

# A Table of Houses for the Latitude of 52. degrees.

| ☽ in ♉ | 10 House | 11 House | 12 House | 1 House | 2 House | 3 House |
|---|---|---|---|---|---|---|
| Time from Noon. | deg. min. | deg. min. | deg. min. | deg. min. | deg. min. | deg. min. |
| Ho. Min. | ♉ | ♊ | ♋ | ♌ | ♍ | ♍ |
| 1 52 | 0 0 | 14 41 | 22 13 | 16 45 | 6 26 | 28 12 |
| 1 55 | 1 0 | 15 38 | 22 57 | 17 25 | 7 8 | 29 1 |
| 1 59 | 2 0 | 16 36 | 23 42 | 18 5 | 7 50 | 29 50 |
| 2 3 | 3 0 | 17 33 | 24 27 | 18 45 | 8 33 | 0 ♎ 40 |
| 2 7 | 4 0 | 18 29 | 25 10 | 19 25 | 9 14 | 1 29 |
| 2 11 | 5 0 | 19 26 | 25 55 | 20 5 | 9 57 | 2 19 |
| 2 15 | 6 0 | 20 22 | 26 38 | 20 45 | 10 39 | 3 8 |
| 2 19 | 7 0 | 21 20 | 27 23 | 21 26 | 11 23 | 3 58 |
| 2 22 | 8 0 | 22 17 | 28 7 | 22 7 | 12 6 | 4 48 |
| 2 26 | 9 0 | 23 13 | 28 51 | 22 47 | 12 48 | 5 38 |
| 2 30 | 10 0 | 24 9 | 29 35 | 23 27 | 13 31 | 6 28 |
| 2 34 | 11 0 | 25 5 | 0 ♌ 19 | 24 8 | 14 14 | 7 19 |
| 2 38 | 12 0 | 26 1 | 1 4 | 24 49 | 14 58 | 8 9 |
| 2 42 | 13 0 | 26 56 | 1 47 | 25 30 | 15 41 | 8 59 |
| 2 46 | 14 0 | 27 51 | 2 32 | 26 12 | 16 25 | 9 50 |
| 2 50 | 15 0 | 28 46 | 3 16 | 26 53 | 17 8 | 10 40 |
| 2 54 | 16 0 | 29 41 | 4 1 | 27 24 | 17 52 | 11 32 |
| 2 58 | 17 0 | 0 ♋ 38 | 4 46 | 28 17 | 18 36 | 12 24 |
| 3 2 | 18 0 | 1 32 | 5 30 | 28 58 | 19 21 | 13 14 |
| 3 6 | 19 0 | 2 27 | 6 15 | 29 40 | 20 5 | 14 6 |
| 3 10 | 20 0 | 3 22 | 7 0 | 0 ♍ 23 | 20 50 | 14 57 |
| 3 14 | 21 0 | 4 17 | 7 45 | 1 5 | 21 34 | 15 49 |
| 3 18 | 22 0 | 5 11 | 8 30 | 1 47 | 22 19 | 16 40 |
| 3 22 | 23 0 | 6 5 | 9 15 | 2 29 | 23 4 | 17 32 |
| 3 26 | 24 0 | 6 59 | 10 0 | 3 12 | 23 49 | 18 24 |
| 3 30 | 25 0 | 7 53 | 10 44 | 3 54 | 24 35 | 19 16 |
| 3 35 | 26 0 | 8 48 | 11 30 | 4 37 | 25 20 | 20 8 |
| 3 39 | 27 0 | 9 43 | 12 15 | 5 20 | 26 6 | 21 1 |
| 3 43 | 28 0 | 10 36 | 13 1 | 6 3 | 26 51 | 21 53 |
| 3 47 | 29 0 | 11 30 | 13 46 | 6 46 | 27 31 | 22 46 |
| 3 51 | 30 0 | 12 24 | 14 31 | 7 29 | 28 23 | 23 38 |

R 2

# A Table of Houses for the Latitude of 52. degrees.

| ⊙ in Ⅱ Time from Noon. Ho. Min. | 10 House deg. m. in. Ⅱ | 11 House deg. min. ♋ | 12 House deg. min. ♌ | 1 House deg. min. ♍ | 2 House deg. min. ♍ | 3 House deg. min. ♎ |
|---|---|---|---|---|---|---|
| 2 51 | 0 0 | 12 24 | 14 31 | 7 29 | 28 23 | 23 28 |
| 3 55 | 1 0 | 13 19 | 15 17 | 8 13 | 29 9 | 24 31 |
| 4 0 | 2 0 | 14 14 | 16 ?8 | 8 57 | 29 55 | 25 24 |
| 4 4 | 3 0 | 15 8 | 16 49 | 9 41 | 0 ♎ 42 | 26 17 |
| 4 8 | 4 0 | 16 2 | 17 35 | 10 25 | 1 28 | 27 0 |
| 4 12 | 5 0 | 16 56 | 18 21 | 11 9 | 2 15 | 28 2 |
| 4 16 | 6 0 | 17 50 | 19 7 | 11 53 | 3 1 | 28 56 |
| 4 21 | 7 0 | 18 44 | 19 53 | 12 37 | 3 48 | 29 49 |
| 4 25 | 8 0 | 19 38 | 20 40 | 13 22 | 4 35 | 0 ♏ 43 |
| 4 29 | 9 0 | 20 31 | 21 25 | 14 6 | 5 21 | 1 36 |
| 4 33 | 10 0 | 21 25 | 22 11 | 14 51 | 6 9 | 2 29 |
| 4 38 | 11 0 | 22 19 | 22 58 | 15 35 | 6 56 | 3 23 |
| 4 42 | 12 0 | 23 14 | 23 45 | 16 21 | 7 44 | 4 17 |
| 4 46 | 13 0 | 24 8 | 24 31 | 17 5 | 8 31 | 5 11 |
| 4 50 | 14 0 | 25 2 | 25 18 | 17 50 | 9 18 | 6 5 |
| 4 55 | 15 0 | 25 37 | 26 5 | 18 35 | 10 6 | 6 59 |
| 4 59 | 16 0 | 26 51 | 26 52 | 19 21 | 10 54 | 7 53 |
| 5 3 | 17 0 | 27 44 | 27 39 | 20 6 | 11 41 | 8 47 |
| 5 8 | 18 0 | 28 38 | 28 27 | 20 51 | 12 28 | 9 40 |
| 5 12 | 19 0 | 29 42 | 29 14 | 21 37 | 13 16 | 10 34 |
| 5 16 | 20 0 | 0 ♌ 2 | 0 ♍ 2 | 22 22 | 14 3 | 11 28 |
| 5 21 | 21 0 | 1 21 | 0 50 | 23 8 | 14 51 | 12 22 |
| 5 25 | 22 0 | 2 15 | 1 37 | 23 53 | 15 39 | 13 17 |
| 5 29 | 23 0 | 3 9 | 2 24 | 24 39 | 16 26 | 14 11 |
| 5 34 | 24 0 | 4 4 | 3 12 | 25 25 | 17 14 | 15 6 |
| 5 38 | 25 0 | 4 57 | 4 0 | 26 10 | 18 2 | 15 59 |
| 5 42 | 26 0 | 5 52 | 4 47 | 26 56 | 18 50 | 16 53 |
| 5 47 | 27 0 | 6 47 | 5 35 | 27 43 | 19 38 | 17 47 |
| 5 51 | 28 0 | 7 41 | 6 23 | 28 28 | 20 25 | 18 42 |
| 5 56 | 29 0 | 8 35 | 7 10 | 29 13 | 21 13 | 19 36 |
| 6 0 | 30 0 | 9 29 | 7 58 | 0 ♎ 0 | 22 1 | 20 30 |

# A Table of Houses for the Latitude of 52. degrees.

⊙ in ♋

| Time from Noon | | 10 House | | 11 House | | 12 House | | 1 House | | 2 House | | 3 House | |
|---|---|---|---|---|---|---|---|---|---|---|---|---|---|
| Ho | Min | ♋ deg | min | ♌ deg | min | ♍ deg | min | ♎ deg | min | ♎ deg | min | ♏ deg | min |
| 6 | 0 | 0 | 0 | 9 | 29 | 7 | 58 | 0 | 0 | 22 | 1 | 20 | 30 |
| 6 | 4 | 1 | 0 | 10 | 24 | 8 | 47 | 0 | 45 | 22 | 50 | 21 | 25 |
| 6 | 9 | 2 | 0 | 11 | 18 | 9 | 34 | 1 | 22 | 23 | 37 | 22 | 19 |
| 6 | 13 | 3 | 0 | 12 | 12 | 10 | 22 | 2 | 17 | 24 | 24 | 23 | 12 |
| 6 | 18 | 4 | 0 | 13 | 7 | 11 | 10 | 3 | 4 | 25 | 12 | 24 | 7 |
| 6 | 22 | 5 | 0 | 14 | 1 | 11 | 58 | 3 | 49 | 26 | 0 | 25 | 2 |
| 6 | 26 | 6 | 0 | 14 | 54 | 12 | 45 | 4 | 35 | 26 | 47 | 25 | 56 |
| 6 | 31 | 7 | 0 | 15 | 49 | 13 | 33 | 5 | 21 | 27 | 35 | 26 | 51 |
| 6 | 35 | 8 | 0 | 16 | 43 | 14 | 21 | 6 | 7 | 28 | 23 | 27 | 45 |
| 6 | 39 | 9 | 0 | 17 | 37 | 15 | 9 | 6 | 52 | 29 | 10 | 28 | 39 |
| 6 | 44 | 10 | 0 | 18 | 22 | 15 | 56 | 7 | 37 | 29 | 58 | 29 | 33 |
| 6 | 48 | 11 | 0 | 19 | 26 | 16 | 44 | 8 | 23 | 0 ♏ | 45 | 0 ♐ | 27 |
| 6 | 52 | 12 | 0 | 20 | 20 | 17 | 31 | 9 | 8 | 1 | 33 | 1 | 22 |
| 6 | 57 | 13 | 0 | 21 | 13 | 18 | 19 | 9 | 54 | 2 | 20 | 2 | 16 |
| 7 | 1 | 14 | 0 | 22 | 7 | 19 | 6 | 10 | 39 | 3 | 7 | 3 | 9 |
| 7 | 5 | 15 | 0 | 23 | 1 | 19 | 54 | 11 | 24 | 3 | 55 | 4 | 3 |
| 7 | 10 | 16 | 0 | 23 | 55 | 20 | 42 | 12 | 10 | 4 | 42 | 4 | 57 |
| 7 | 14 | 17 | 0 | 24 | 49 | 21 | 28 | 12 | 54 | 5 | 28 | 5 | 51 |
| 7 | 18 | 18 | 0 | 25 | 42 | 22 | 15 | 13 | 39 | 6 | 15 | 6 | 46 |
| 7 | 22 | 19 | 0 | 26 | 37 | 23 | 4 | 14 | 24 | 7 | 2 | 7 | 40 |
| 7 | 27 | 20 | 0 | 27 | 30 | 23 | 51 | 15 | 9 | 7 | 48 | 8 | 35 |
| 7 | 31 | 21 | 0 | 28 | 24 | 24 | 38 | 15 | 54 | 8 | 35 | 9 | 29 |
| 7 | 35 | 22 | 0 | 29 | 17 | 25 | 25 | 16 | 37 | 9 | 20 | 10 | 22 |
| 7 | 39 | 23 | 0 | 0 ♍ | 11 | 26 | 12 | 17 | 22 | 10 | 6 | 11 | 16 |
| 7 | 44 | 24 | 0 | 1 | 4 | 26 | 58 | 18 | 7 | 10 | 53 | 12 | 10 |
| 7 | 48 | 25 | 0 | 1 | 57 | 27 | 45 | 18 | 51 | 11 | 39 | 13 | 3 |
| 7 | 52 | 26 | 0 | 2 | 51 | 28 | 21 | 19 | 35 | 12 | 25 | 13 | 57 |
| 7 | 55 | 27 | 0 | 3 | 43 | 29 | 18 | 20 | 19 | 13 | 11 | 14 | 51 |
| 8 | 0 | 28 | 0 | 4 | 36 | 0 ♎ | 4 | 21 | 3 | 13 | 57 | 15 | 46 |
| 8 | 5 | 29 | 0 | 5 | 29 | 0 | 51 | 21 | 47 | 14 | 43 | 16 | 41 |
| 8 | 9 | 30 | 0 | 6 | 22 | 1 | 37 | 22 | 31 | 15 | 29 | 17 | 31 |

d

# A Table of Houses for the Latitude of 52. degrees.

| ⊙ in ♌ | 10 House | 11 House | 12 House | 1 House | 2 House | 3 House |
|---|---|---|---|---|---|---|
| Time from Noon. | deg. min. | deg. min. | deg. min. | deg. min. | deg. min. | deg. min. |
| Ho. min. | ♌ | ♍ | ♎ | ♎ | ♏ | ♐ |
| 8  9 | 0  0 | 6  22 | 1  37 | 22  21 | 15  29 | 17  8 |
| 8  13 | 1  0 | 7  14 | 2  2 | 23  14 | 16  14 | 18  2 |
| 8  17 | 2  0 | 8  7 | 3  9 | 23  57 | 16  59 | 19  22 |
| 8  21 | 3  0 | 8  59 | 3  54 | 24  40 | 17  44 | 20  17 |
| 8  25 | 4  0 | 9  51 | 4  25 | 25  23 | 18  30 | 21  12 |
| 8  30 | 5  0 | 10  44 | 5  25 | 26  6 | 19  15 | 22  7 |
| 8  34 | 6  0 | 11  36 | 6  10 | 26  48 | 20  0 | 23  1 |
| 8  38 | 7  0 | 12  28 | 6  55 | 27  31 | 20  44 | 23  55 |
| 8  42 | 8  0 | 13  19 | 7  41 | 28  14 | 21  29 | 24  49 |
| 8  46 | 9  0 | 14  11 | 8  25 | 28  55 | 22  15 | 25  43 |
| 8  50 | 10  0 | 15  2 | 9  10 | 29  37 | 23  0 | 26  37 |
| 8  54 | 11  0 | 15  54 | 9  55 | 0 ♏ 19 | 23  45 | 27  33 |
| 8  58 | 12  0 | 16  45 | 10  39 | 1  1 | 24  29 | 28  27 |
| 9  2 | 13  0 | 17  36 | 11  23 | 1  43 | 25  14 | 29  22 |
| 9  6 | 14  0 | 18  28 | 12  8 | 2  25 | 25  59 | 0 ♑ 18 |
| 9  10 | 15  0 | 19  20 | 12  52 | 3  7 | 26  44 | 1  14 |
| 9  14 | 16  0 | 20  10 | 13  35 | 3  48 | 27  28 | 2  8 |
| 9  18 | 17  0 | 21  1 | 14  19 | 4  29 | 28  12 | 3  4 |
| 9  22 | 18  0 | 21  51 | 15  2 | 5  10 | 28  56 | 3  59 |
| 9  26 | 19  0 | 22  41 | 15  45 | 5  51 | 29  40 | 4  54 |
| 9  30 | 20  0 | 23  32 | 16  28 | 6  32 | 0 ♐ 25 | 5  50 |
| 9  34 | 21  0 | 24  22 | 17  12 | 7  13 | 1  9 | 6  46 |
| 9  38 | 22  0 | 25  12 | 17  54 | 7  53 | 1  52 | 7  42 |
| 9  41 | 23  0 | 26  2 | 18  37 | 8  34 | 2  37 | 8  40 |
| 9  45 | 24  0 | 26  51 | 19  20 | 9  15 | 3  22 | 9  37 |
| 9  49 | 25  0 | 27  41 | 20  3 | 9  55 | 4  5 | 10  33 |
| 9  53 | 25  0 | 28  31 | 20  45 | 10  35 | 4  49 | 11  30 |
| 9  57 | 27  0 | 29  20 | 21  27 | 11  14 | 5  33 | 12  26 |
| 10  1 | 28  0 | 0 ♎ 9 | 22  9 | 11  55 | 6  18 | 13  24 |
| 10  5 | 29  0 | 0  55 | 22  52 | 12  52 | 7  2 | 14  22 |
| 10  8 | 30  0 | 1  48 | 23  33 | 13  14 | 7  47 | 15  19 |

# A Table of Houses for the Latitude of 52. degrees.

☉ in ♍

| Time from Noon. | | 10 House | | 11 House | | 12 House | | 1 House | | 2 House | | 3 House | |
|---|---|---|---|---|---|---|---|---|---|---|---|---|---|
| Ho. | Min. | deg. | min. | deg. | min. | deg. | min. | deg. | min. | deg. | min. | deg. | min. |
| | | ♍ | | ♎ | | ♎ | | ♏ | | ♐ | | ♑ | |
| 10 | 8 | 0 | 0 | 1 | 48 | 23 | 33 | 13 | 14 | 7 | 47 | 15 | 0 |
| 10 | 12 | 1 | 0 | 2 | 37 | 24 | 15 | 13 | 54 | 8 | 31 | 16 | 10 |
| 10 | 16 | 2 | 0 | 3 | 25 | 24 | 56 | 14 | 34 | 9 | 15 | 17 | 15 |
| 10 | 20 | 3 | 0 | 4 | 13 | 25 | 36 | 15 | 14 | 9 | 59 | 18 | 14 |
| 10 | 24 | 4 | 0 | 5 | 2 | 26 | 20 | 15 | 53 | 10 | 44 | 19 | 14 |
| 10 | 27 | 5 | 0 | 5 | 50 | 27 | 1 | 16 | 33 | 11 | 28 | 20 | 14 |
| 10 | 31 | 6 | 0 | 6 | 39 | 27 | 42 | 17 | 12 | 12 | 12 | 21 | 14 |
| 10 | 35 | 7 | 0 | 7 | 27 | 28 | 23 | 17 | 51 | 12 | 57 | 22 | 14 |
| 10 | 39 | 8 | 0 | 8 | 15 | 29 | 4 | 18 | 21 | 13 | 42 | 23 | 14 |
| 10 | 42 | 9 | 0 | 9 | 3 | 29 | 46 | 19 | 10 | 14 | 28 | 24 | 15 |
| 10 | 46 | 10 | 0 | 9 | 51 | 0 ♏ | 27 | 19 | 49 | 15 | 13 | 25 | 15 |
| 10 | 50 | 11 | 0 | 10 | 38 | 1 | 8 | 20 | 29 | 15 | 58 | 26 | 17 |
| 10 | 54 | 12 | 0 | 11 | 26 | 1 | 49 | 21 | 8 | 16 | 44 | 27 | 19 |
| 10 | 57 | 13 | 0 | 12 | 14 | 2 | 30 | 21 | 48 | 17 | 29 | 28 | 21 |
| 11 | 1 | 14 | 0 | 13 | 1 | 3 | 10 | 22 | 27 | 18 | 15 | 29 | 23 |
| 11 | 5 | 15 | 0 | 13 | 49 | 3 | 51 | 23 | 6 | 19 | 1 | 0 ♒ | 26 |
| 11 | 8 | 16 | 0 | 14 | 36 | 4 | 32 | 23 | 45 | 19 | 47 | 1 | 30 |
| 11 | 12 | 17 | 0 | 15 | 23 | 5 | 12 | 24 | 25 | 20 | 33 | 2 | 33 |
| 11 | 16 | 18 | 0 | 16 | 9 | 5 | 52 | 25 | 3 | 21 | 19 | 3 | 37 |
| 11 | 20 | 19 | 0 | 16 | 57 | 6 | 32 | 25 | 43 | 22 | 7 | 4 | 43 |
| 11 | 23 | 20 | 0 | 17 | 43 | 7 | 12 | 26 | 22 | 22 | 54 | 5 | 48 |
| 11 | 27 | 21 | 0 | 18 | 30 | 7 | 52 | 27 | 1 | 23 | 42 | 6 | 54 |
| 11 | 31 | 22 | 0 | 19 | 18 | 8 | 32 | 27 | 41 | 24 | 30 | 8 | 1 |
| 11 | 34 | 23 | 0 | 20 | 4 | 9 | 12 | 28 | 21 | 25 | 18 | 9 | 8 |
| 11 | 38 | 24 | 0 | 20 | 51 | 9 | 52 | 29 | 0 | 26 | 7 | 10 | 16 |
| 11 | 42 | 25 | 0 | 21 | 37 | 10 | 32 | 29 | 39 | 26 | 56 | 11 | 23 |
| 11 | 45 | 26 | 0 | 22 | 24 | 11 | 12 | 0 ♐ | 19 | 27 | 45 | 12 | 31 |
| 11 | 49 | 27 | 0 | 23 | 10 | 11 | 52 | 0 | 58 | 28 | 34 | 13 | 39 |
| 11 | 53 | 28 | 0 | 23 | 57 | 12 | 23 | 1 | 38 | 29 | 23 | 14 | 48 |
| 11 | 56 | 29 | 0 | 24 | 42 | 13 | 12 | 2 | 18 | 0 ♑ | 14 | 15 | 59 |
| 12 | 0 | 30 | 0 | 25 | 29 | 13 | 53 | 2 | 58 | 1 | 5 | 17 | 9 |

# A Table of Houses for the Latitude of 52. degrees.

| ☉ in ≏ Time from Noon. | | 10 House deg. min. | | 11 House deg. min. | | 12 House deg. min. | | 1 House deg. min. | | 2 House deg. min. | | 3 House deg. min. | |
|---|---|---|---|---|---|---|---|---|---|---|---|---|---|
| Ho | Min | ≏ | | ≏ | | ♏ | | ♐ | | ♑ | | ♒ | |
| 12 | 0 | 0 | 0 | 25 | 29 | 13 | 53 | 2 | 58 | 1 | 5 | 17 | 9 |
| 12 | 4 | 1 | 0 | 26 | 15 | 14 | 33 | 3 | 37 | 1 | 56 | 18 | 28 |
| 12 | 7 | 2 | 0 | 27 | 1 | 15 | 13 | 4 | 17 | 2 | 48 | 19 | 32 |
| 12 | 11 | 3 | 0 | 27 | 47 | 15 | 53 | 4 | 58 | 3 | 40 | 20 | 44 |
| 12 | 15 | 4 | 0 | 28 | 34 | 16 | 22 | 5 | 28 | 4 | 33 | 21 | 57 |
| 12 | 18 | 5 | 0 | 29 | 20 | 17 | 1 | 5 | 10 | 5 | 26 | 23 | 12 |
| 12 | 22 | 6 | 0 | 0 ♏ | 6 | 17 | 53 | 7 | 1 | 6 | 20 | 24 | 24 |
| 12 | 26 | 7 | 0 | 0 | 52 | 18 | 33 | 7 | 41 | 7 | 15 | 25 | 38 |
| 12 | 29 | 8 | 0 | 1 | 38 | 19 | 14 | 8 | 22 | 8 | 10 | 26 | 53 |
| 12 | 33 | 9 | 0 | 2 | 25 | 19 | 55 | 9 | 4 | 9 | 6 | 28 | 11 |
| 12 | 37 | 10 | 0 | 3 | 12 | 20 | 35 | 9 | 45 | 10 | 2 | 29 | 26 |
| 12 | 40 | 11 | 0 | 3 | 57 | 21 | 15 | 10 | 27 | 10 | 59 | 0 ♓ | 43 |
| 12 | 44 | 12 | 0 | 4 | 44 | 21 | 57 | 11 | 10 | 11 | 58 | 2 | 1 |
| 12 | 48 | 13 | 0 | 5 | 30 | 22 | 38 | 11 | 51 | 12 | 57 | 3 | 19 |
| 12 | 52 | 14 | 0 | 6 | 17 | 23 | 18 | 12 | 34 | 13 | 56 | 4 | 37 |
| 12 | 55 | 15 | 0 | 7 | 3 | 24 | 0 | 13 | 17 | 14 | 57 | 5 | 57 |
| 12 | 59 | 16 | 0 | 7 | 50 | 24 | 41 | 14 | 1 | 15 | 58 | 7 | 17 |
| 13 | 3 | 17 | 0 | 8 | 36 | 25 | 22 | 14 | 44 | 16 | 59 | 8 | 37 |
| 13 | 6 | 18 | 0 | 9 | 22 | 26 | 4 | 15 | 27 | 18 | 2 | 9 | 58 |
| 13 | 10 | 19 | 0 | 10 | 8 | 26 | 45 | 15 | 12 | 19 | 7 | 11 | 19 |
| 13 | 14 | 20 | 0 | 10 | 55 | 27 | 27 | 16 | 55 | 20 | 13 | 12 | 42 |
| 13 | 18 | 21 | 0 | 11 | 42 | 28 | 9 | 17 | 41 | 21 | 20 | 14 | 4 |
| 13 | 21 | 22 | 0 | 12 | 29 | 28 | 51 | 18 | 27 | 22 | 29 | 15 | 29 |
| 13 | 25 | 23 | 0 | 13 | 16 | 29 | 33 | 19 | 12 | 23 | 37 | 16 | 52 |
| 13 | 29 | 24 | 0 | 14 | 2 | 0 ♐ | 15 | 19 | 57 | 24 | 45 | 18 | 16 |
| 13 | 33 | 25 | 0 | 14 | 50 | 0 | 58 | 20 | 44 | 25 | 56 | 19 | 40 |
| 13 | 36 | 26 | 0 | 15 | 37 | 1 | 40 | 21 | 32 | 27 | 9 | 21 | 6 |
| 13 | 40 | 27 | 0 | 16 | 24 | 2 | 23 | 22 | 19 | 28 | 23 | 22 | 31 |
| 13 | 44 | 28 | 0 | 17 | 11 | 2 | 7 | 23 | 7 | 29 | 33 | 23 | 57 |
| 13 | 48 | 29 | 0 | 17 | 58 | 3 | 49 | 23 | 56 | 0 ♒ | 55 | 25 | 21 |
| 13 | 52 | 20 | 0 | 18 | 46 | 4 | 32 | 24 | 44 | 2 | 12 | 26 | 49 |

g

# A Table of Houſes for the Latitude of 52. degrees.

| ☉ in ♏ | 10 Houſe | | 11 Houſe | | 12 Houſe | | 1 Houſe | | 2 Houſe | | 3 Houſe | |
|---|---|---|---|---|---|---|---|---|---|---|---|---|
| **Time from Noon.** | deg. | min. | deg. | min. | d g. | min. | deg. | min. | deg. | min. | deg. | min. |
| **Ho. Min.** | ♏ | | ♏ | | ♐ | | ♐ | | ♒ | | ♓ | |
| 13 52 | 0 | 0 | 18 | 46 | 4 | 32 | 24 | 44 | 2 | 12 | 26 | 49 |
| 13 55 | 1 | 0 | 19 | 33 | 5 | 16 | 25 | 34 | 3 | 32 | 28 | 15 |
| 13 59 | 2 | 0 | 20 | 21 | 6 | 1 | 26 | 25 | 4 | 54 | 20 | 43 |
| 14 3 | 3 | 0 | 21 | 9 | 6 | 45 | 27 | 16 | 6 | 19 | ♈ 1 | 11 |
| 14 7 | 4 | 0 | 21 | 57 | 7 | 29 | 28 | 7 | 7 | 42 | 2 | 37 |
| 14 11 | 5 | 0 | 22 | 44 | 8 | 14 | 28 | 59 | 9 | 7 | 4 | 6 |
| 14 15 | 6 | 0 | 23 | 32 | 8 | 59 | 29 | 52 | 10 | 35 | 5 | 33 |
| 14 19 | 7 | 0 | 24 | 22 | 9 | 45 | 0 ♑ 46 | | 12 | 6 | 7 | 1 |
| 14 22 | 8 | 0 | 25 | 11 | 10 | 31 | 1 | 41 | 12 | 38 | 8 | 30 |
| 14 26 | 9 | 0 | 25 | 59 | 11 | 16 | 2 | 36 | 15 | 10 | 9 | 57 |
| 14 30 | 10 | 0 | 26 | 48 | 12 | 3 | 2 | 32 | 16 | 45 | 11 | 25 |
| 14 34 | 11 | 0 | 27 | 38 | 12 | 49 | 4 | 29 | 18 | 23 | 12 | 52 |
| 14 38 | 12 | 0 | 28 | 27 | 13 | 37 | 5 | 26 | 20 | 3 | 14 | 20 |
| 14 42 | 13 | 0 | 29 | 16 | 14 | 24 | 6 | 25 | 21 | 45 | 15 | 48 |
| 14 46 | 14 | 0 | 0 ♐ 6 | | 15 | 12 | 7 | 25 | 23 | 30 | 17 | 16 |
| 14 50 | 15 | 0 | 0 | 55 | 16 | 0 | 8 | 26 | 25 | 14 | 18 | 44 |
| 14 54 | 16 | 0 | 1 | 45 | 16 | 48 | 9 | 28 | 27 | 2 | 20 | 10 |
| 14 58 | 17 | 0 | 2 | 36 | 17 | 38 | 10 | 23 | 28 | 54 | 21 | 38 |
| 15 2 | 18 | 0 | 3 | 26 | 18 | 28 | 11 | 28 | 0 ♓ 45 | | 23 | 6 |
| 15 6 | 19 | 0 | 4 | 16 | 19 | 17 | 12 | 43 | 2 | 37 | 24 | 31 |
| 15 10 | 20 | 0 | 5 | 7 | 20 | 8 | 12 | 51 | 4 | 33 | 25 | 58 |
| 15 14 | 21 | 0 | 5 | 58 | 20 | 59 | 15 | 0 | 6 | 31 | 27 | 24 |
| 15 18 | 22 | 0 | 5 | 50 | 21 | 51 | 16 | 10 | 8 | 21 | 28 | 50 |
| 15 22 | 23 | 0 | 7 | 41 | 22 | 43 | 17 | 21 | 10 | 32 | 0 ♉ 15 | |
| 15 26 | 4 | 0 | 8 | 33 | 23 | 35 | 18 | 23 | 12 | 25 | 1 | 39 |
| 15 30 | 25 | 0 | 9 | 24 | 24 | 29 | 19 | 48 | 14 | 39 | 3 | 4 |
| 15 35 | 26 | 0 | 10 | 17 | 25 | 23 | 21 | 5 | 16 | 47 | 4 | 28 |
| 15 39 | 27 | 0 | 11 | 9 | 26 | 17 | 22 | 23 | 18 | 56 | 5 | 52 |
| 15 4 | 28 | 0 | 12 | 2 | 27 | 12 | 23 | 4 | 21 | 4 | 7 | 15 |
| 15 47 | 29 | 0 | 12 | 54 | 28 | 8 | 25 | 5 | 23 | 12 | 8 | 36 |
| 15 51 | 30 | 0 | 13 | 47 | 29 | 3 | 26 | 30 | 25 | 21 | 0 | 50 |

*h*

# A Table of Houses for the Latitude of 52. degrees.

| ☉ in ♐ | | 10 House ♐ | | 11 House ♐ | | 12 House ♐ | | 1 House ♑ | | 2 House ♓ | | 3 House ♉ | |
|---|---|---|---|---|---|---|---|---|---|---|---|---|---|
| Time from Noon. | | deg. min | | deg. min. | | deg. min. | | deg. min. | | deg. min. | | deg. min. | |
| Ho. | Min. | | | | | | | | | | | | |
| 15 | 51 | 0 | 0 | 13 | 47 | 29 | 3 | 26 | 20 | 25 | 21 | 9 | 59 |
| 15 | 55 | 1 | 0 | 14 | 41 | 0 ♑ | 1 | 27 | 57 | 27 | 33 | 11 | 21 |
| 16 | 0 | 2 | 0 | 15 | 35 | 0 | 59 | 29 | 26 | 29 | 49 | 12 | 43 |
| 16 | 4 | 3 | 0 | 16 | 30 | 1 | 58 | 0 ♒ | 57 | 2 ♈ | 2 | 14 | 4 |
| 16 | 8 | 4 | 0 | 17 | 25 | 2 | 57 | 2 | 31 | 4 | 14 | 15 | 24 |
| 16 | 12 | 5 | 0 | 18 | 20 | 3 | 57 | 4 | 8 | 6 | 26 | 16 | 43 |
| 16 | 16 | 6 | 0 | 19 | 15 | 4 | 58 | 5 | 46 | 8 | 35 | 18 | 1 |
| 16 | 21 | 7 | 0 | 20 | 10 | 6 | 1 | 7 | 29 | 10 | 47 | 19 | 19 |
| 16 | 25 | 8 | 0 | 21 | 7 | 7 | 4 | 9 | 13 | 13 | 0 | 20 | 38 |
| 16 | 29 | 9 | 0 | 22 | 2 | 8 | 7 | 11 | 0 | 15 | 10 | 21 | 55 |
| 16 | 33 | 10 | 0 | 22 | 59 | 9 | 11 | 12 | 51 | 17 | 21 | 23 | 12 |
| 16 | 38 | 11 | 0 | 23 | 56 | 10 | 16 | 14 | 42 | 19 | 30 | 24 | 28 |
| 16 | 42 | 12 | 0 | 24 | 53 | 11 | 24 | 16 | 41 | 21 | 39 | 25 | 45 |
| 16 | 46 | 13 | 0 | 25 | 50 | 12 | 32 | 18 | 41 | 23 | 44 | 27 | 0 |
| 16 | 50 | 14 | 0 | 26 | 47 | 13 | 41 | 20 | 44 | 25 | 48 | 28 | 14 |
| 16 | 55 | 15 | 0 | 27 | 46 | 14 | 51 | 22 | 52 | 27 | 52 | 29 | 28 |
| 16 | 59 | 16 | 0 | 28 | 45 | 16 | 2 | 25 | 0 | 29 | 52 | 0 ♊ | 41 |
| 17 | 3 | 17 | 0 | 29 | 44 | 17 | 13 | 27 | 12 | 1 ♉ | 49 | 1 | 53 |
| 17 | 8 | 18 | 0 | 0 ♑ | 44 | 18 | 28 | 29 | 28 | 3 | 47 | 3 | 5 |
| 17 | 12 | 19 | 0 | 1 | 44 | 19 | 43 | 1 ♓ | 49 | 5 | 44 | 4 | 17 |
| 17 | 16 | 20 | 0 | 2 | 44 | 21 | 1 | 4 | 11 | 7 | 28 | 5 | 28 |
| 17 | 21 | 21 | 0 | 3 | 45 | 22 | 19 | 6 | 35 | 9 | 31 | 6 | 34 |
| 17 | 25 | 22 | 0 | 4 | 46 | 23 | 28 | 9 | 2 | 11 | 22 | 7 | 47 |
| 17 | 29 | 23 | 0 | 5 | 47 | 24 | 57 | 11 | 32 | 13 | 10 | 8 | 57 |
| 17 | 34 | 24 | 0 | 6 | 50 | 26 | 20 | 14 | 7 | 14 | 57 | 10 | 6 |
| 17 | 38 | 25 | 0 | 7 | 53 | 27 | 44 | 16 | 42 | 16 | 38 | 11 | 14 |
| 17 | 42 | 26 | 0 | 8 | 56 | 29 | 11 | 19 | 21 | 18 | 21 | 12 | 23 |
| 17 | 47 | 27 | 0 | 10 | 0 | 0 ♒ | 37 | 21 | 57 | 20 | 1 | 13 | 30 |
| 17 | 51 | 28 | 0 | 11 | 4 | 2 | 5 | 24 | 27 | 21 | 28 | 14 | 36 |
| 17 | 56 | 29 | 0 | 12 | 8 | 3 | 36 | 27 | 17 | 23 | 13 | 15 | 41 |
| 18 | 0 | 30 | 0 | 13 | 13 | 5 | 10 | 0 ♈ | 0 | 24 | 50 | 16 | 47 |

## A Table of Houſes for the Latitude of 52. degrees.

| ☉ in ♑ Time from Noon Ho. min. | 10 Houſe deg. min. ♑ | | 11 Houſe deg. min. ♑ | | 12 Houſe deg. min. ♒ | | 1 Houſe deg. min. ♈ | | 2 Houſe deg. min. ♊ | | 3 Houſe deg. min. ♉ | |
|---|---|---|---|---|---|---|---|---|---|---|---|---|
| 18 0 | 0 | 0 | 13 | 13 | 5 | 10 | 0 | 0 | 24 | 50 | 16 | 47 |
| 18 4 | 1 | 0 | 14 | 19 | 6 | 47 | 2 | 42 | 26 | 24 | 17 | 52 |
| 18 9 | 2 | 0 | 15 | 24 | 8 | 22 | 5 | 22 | 27 | 54 | 18 | 56 |
| 18 13 | 3 | 0 | 16 | 29 | 9 | 58 | 8 | 2 | 29 | 23 | 20 | 0 |
| 18 18 | 4 | 0 | 17 | 38 | 11 | 40 | 10 | 40 | 0 ♊ 51 | | 21 | 4 |
| 18 22 | 5 | 0 | 18 | 45 | 13 | 21 | 13 | 17 | 2 | 16 | 22 | 7 |
| 18 26 | 6 | 0 | 19 | 54 | 15 | 2 | 15 | 52 | 3 | 39 | 23 | 9 |
| 18 31 | 7 | 0 | 21 | 3 | 16 | 50 | 18 | 28 | 5 | 2 | 24 | 12 |
| 18 35 | 8 | 0 | 22 | 13 | 18 | 38 | 20 | 58 | 6 | 21 | 25 | 14 |
| 18 39 | 9 | 0 | 23 | 22 | 20 | 29 | 23 | 24 | 7 | 40 | 26 | 15 |
| 18 44 | 10 | 0 | 24 | 32 | 22 | 22 | 25 | 49 | 8 | 59 | 27 | 16 |
| 18 48 | 11 | 0 | 25 | 42 | 24 | 16 | 28 | 11 | 10 | 17 | 28 | 16 |
| 18 52 | 12 | 0 | 26 | 54 | 26 | 12 | 0 ♉ 32 | | 11 | 32 | 29 | 16 |
| 18 57 | 13 | 0 | 28 | 7 | 28 | 11 | 2 | 47 | 12 | 45 | 0 ♋ 16 | |
| 19 1 | 14 | 0 | 29 | 19 | 0 ♓ 7 | | 5 | 0 | 13 | 58 | 1 | 14 |
| 19 5 | 15 | 0 | 0 ♒ 31 | | 2 | 8 | 7 | 8 | 15 | 9 | 2 | 13 |
| 19 10 | 16 | 0 | 1 | 46 | 4 | 11 | 9 | 15 | 16 | 19 | 3 | 12 |
| 19 14 | 17 | 0 | 3 | 0 | 6 | 15 | 11 | 19 | 17 | 28 | 4 | 10 |
| 19 18 | 18 | 0 | 4 | 15 | 8 | 21 | 13 | 19 | 18 | 36 | 5 | 7 |
| 19 22 | 19 | 0 | 5 | 32 | 10 | 30 | 15 | 17 | 19 | 43 | 6 | 4 |
| 19 27 | 20 | 0 | 6 | 48 | 12 | 39 | 17 | 9 | 20 | 49 | 7 | 1 |
| 19 31 | 21 | 0 | 8 | 5 | 14 | 49 | 19 | 0 | 21 | 53 | 7 | 50 |
| 19 35 | 22 | 0 | 9 | 2 | 17 | 0 | 20 | 47 | 22 | 56 | 8 | 52 |
| 19 39 | 23 | 0 | 10 | 4 | 19 | 12 | 22 | 31 | 23 | 59 | 9 | 50 |
| 19 44 | 24 | 0 | 11 | 59 | 21 | 25 | 24 | 14 | 25 | 2 | 10 | 45 |
| 19 48 | 25 | 0 | 13 | 1 | 23 | 34 | 25 | 52 | 26 | 3 | 11 | 40 |
| 19 52 | 26 | 0 | 14 | 3 | 25 | 45 | 27 | 28 | 27 | 3 | 12 | 35 |
| 19 56 | 27 | 0 | 15 | 1 | 27 | 58 | 29 | 30 | 28 | 2 | 13 | 29 |
| 20 0 | 28 | 0 | 17 | 1 | 0 ♈ 12 | | 0 ♊ 34 | | 29 | 1 | 14 | 24 |
| 20 5 | 29 | 0 | 18 | 38 | 2 | 27 | 2 | 3 | 29 | 59 | 15 | 19 |
| 20 9 | 30 | 0 | 0 | 1 | 4 | 39 | 3 | 30 | 0 ♋ 56 | | 16 | 13 |

# A Table of Houses for the Latitude of 52. degrees.

| ☉ in ♒ Time from Noon. Ho. min. | 10 House deg. min. ♒ | | 11 House deg. min. ♒ | | 12 House deg. min. ♈ | | 1 House deg. min. ♊ | | 2 House deg. min. ♋ | | 3 House deg. min. ♋ | |
|---|---|---|---|---|---|---|---|---|---|---|---|---|
| 20  9 | 0 | 0 | 20 | 1 | 4 | 39 | 3 | 30 | 0 | 56 | 16 | 13 |
| 20 13 | 1 | 0 | 21 | 23 | 6 | 48 | 4 | 54 | 1 | 52 | 17 | 6 |
| 20 17 | 2 | 0 | 22 | 4c | 8 | 5c | 6 | 17 | 2 | 47 | 17 | 58 |
| 20 21 | 3 | 0 | 24 | ♉ 8 | 11 | 4 | 7 | 37 | 3 | 43 | 18 | 51 |
| 20 25 | 4 | 0 | 25 | 31 | 13 | 1? | 8 | 55 | 4 | 27 | 19 | 43 |
| 20 30 | 5 | 0 | 26 | 56 | 15 | 21 | 10 | 12 | 5 | 31 | 20 | 35 |
| 20 34 | 6 | 0 | 28 | 20 | 17 | 2c | 11 | 26 | 6 | 24 | 21 | 27 |
| 20 38 | 7 | 0 | 29 | 45 | 19 | 2b | 12 | 39 | 7 | 17 | 22 | 18 |
| 20 42 | 8 | 0 | ♓ 1 | 1 | 21 | 29 | 13 | 49 | 8 | 9 | 23 | 10 |
| 20 46 | 9 | 0 | 2 | 30 | 23 | 2c | 15 | 0 | 9 | 1 | 24 | 2 |
| 20 50 | 10 | 0 | 4 | 1 | 25 | 27 | 16 | 9 | 9 | 52 | 24 | 53 |
| 20 54 | 11 | 0 | 5 | 28 | 27 | 2? | 17 | 16 | 10 | 42 | 25 | 44 |
| 20 58 | 12 | 0 | 6 | 54 | 29 | 15 | 18 | 22 | 11 | 32 | 26 | 34 |
| 21  2 | 13 | 0 | 8 | 21 | ♉ 1 | 5 | 19 | 27 | 12 | 21 | 27 | 24 |
| 21  6 | 14 | 0 | 9 | 5c | 2 | 56 | 20 | 31 | 13 | 11 | 28 | 1? |
| 21 10 | 15 | 0 | 11 | 16 | 4 | 45 | 21 | 34 | 14 | 0 | 29 | 5 |
| 21 14 | 16 | 0 | 12 | 43 | 6 | 3c | 22 | 34 | 14 | 48 | 29 | 54 |
| 21 18 | 17 | 0 | 14 | 12 | 8 | 14 | 23 | 35 | 15 | 36 | ♋ 0 | 44 |
| 21 22 | 18 | 0 | 15 | 39 | 9 | 56 | 24 | 23 | 16 | 23 | 1 | 32 |
| 21 26 | 19 | 0 | 17 | 7 | 11 | 37 | 25 | 31 | 17 | 10 | 2 | 22 |
| 21 30 | 20 | 0 | 18 | 35 | 13 | 14 | 26 | 27 | 17 | 56 | 3 | 12 |
| 21 34 | 21 | 0 | 20 | 3 | 14 | 5c | 27 | 23 | 18 | 43 | 4 | 1 |
| 21 38 | 22 | 0 | 21 | 2c | 16 | 21 | 28 | 19 | 19 | 29 | 4 | 48 |
| 21 41 | 23 | 0 | 22 | 5c | 17 | 54 | 29 | 14 | 20 | 15 | 5 | 38 |
| 21 45 | 24 | 0 | 24 | 2? | 19 | 24 | ♋ 0 | 8 | 21 | 1 | 6 | 27 |
| 21 49 | 25 | 0 | 25 | 54 | 10 | 52 | 1 | 1 | 21 | 45 | 7 | 15 |
| 21 53 | 25 | 0 | 27 | 2? | 12 | 17 | 1 | 5? | 22 | 20 | 8 | 3 |
| 21 57 | 27 | 0 | 18 | 4c | 13 | 41 | 2 | 44 | 23 | 14 | 8 | 51 |
| 22  1 | 28 | 0 | ♈ 1c | 15 | 6 | | 3 | 35 | 23 | 59 | 9 | 31 |
| 22  5 | 29 | 0 | 1 | 4c | 6 | 28 | 4 | 26 | 24 | 44 | 10 | 27 |
| 22  8 | 30 | 0 | 2 | 1 | 17 | 47 | 5 | 15 | 25 | 27 | 11 | 14 |

*k*

# A Table of Houſes for the Latitude of 52. degrees.

| ☉ in ♓ Time from Noon. | | 10 Houſe ♓ | | 11 Houſe ♈ | | 12 Houſe ♉ | | 1 Houſe ♋ | | 2 Houſe ♋ | | 3 Ho.ſe ♌ | |
|---|---|---|---|---|---|---|---|---|---|---|---|---|---|
| Ho. | Mi. | deg. | min | deg. | min | deg. | min | deg. | min | deg. | min | deg. | min |
| 22 | 8 | 0 | 0 | 3 | 11 | 27 | 47 | 5 | 15 | 25 | 27 | 11 | 14 |
| 22 | 12 | 1 | 0 | 4 | 37 | 29 | 5 | 6 | 4 | 26 | 10 | 12 | 1 |
| 22 | 16 | 2 | 0 | 6 | 3 | 0 ♉ | 21 | 6 | 52 | 26 | 53 | 12 | 48 |
| 22 | 20 | 3 | 0 | 7 | 26 | 1 | 36 | 7 | 40 | 27 | 36 | 13 | 36 |
| 22 | 24 | 4 | 0 | 8 | 54 | 2 | 51 | 8 | 28 | 28 | 19 | 14 | 27 |
| 22 | 27 | 5 | 0 | 10 | 19 | 4 | 4 | 9 | 15 | 29 | 2 | 15 | 10 |
| 22 | 31 | 6 | 0 | 11 | 44 | 5 | 15 | 10 | 2 | 29 | 45 | 15 | 57 |
| 22 | 35 | 7 | 0 | 13 | 7 | 6 | 23 | 10 | 48 | 0 ♌ | 27 | 16 | 44 |
| 22 | 39 | 8 | 0 | 14 | 31 | 7 | 30 | 11 | 33 | 1 | 9 | 17 | 31 |
| 22 | 42 | 9 | 0 | 15 | 55 | 8 | 39 | 12 | 19 | 1 | 51 | 18 | 18 |
| 22 | 46 | 10 | 0 | 17 | 18 | 9 | 47 | 13 | 4 | 2 | 32 | 19 | 5 |
| 22 | 50 | 11 | 0 | 18 | 41 | 10 | 53 | 13 | 47 | 3 | 15 | 19 | 52 |
| 22 | 54 | 12 | 0 | 20 | 1 | 11 | 58 | 14 | 31 | 3 | 56 | 20 | 38 |
| 22 | 57 | 13 | 0 | 21 | 23 | 13 | 1 | 15 | 16 | 4 | 38 | 21 | 24 |
| 23 | 1 | 14 | 0 | 22 | 42 | 14 | 2 | 15 | 59 | 5 | 18 | 22 | 10 |
| 23 | 5 | 15 | 0 | 24 | 3 | 15 | 3 | 16 | 43 | 6 | 0 | 22 | 57 |
| 23 | 8 | 16 | 0 | 25 | 22 | 16 | 4 | 17 | 26 | 6 | 41 | 23 | 43 |
| 23 | 12 | 17 | 0 | 26 | 40 | 17 | 3 | 18 | 8 | 7 | 22 | 24 | 29 |
| 23 | 16 | 18 | 0 | 27 | 58 | 18 | 2 | 18 | 50 | 8 | 3 | 25 | 16 |
| 23 | 20 | 19 | 0 | 29 | 17 | 19 | 1 | 19 | 32 | 8 | 44 | 26 | 2 |
| 23 | 23 | 20 | 0 | 0 ♉ | 33 | 19 | 50 | 20 | 14 | 9 | 25 | 26 | 48 |
| 23 | 27 | 21 | 0 | 1 | 49 | 20 | 54 | 20 | 55 | 10 | 5 | 27 | 35 |
| 23 | 31 | 22 | 0 | 3 | 7 | 21 | 50 | 21 | 37 | 10 | 46 | 28 | 22 |
| 23 | 34 | 23 | 0 | 4 | 22 | 22 | 44 | 22 | 18 | 11 | 26 | 29 | 7 |
| 23 | 38 | 24 | 0 | 5 | 36 | 23 | 39 | 22 | 59 | 12 | 6 | 29 | 54 |
| 23 | 42 | 25 | 0 | 6 | 49 | 24 | 33 | 23 | 40 | 12 | 47 | 0 ♍ | 40 |
| 23 | 45 | 26 | 0 | 8 | 2 | 25 | 27 | 24 | 21 | 13 | 27 | 1 | 26 |
| 23 | 49 | 27 | 0 | 9 | 15 | 26 | 20 | 25 | 2 | 14 | 7 | 2 | 13 |
| 23 | 53 | 28 | 0 | 10 | 27 | 27 | 12 | 25 | 42 | 14 | 47 | 2 | 52 |
| 23 | 56 | 29 | 0 | 11 | 39 | 28 | 4 | 26 | 22 | 15 | 27 | 3 | 45 |
| 24 | 0 | 30 | 0 | 12 | 51 | 28 | 55 | 27 | 2 | 16 | 7 | 4 | 31 |

4.12 and 4.16: we want a value corresponding to 4.15. In four minutes of time the value for the 3rd house increases by 54' of arc (28° 02' − 28° 56'). In three minutes of time the value will therefore increase by 3 × 54' /4, or 40' 30" of arc. We discard the 30" and add 40' to the value against 4.12 hrs., to obtain Libra 28° 42' for the 3rd house.

## 2 Excursus: Using Tables of Oblique Ascension

What of the situation when no appropriate table of houses was to hand? Before the astrologer was reduced to calculating from scratch, he had another resort. He could look (with rather more effort) at an appropriate set of Tables of Oblique Ascension. These list, for given latitudes, the degrees of the celestial equator that come to the ascendant with given degrees of the zodiac. From these tabulations it is still possible to set up the basic diagram for the horoscope on the Regiomontanus system. The tables to be consulted for houses 12 and 2 at latitude $x$ are determined by the formula $\tan y = \tan x \cos 30°$; the tables to be consulted for houses 11 and 3 at latitude $x$ are determined by the formula $\tan y' = \tan x \cos 60$. For the first house consult table $x$ directly.

Here again an example will assist: let the latitude be 53°, and let Libra 0 be on the meridian. How do we find values for the 11th and the 3rd houses?

If Libra 0 is in the 10th, the right ascension of the meridian will be 180° (12.00 hrs.). On the Regiomontanus system this means that 210° will lead to the 11th house, 240° to the 12th, . . . and 330° to the 3rd. For the 11th and 3rd houses, then, the values 210° and 330° will lead to the appropriate longitudes in a table compiled for latitude 34°, since $\tan 53°$ times $\cos 60°$ rounds up to that. The nearest oblique ascension one would find in such a table that answered to 210° even, would probably be in the order of 210° 58'. The equivalent longitude would be Libra 26, and since 210° 58' is too high, we could be content to say that Libra 25 defines the 11th house. Similarly for the 3rd house: the value closest to 330° that Lilly tabulates (sig. Qqq4$^r$) is 329° 41', to which Aquarius 16 answers. Since Aquarius 17 does not enter the table until the oblique ascension rises to 330° 27', Aquarius 16 will do for the 3rd house on this form of approximation.

It is, of course, possible to 'refine' the data by using the rule of three; but even then not much will be gained, if one considers that many a table of houses was content to operate to the nearest degree.

## II. 6  Finding Time from Day and House

One would normally enter a table of houses armed with a given day (converted into a noon position for the sun) and a given time of day. We have already seen how we would then use the tables to define our horoscope. There will be occasions, however, on which we want to work the system in reverse. Suppose, for instance, that we have been told by a mid-sixteenth century text only that it is 4 p.m. and that Gemini 10 is rising. What day of the year is it?

The answer is readily found. The Time from Noon answering to Gemini 10 in the 1st house is 20.30 hrs. Our *clock* time from noon, however, is 4.00 hrs. The difference is 16.30 hrs.—which answers to the sun's being at Sagittarius 9. Inspection of the relevant tables (an almanac, say) will show us that the sun was there on 22 November.

## II. 7  Accuracy of Tables of Houses

In an attempt to judge the accuracy of renaissance tables of houses I have looked at those of Joseph Blagrave in his *Introduction to Astrology* (1682). I checked all 1,800 places in his tabulation against values derived from using the appropriate trigonometrical formulas in a calculator programme.

I chose Blagrave not only because he gives both degrees and minutes for each house, but also because he specifies his latitude and his value for the obliquity of the ecliptic precisely. This means that all the variables in the required equations are determined exactly, so that only the rounding of seconds to minutes can make a difference between his tabulation and one's own attempt to reproduce his values.

The result of this investigation was that of the 1,800 places for which Blagrave had to specify a value, only 96 differed at all, and only 60 differed by more than one minute of arc. The degree of compatibility, in other words, was very high. Indeed it is worth noting that a large number of the differences were multiples of ten: Blagrave, for instance, exhibits

'13 19' for the 12th house alongside Leo 16, whereas the correct value is 13° 39'. It seems reasonable, then, to blame the printer for at least a certain proportion of the differences. Indeed, there is only one occasion on which the correct value is 29° 58' and Blagrave exhibits '30 00'—a difference that cannot be typographical.

## ERECTING THE FIGURE

### II. 8 The Diagram

When a horoscope is to be constructed, three procedural stages are involved. The positions of the planets must be

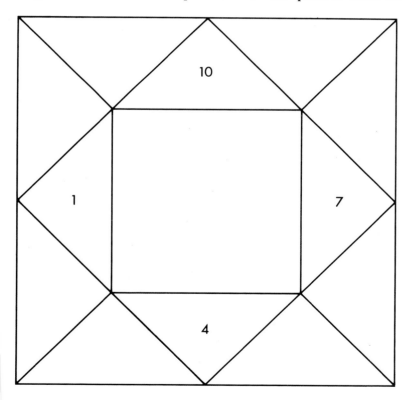

FIG. 5

determined, the relation of the zodiac to the astrological houses must be sought, and then the two sets of information must be brought together in the astrological diagram. In its commonest form this diagram consists of a series of triangles with a square at the centre (Fig. 5). The triangle at '9 o'clock' conventionally represents the 1st house, so that the one at '3 o'clock' correspondingly represents the 7th house. Because of the design of the figure, however, the cusps of the main houses cannot lie in the horizontal and the vertical, which makes the figure difficult to assimilate upon first acquaintance. The ordering of the houses, however, sufficiently indicates which of its boundaries must be its cusp—it is always the one at the clockwise end.

The degrees of the zodiac that define the cusps of the houses are conventionally written inside the leading edge of the triangle; the planets, in turn, are plotted in the approximate position that answers to their longitude; and the place, date, and time are conventionally entered in the centre square, where sometimes the aspects the planets bear to each other are also noted.

## II. 9 Tabulating the Planets

The second task is to determine where the planets are at the particular time for which the horoscope is cast. The need for this information, of course, makes astrology parasitic on astronomy. Usually the astrologer would turn to an ephemeris. But just as he might not always have a table of houses to hand and so need to look at a table of oblique ascensions, so he might also not have an ephemeris available, and so need to have the knowledge that would permit him to make his calculations from scratch.

This is not an artificial supposition. The horoscope of his own nativity that Robert Burton recorded in his Diary survives to us (see illustration), and in the Diary we also find him making a calculation for his brother's horoscope which, 'exempli causa', involves him in making his own computation of the sun's position. For this he used Tycho's *Astronomiae Instauratae Progymnasmata* (1602)—a major contemporary text, sections of which he had copied out.

We may now adopt Burton as a case history and attempt

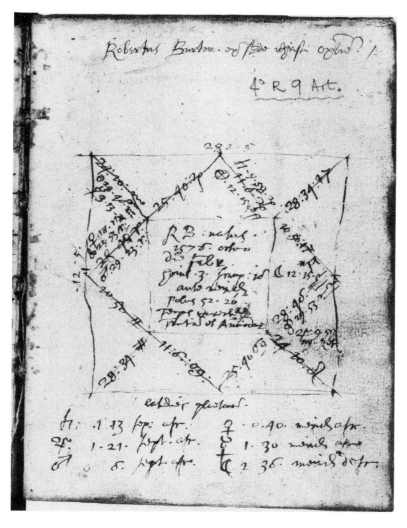

Robert Burton's Horoscope

to trace his steps. Can we verify the values he adopted and follow his procedures? Let us begin by looking at where Burton thought the planets were when he was born. Our first task is to determine from Tuckerman (I. 21. 2) what were their longitudes at the time concerned, and to compare them with those that Burton gives.

Tuckerman's values are here converted from decimals of a degree to degrees and minutes of a sign.

The time we seek is 8.44 a.m., 8 February 1576/7:

|         | Tuckerman |          | Burton |          |
|---------|-----------|----------|--------|----------|
| Saturn  | Cap.      | 9° 30'   | Cap.   | 9° 58'   |
| Jupiter | Vir.      | 9° 47'   | Vir.   | 9° 59'   |
| Mars    | Ar.       | 29° 35'  | Ar.    | 29° 23'  |
| sun     | Aqu.      | 29° 39'  | Aqu.   | 28° 46'  |
| Venus   | Ar.       | 1° 27'   | Ar.    | 1° 07'   |
| Mercury | Aqu.      | 28° 19'  | Pis.   | 3° 13'   |
| moon    | Sco.      | 11° 59'  | Sco.   | 12° 15'. |

What of the extent of the agreement here? It is satisfactory in the case of Saturn, Jupiter, Mars, Venus, and the moon. (The maximum difference is less than half a degree.)

Mercury, admittedly, is nearly 5 degrees out according to modern computation. But such discrepancies are not uncommon. Indeed there were serious astronomers who confessed they had never seen Mercury since it lies always so close to the sun.

Even if the agreement is not perfect, it is still true that the figures Burton gives uniquely identify a date over a period of several thousand years—or would do, were it not that the value he gives for the sun's position is at such serious variance with its actual position.

We recall that one degree of motion in the sun represents 24 hours in time.

Burton copied from Tycho a wealth of information, including the 'Epochae mediorum motuum solis' ('the epochs of the mean motion of the sun'), Tycho's value for the 'Vera anni quantitas' ('the true extent of the year'), and the length of the day (to seven sexagesimal places), together with the

length of the leap year. Much of this information was required
if one was to determine exactly the position of the sun or of
a planet at a given time.

Then on one occasion he set out to define where the sun
was when his brother was born, as a means of testing himself.
This is fortunate, since in attempting to reproduce Burton's
value for the sun at his own nativity, we can use these values
(marked * below) supplying the remaining figures from the
*Rudolphine Tables.*

To set out the calculation will also give some indication of
how cumbersome the procedures were (9 s(igns) 08° equals
278°, and so on).

Sun's mean longitude:

| | | | | | | |
|---|---|---|---|---|---|---|
| *epocha Christi | 9s | 08° | 38′ | 45″ | 0iii | 0iv |
| *1000 | | 07 | 42 | 0 | 11 | 52 |
| *500 | | 03 | 51 | 0 | 05 | 56 |
| *70 | | | 02 | 46 | 14 | 53 |
| 6 yrs. | 11 | 29 | 33 | 12 | 09 | 20 |
| Jan. | 1 | 0 | 33 | 18 | 14 | 46 |
| 7 days | | | 06 | 53 | 58 | 18 | 49 |
| 21 hrs | | | 51 | 44 | 46 | 49 |
| 8 mins | | | | 19 | 42 | 47 |
| | 10 | 28 | 07 | 04 | 45 | 12 |

Sun's apogee:

| | | | | |
|---|---|---|---|---|
| *epocha Christi | 2 | 15 | 39 | 45 |
| *1000 | | 12 | 30 | 00 |
| *500 | | 06 | 15 | 00 |
| *70 | | | 52 | 30 |
| 6 | | | 04 | 30 |
| Jan. | | | | 04 |
| | 3 | 05 | 21 | 49 |

mean longitude minus apogee equals 7s 22° 46′, which yields
for equation of centre: 1° 40′ 12″.

| | | | | | | |
|---|---|---|---|---|---|---|
| mean longitude: | 10s | 28° | 07′ | 04″ | 45 | 12 |
| equation: | | 01 | 40 | 12 | 00 | 00 |
| sun's true place: | 10 | 29 | 47 | 16 | | |

= Aquarius 29° 47′.

We should be aware, here, of the supposed precision involved. There are sixty minutes of arc in a degree, sixty seconds of arc in a minute of arc, sixty thirds in a second . . . and Burton is calculating to fourths! But there are 216,000 thirds of arc in a degree, and so 900 thirds of arc turn over in each second of time! Precision of this kind could, of course, only be mathematically based in Burton's day.

The value we derived from Tuckerman for the position of the sun at Burton's birth was Aquarius 29° 39', while the figure we derived from using a combination of Burton's values and the *Rudolphine Tables* was Aquarius 29° 47'—the difference is only 8' of arc. The difference, however, between Tuckerman and Burton himself is 52' of arc. I am tempted to believe that at some stage Burton (or whoever did the calculation) arrived at 29° 46' for the sun's position and that this was misread in the copying. In any event, the value Burton actually recorded for the sun does not square with the values for the rest of the planets, in particular the moon.

## II. 10  Defining the Cusps

We saw in II. 5 something of how Tables of Houses are used. Here we may tabulate Burton's values for the astrological houses against those available in a standard book of reference. It will at once be apparent that Burton, like Lilly, was using the Regiomontanus method—any other system would produce much wider disprepancies:

| Burton | | Lilly | |
|---|---|---|---|
| 10 Cap. | 11° 06' | Cap. | 11° 00' |
| 11 Cap. | 25° 40' | Cap. | 25° 42' |
| 12 Aqu. | 24° 10' | Aqu. | 24° 16' |
| 1 Ar. | 28° 46' | Ar. | 28° 11' |
| 2 Gem. | 10° 50' | Gem. | 10° 16' |
| 3 Gem. | 28° 34' | [Gem.] | 28° 16'. |

There are two things to note here: firstly that Lilly's value for the 10th house is an even degree—as is inevitable from the way in which the houses were tabulated; and secondly that Lilly's latitude is expressed as 52° while Burton's is 52° 10'. These things considered, the agreement is very close.

## II. 11 Plotting the Figure

We are now at last able to examine the planetary positions as plotted against the astrological houses in the diagram. We will adopt the values Burton records, except in one case where a patent transcription error is involved.

The Dragon's Head, in the 12th house, is clearly specified by Burton as being at '23.53' Aries, while the Dragon's Tail in the 6th house is placed at '29.53' Libra. One of these figures must be wrong. In the circumstances, it is easy to tell which is in error. The cusp of the 7th house is defined by Libra '28.46', so that if the value for the Dragon's Tail was right, it would have to lie in the 7th house, not the 6th.

*1* Pars fortunae, *and the Dragon's Head/Tail*

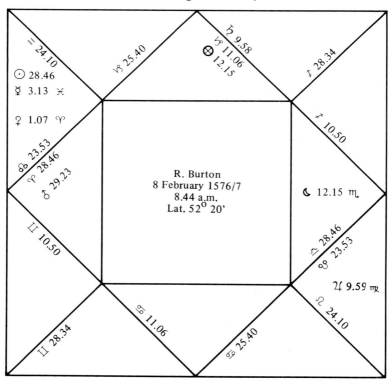

FIG. 6

In addition to the planetary symbols three other non-zodiacal symbols may be found in the diagram (Fig. 6). That in the 10th house (against Capricorn 12° 15') represents *pars fortunae*. The significance of this notional point will become clear when we eventually examine what is known as the 'hyleg' (II. 30). For the moment, we may say that the position of *pars fortunae* is found internally, and is an extremely useful check, since it has to tally with three other values in the figure. To find it, subtract the sun's longitude from the moon's longitude, and add the longitude of the ascendant to the result. In the present case the figures work out exactly: 222° 15' (moon) minus 328° 46' (sun), plus 28° 46' (ascendant) equals 282° 15', as required.

The *Dragon's Head* marks the point on the ecliptic where the moon will cross it going north: it is the 'ascending node' of the moon. The Dragon's Tail, opposite, is the descending node. Renaissance ephemerides usually include the position of the Dragon's Head, but calculation of its position may also be made from modern planetary tables—with a certain degree of approximation.

It is desirable to have one of the two latitudinal positions of the moon as close as possible to zero, in order to minimise distortion.

## DIGNITIES AND DEBILITIES

### II. 12 Essential and Accidental

Now begins the task of analysing and interpreting the scheme. Fortunately we do not need to examine all the ramifications, but we do need to consider the main components of the procedure. And even this task is not slight.

All the planets have sets of what are known as 'essential' and 'accidental' dignities: their essential dignities derive from their relation to the zodiacal signs—they are essential in the sense of being permanent. Their accidental dignities derive from their particular situation within the astrological houses —they are accidental in the sense that they depend on the circumstances of the moment. To facilitate the assessment of the relative strengths of the planets and their relative weaknesses, a points system was developed—plus for *dignities* of either kind, and minus for *debilities* of either kind.

### II. 13  Essential Dignities: Mansion (opposed by Detriment), *Gaudium*

Consider: you have twelve zodiacal signs and seven planets. How are you to distribute one among the other? Break the circle of the signs between Cancer and Leo, and give Cancer to the moon and Leo to the sun. (See Fig. 7.) You now have

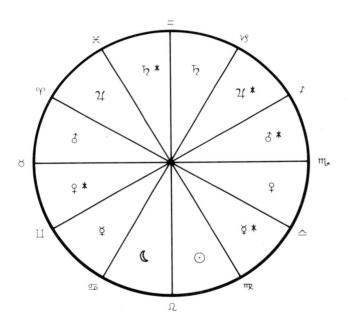

FIG. 7

ten signs and five planets remaining. It will be obvious that each remaining planet may be given two signs. But on what principle? The 'rational' answer is to reflect the Ptolemaic order of the planets. Given the force of 'opposition' in astrology, it will also be rational to make a planet's *'detriment'* the sign that lies opposite its mansion, or 'proper' sign:

|         | mansion/sign              | detriment                |
|---------|---------------------------|--------------------------|
| moon    | Cancer                    | Capricorn                |
| Mercury | Gemini and Virgo*         | Sagittarius and Pisces   |
| Venus   | Taurus* and Libra         | Scorpio and Aries        |
| sun     | Leo                       | Aquarius                 |
| Mars    | Aries and Scorpio*        | Libra and Taurus         |
| Jupiter | Pisces and Sagittarius*   | Virgo and Gemini         |
| Saturn  | Capricorn and Aquarius*   | Cancer and Leo.          |

If Saturn, say, is in Capricorn, authors will often refer to its being 'in its mansion'. The use of the singular here does not imply a supposition that Saturn has only one mansion—such a phrase is shorthand for 'one of its mansions'.

We can see the reciprocity in this distribution: Mercury's mansions are Jupiter's detriments, and vice versa; Venus's mansions are Mars's detriments, and vice versa; while Saturn exchanges with the sun and the moon. Astrology is full of such orderliness, some of it having an attractive ingenuity.

The sign marked above with an asterisk is the appropriate planet's *gaudium*, the one in which it particularly rejoices.

For being in its mansion a planet receives five 'dignities' or 'fortitudes' (plus points); for being in its detriment it receives five 'debilities' (minus points).

## 1 Aspect (Definition of)

It will be seen that there is some sophistication in the distribution of mansions, when it is realized that it also accommodates the aspects of the planets.

*Aspect* is angular separation (in celestial longitude) of one body from another—latitude not being taken into account. Except for conjunction, they are measured in multiples of 30°:

| | |
|---|---|
| opposition | 180° |
| trine | 120° |
| square (quartile) | 90° |
| sestile (sextile) | 60° |
| conjunction | 0°. |

Opposition and square are malign aspects, and Saturn and Mars are malevolent planets; trine and sestile are benign aspects, and

Jupiter and Venus are benign planets. Mercury, the sun, and the moon, are neutral, though some say Mercury is 'common' —good with good and bad with bad.

In the diagram of the mansions we can see that Saturn is in opposition to the sun on one side (from Aquarius) and in opposition to the moon from the other (from Capricorn). Mars, on the other hand, is square to the sun from Scorpio and square to the moon from Aries. So much for bad with bad. Jupiter, on the other hand, is trine to the sun from Sagittarius and trine to the moon from Pisces; while Venus is sestile to the sun from Libra and sestile to the moon from Taurus. This is all rather ingenious—it means that the greater aspects (opposition and trine) are occupied by the 'major infortune' (Saturn) and the 'major fortune' (Jupiter), while the lesser aspects (square and sestile) are occupied by the 'lesser infortune' (Mars) and the 'lesser fortune' (Venus).

It should be carefully noted, here, that this model is static and schematic—as an astrologer would say, it is 'essential'. Aspects, however, were commonly read in an 'accidental' sense, i.e. the actual angular separations in particular configurations were what really mattered.

In some contexts, when one planet is described as being able to 'see' another, or to 'view' it, the implication will be that they are in a set aspectual relation with each other. In a standard representation, one with the planets distributed round the zodiacal circle, it may appear that all the planets can 'see' each other. But in some uses of the word, it seems to be implied that the aspects provided a sort of tunnel or sight-line along which one planet would regard another.

Given that the ecliptic is a circle, it is not surprising that aspects were read in both directions. If the moon was in Aries, then Mars would be sestile to it in either Gemini or Aquarius, square to it in either Cancer or Capricorn, and trine to it in either Leo or Sagittarius. It would not 'see' the moon, however, in Taurus, Virgo, Scorpio, or Pisces: in Taurus and Pisces it would be only 30° away, and in Virgo and Sagittarius it would be 150° away, neither of which were generally recognized aspects.

## 2 *Antiscions*

Antiscions are pairs of degrees in the zodiac which are at an equal distance from the first points of Cancer or Capricorn. Thus: Gemini 20, being 10° distant from the beginning of Cancer, 'casts its antiscion' to Cancer 10; while Aquarius 10, being 40° past the beginning of Capricorn, casts its antiscion to Scorpio 20, which lies 40° away from the beginning of Capricorn (see Fig. 8).

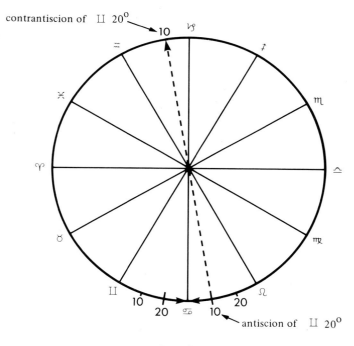

contrantiscion of Ⅱ 20°

antiscion of Ⅱ 20°

FIG. 8

The doctrinal point here is that a planet imparts its influence to any other planet that is in its antiscion—or, indeed, to any planet that is in aspect with its antiscion. This may seem to us already like the more remote imaginings of the subject; but we must not be too hasty—there were also such things as *contrantiscions*. Our sense of the schematization of the subject, however, would lead us to guess, correctly, that a contrantiscion is merely the degree lying diametrically opposite an antiscion (Fig. 8). We could also guess, correctly, that to lie in an antiscion was benign, to lie in a contrantiscion was malign.

Already we sense a peculiar kind of tension: the geometry is mundane, but its possible ramifications seem to be innumerable. They seem to give the astrologer an infinite amount of room to manœuvre. The responsible astrologer could not say just whatever he felt like, but he was able to say almost anything and still stay within the intricate confines of his pseudo-discipline.

## II. 14  Essential Dignities: Exaltation (opposed by Fall)

Next in importance to a planet's lying in one of its mansions comes its being located in its *exaltation*. This is, properly speaking, a specific degree of a given sign, in which the planet is accorded an access of power. Many authors, however, are content if the planet simply lies within the sign in which its exaltation occurs; while the opposite point, the *fall*, even more generally embraces the whole sign. The allocation is as follows:

|          | Exaltation:   | Fall (Depression): |
|----------|---------------|--------------------|
| moon     | Taurus 3      | Scorpio            |
| Mercury  | Virgo 15      | Pisces             |
| Venus    | Pisces 27     | Virgo              |
| sun      | Aries 19      | Libra              |
| Mars     | Capricorn 28  | Cancer             |
| Jupiter  | Cancer 15     | Capricorn          |
| Saturn   | Libra 21      | Aries              |

| Dragon's Head | Gemini 3       |
|---------------|----------------|
| Dragon's Tail | Sagittarius 3  |

The Dragon's Head and Tail could readily be thought of as having each other's exaltation for their fall, but the handbooks do not, in my experience, adopt this expedient.

Only Mercury has its exaltation in a sign that is also one of its mansions. From which it follows, of course, that no other planet can properly be said to be in both simultaneously.

Ptolemy (*Tetrabiblos*, I. 19) explains the allocation of exaltations as follows: Aries is given to the sun because when in that sign his power of warming the earth begins to increase. Saturn is placed opposite the sun, as was the case with his solar mansion. Jupiter, whom Ptolemy calls bringer of north winds, reaches his furthest point of travel north in Cancer (as do all the others!), while Mars becomes most fiery when furthest south, and so is allocated Capricorn. Venus, who is moist, increases her power in Pisces, which begins the moist Spring. While Mercury is drier and so has an autumn sign. Finally, the moon, says Ptolemy, when new in the sun's exaltation, Aries, will begin her first phase in Taurus, the first sign of her triplicity (II. 15), and so is given Taurus.

By comparison with the schematic elegance which accompanied the allocation of mansions, these justifications look lame indeed. There is a falling-off of ingenuity here, and Ptolemy's arguments are, to my knowledge, seldom reproduced.

For being in its exaltation a planet receives four plus points; for being in its fall it receives four minus points.

## II. 15 Essential Dignities: Triplicity

The circle of the zodiac is divided into four 'triplicities' sometimes called 'trigons', each of them having properties drawn from the theory of elements and of humours. They are ruled as indicated:

the Aries Triangle (fiery, choleric)

| Aries | |
|---|---|
| Leo | sun by day |
| Sagittarius | Jupiter by night |

the Taurus Triangle (earthy, melancholic)

| Taurus | |
|---|---|
| Virgo | Venus by day |
| Capricorn | moon by night |

the Gemini Triangle (airy, sanguine)

| Gemini | |
|---|---|
| Libra | Saturn by day |
| Aquarius | Mercury by night |

the Cancer Triangle (watery, phlegmatic)

Cancer  
Scorpio  } Mars by day and night  
Pisces  

By being in its triplicity a planet acquires three plus points.

## 1  The Natures of the Planets

The planets are considered to have a 'complexion' that imparts to the individual his 'temperament'. The characteristics were as follows:

| | | |
|---|---|---|
| Saturn | Cold and Dry | (melancholic) |
| Jupiter | Hot and Moist | (sanguine) |
| Mars | Hot and Dry | (choleric) |
| sun | Hot and Dry | (choleric) |
| Venus | Cold and Moist | (phlegmatic) |
| Mercury | common | |
| moon | Cold and Moist | (phlegmatic) |

Mercury was considered to take on the properties of the body most strongly influencing him. Thus he is 'drying' when with the sun and 'humidifying' when with the moon.

The only point at which the nature of the planet is matched by the nature of the triplicity it governs is where the sun rules the Aries triangle. The remaining planets are out of kilter: the melancholic Saturn, for instance, governs the sanguine Gemini triangle, while the choleric Mars governs the phlegmatic Cancer triangle.

Ptolemy (*Tetrabiblos*, I. 18) explains the allocation of planets as rulers in terms of the mansions included in each triangle and the sex of the signs. The Aries triangle, for instance, includes the mansions of Mars, the sun, and Jupiter; but only two planets are required—one for day and one for night. Mars cedes to the other two. The Taurus triangle was easier to rationalize, since Taurus, Virgo, and Capricorn are all 'feminine' (even-numbered) signs, and there are only two female planets. The Gemini triangle contains three 'masculine' signs, of which Gemini is Mercury's mansion, Libra is Venus's mansion, and Aquarius is Saturn's mansion. Venus, however, has already been accommodated in the Taurus triangle. The Cancer triangle is the most untidy—it consists of feminine signs and contains the mansions of the moon, Mars, and Jupiter. But Mars has so far failed to stake a claim, and so the entire government passes to him.

## II. 16 Essential Dignities: Terms and Faces

*Terms* are uneven divisions of the zodiacal signs, none being accorded either to the sun or to the moon. There are two main systems, the 'Ptolemaic' and the 'Egyptian' (a third, the 'Chaldean', was largely ignored by later writers).

Ptolemaic Terms (*Tetrabiblos*, I. 21):

|        | I     | II      | III     | IV      | V       |
|--------|-------|---------|---------|---------|---------|
| Aries  | 1–6J  | 7–14V   | 15–21Me | 22–26Ma | 27–30S  |
| Taurus | 1–8V  | 9–15Me  | 16–22J  | 23–24S  | 25–30Ma |
| Gemini | 1–7Me | 8–13J   | 14–20V  | 21–26Ma | 27–30S  |
| Cancer | 1–6Ma | 7–13J   | 14–20Me | 21–27V  | 28–30S  |
| Leo    | 1–6J  | 7–13Me  | 14–19S  | 20–25V  | 26–30Ma |
| Virgo  | 1–7Me | 8–13V   | 14–18J  | 19–24S  | 25–30Ma |
| Libra  | 1–6S  | 7–11V   | 12–16Me | 17–24J  | 25–30Ma |
| Scorpio| 1–6Ma | 7–13V   | 14–21J  | 22–27Me | 28–30S  |
| Sagittarius | 1–8J | 9–14V | 15–19Me | 20–25S | 26–30Ma |
| Capricorn | 1–6V | 7–12Me | 13–19J  | 20–25S  | 26–30Ma |
| Aquarius | 1–6S | 7–12Me | 13–20V  | 21–25J  | 26–30Ma |
| Pisces | 1–8V  | 9–14J   | 15–20Me | 21–25Ma | 26–30S  |

Egyptian Terms (*Tetrabiblos*, I. 20)

|        | I      | II      | III     | IV      | V       |
|--------|--------|---------|---------|---------|---------|
| Aries  | 1–6J   | 7–12V   | 13–20Me | 21–25Ma | 26–30S  |
| Taurus | 1–8V   | 9–14Me  | 15–22J  | 23–27S  | 28–30Ma |
| Gemini | 1–6Me  | 7–12J   | 13–17V  | 18–24Ma | 25–30S  |
| Cancer | 1–7Me  | 8–13V   | 14–19Me | 20–26J  | 27–30S  |
| Leo    | 1–6J   | 7–11Me  | 12–18S  | 19–24V  | 25–30S  |
| Virgo  | 1–7Me  | 8–17V   | 18–21J  | 22–28Ma | 29–30S  |
| Libra  | 1–6S   | 7–14Me  | 15–21J  | 22–28V  | 29–30Ma |
| Scorpio| 1–7Ma  | 8–11V   | 12–19Me | 20–24J  | 25–30S  |
| Sagittarius | 1–12J | 13–17V | 18–21Me | 22–26S | 27–30Ma |
| Capricorn | 1–7Me | 8–14J  | 15–22V  | 23–26S  | 27–30Ma |
| Aquarius | 1–7Me | 8–13V  | 14–20J  | 21–25Ma | 26–30S  |
| Pisces | 1–12V  | 13–16J  | 17–19Me | 20–28Ma | 29–30S  |

Some historians of astrology (e.g. North, p. 264) assert that the Egyptian system was the one most commonly employed in the

Middle Ages and the Renaissance. But only one handbook (Searle's) of the six consulted here for their tables of terms uses that system. All the others (Lilly, Middleton, Partridge, Blagrave, and Ball) use the Ptolemaic system. There are some minor differences, of course, as one would expect with different lines of transmission and different printing houses, but there is no doubt of its being the Ptolemaic system. It is true that Haly (Pt. I, cap. 5) says 'few use Ptolemy's terms'; but by the end of the sixteenth century in England, this was no longer the case.

As if this were not a sufficient complication, the planets were also accorded *faces*, another mode of dividing up the zodiac among the planets. This system, however, is simpler in its organization: merely divide each of the signs into three equal sections and distribute the planets in Ptolemaic order:

|             | 1–10°   | 11–20°  | 21–30°  |
|-------------|---------|---------|---------|
| Aries       | Mars    | Sun     | Venus   |
| Taurus      | Mercury | Moon/   | Saturn  |
| Gemini      | Jupiter | Mars    | Sun     |
| Cancer      | Venus   | Mercury | Moon/   |
| Leo         | Saturn  | Jupiter | Mars    |
| Virgo       | Sun     | Venus   | Mercury |
| Libra       | Moon/   | Saturn  | Jupiter |
| Scorpio     | Mars    | Sun     | Venus   |
| Sagittarius | Mercury | Moon/   | Saturn  |
| Capricorn   | Jupiter | Mars    | Sun     |
| Aquarius    | Venus   | Mercury | Moon/   |
| Pisces      | Saturn  | Jupiter | Mars    |

The theorist's problem here is how to determine the point of entry into the loop. There are seven planets and thirty-six divisions—one planet must get an extra turn. One sees it is Mars, who both begins and ends the sequence, when it is set out (as it traditionally was) according to the order of signs. One can at least say that Aries is Mars's mansion (II. 13), so that it is reasonable to accord him the first section of Aries; but whether there are other subtleties is open to debate.

A planet acquires two plus points for being located in one of its terms, and one plus point for being located in one of its faces.

## 1 Reception

This condition occurs when two planets exchange with each other any one (strictly, the same one) of their essential dignities. Reception is therefore possible by mansion, exaltation, triplicity, term, or face. It counts, with some authorities, for as much as the dignity itself.

> It is occasionally uncertain whether reception is thought of as being strictly reciprocal, or whether it is sufficient for one planet to be located in the dignity of another. Venus in Leo, for example, might be described as being 'received' into the sun's mansion, without its being clear whether the sun was also located in either Taurus or Libra. It seems likely that strict reciprocity was not always insisted upon.

## 2 Further Division of the Ecliptic: Signs

Just as the planets had their individual natures, so the signs of the zodiac were invested with a variety of characteristics in addition to those they possessed as members of triplicities (II. 15) or as grouped by seasons (I. 13). There were, of course, some variations, both in the grouping and in the values assigned. But there was substantial agreement, not only because the doctrinal foundations of the subject were fixed (and few would be so bold as to rewrite them), but also because many a handbook was simply a compilation from its predecessors.

The chief modes of division were as follows:

### (a) Masculine/Feminine Signs

The masculine are the alternate signs commencing with Aries; the feminine are the alternate signs commencing with Taurus:

| masculine | feminine |
|---|---|
| Aries | Taurus |
| Gemini | Cancer |
| Leo | Virgo |
| Libra | Scorpio |
| Sagittarius | Capricorn |
| Aquarius | Pisces |

Here the mania for order takes over, it is particularly the signs on the 'feminine' side that suffer—the femaleness of the Bull and the Goat, for instance, were never reflected in the iconography of the constellations.

(b) *Northern/Southern Signs*
This division was more rational: the northern signs are simply those in which the sun lies when north of the celestial equator: they are also known as 'boreal' (Latin: 'Boreas', the north wind) or as 'septentrional', the seven (*septem*) stars of the Bear being so famous as to make their name equivalent to 'northern'.

(c) *Movable, fixed, and common signs*
The movable signs were the 'cardinal' ones: Aries, Cancer, Libra, Capricorn. The 'fixed' were those that followed in each quadrant: Taurus, Leo, Scorpio, and Aquarius. The 'common' are the remainder: Gemini, Virgo, Sagittarius, and Pisces.

> Lilly (p. 88) is typical in his rationalizing of this division. The 'movable' signs, he says, are those in which the sun lies when the seasons change. If a child is born in a movable sign, though, it is a token (simultaneously) that it will be fickle.

(d) *Signs commanding or obeying*
The signs which 'command' are the northern signs; those which 'obey' are the southern signs—a fine example of northern hemisphere discrimination.

(e) *Signs of long or short ascension*
The signs of long ascension are those between Cancer and Sagittarius, the point being that these signs rise more steeply (more 'directly') over the horizon. Since their angle to the horizon is greater, they must take longer to rise. The signs of short ascension are those between Capricorn and Gemini. Their angle to the horizon is more shallow, and so they rise more rapidly (more 'obliquely').

> Virgo and Libra are the most direct of the signs; Pisces and Aries are the most oblique. The length of time each sign occupies in rising may easily be determined by consulting a Table of Houses: take the interval in 'Time from Noon' answering to the beginning and to the end of a given sign's transit through the 1st house.

## 3 *Further Division of the Ecliptic: Degrees*

Not only the signs, but the very degrees of a sign were invested with properties. Some of them, indeed, had more than one. At this level (one of very fine detail, we would think) two systems were employed: one under which every degree of the zodiac had one or another characteristic; and the other, under which only a certain number of the degrees were singled out.

### (a) *Degrees masculine and feminine*

When the 'testimonies' of the signs or the houses were equal —for instance, if both Mars and Venus were in the house of children, the 5th, one might look to see whether the degree on the cusp of the 5th was masculine or feminine.

The distribution was as follows:

|  | masculine | feminine |
|---|---|---|
| Aries | 1–8, 10–15, 23–30 | 9, 16–22 |
| Taurus | 6–11, 18–21, 25–30 | 1–5, 12–17, 22–4 |
| Gemini | 6–16, 23–6 | 1–5, 17–22, 27–30 |
| Cancer | 1–2, 9–10, 13–23, 28–30 | 3–8, 11–12, 24–7 |
| Leo | 1–5, 9–15, 24–30 | 6–8, 16–23 |
| Virgo | 9–12, 21–30 | 1–8, 13–20 |
| Libra | 1–5, 16–20, 28–30 | 6–15, 21–7 |
| Scorpio | 1–4, 15–17, 26–30 | 5–14, 18–25 |
| Sagittarius | 1–12, 25–30 | 13–24 |
| Capricorn | 1–11, 20–30 | 12–19 |
| Aquarius | 1–5, 16–21, 26–7 | 6–15, 22–5, 28–30 |
| Pisces | 1–10, 21–3, 29–30 | 11–20, 24–8. |

### (b) *Degrees dark, light, void, and smoky*

These had chiefly to do with a person's colouring, 'smoky' being intermediate between dark and light; 'void', however, is an interloper, in that it applies rather to the intelligence. The distribution was as follows:

|  | dark | light | void | smoky |
|---|---|---|---|---|
| Aries | 1–3, 9–16 | 4–8, 17–20, 25–9 | 21–4, 30 |  |
| Taurus | 1–3, 29–30 | 4–7, 13–15, 21–8 | 8–12, 16–20 |  |

72  *Astrology*

|         | dark              | light                | void            | smoky   |
|---------|-------------------|----------------------|-----------------|---------|
| Gemini  | 5-7, 23-7         | 1-4, 8-12, 17-22     | 13-16, 28-30    |         |
| Cancer  | 13-14             | 1-12, 21-8           | 15-18, 29-30    | 19-20   |
| Leo     | 1-10              | 26-30                | 21-5            | 11-20   |
| Virgo   | 1-5, 28-30        | 6-8, 11-16           | 9-10, 23-7      | 17-22   |
| Libra   | 6-10, 19-21       | 1-5, 11-18, 22-7     | 28-30           |         |
| Scor.   | 1-3, 30           | 4-8, 15-22           | 9-14, 25-9      | 23-4    |
| Sagitt. | 10-12             | 1-9, 13-19, 24-30    |                 | 20-3    |
| Cap.    | 1-5, 20-2, 26-30  | 6-10, 16-19          | 23-5            | 11-15   |
| Aquar.  | 9-13              | 5-8, 14-21, 26-30    | 22-5            | 1-4     |
| Pisces  | 1-5, 13-18, 29-30 | 6-12, 19-22, 26-8    | 23-5            |         |

(c) *Degrees pitted, lame, or increasing fortune*

'Pitted' degrees showed that the matter stood in doubt, since a *'puteus'* is a well or pit. These degrees, as Lilly says (p. 118), show that the querent is 'as a man cast into a Ditch'. The implication is that they relate more to judicial astrology than to nativities.

'Lame' degrees are those showing that some party in the affair (the thief?, the prospective husband?) is maimed in some way. Or alternatively, if the inquirer is maimed, the astrologer may conclude that one of these degrees was in the ascendant at the inquirer's birth.

Degrees 'increasing fortune' (in a somewhat miserly fashion) were considered only as they related to the 2nd house, or to the lord of that house, or to the position occupied by *pars fortunae*. In defence of this limitation we may note that the 2nd house was conventionally the house of riches.

Whereas all degrees were either male or female, only certain of the degrees had the effects indicated below—and some degrees were allowed two qualities at once.

| | pitted | lame | increasing fortune |
|---|---|---|---|
| Aries | 6, 11, 16, 23, 29; | | 19; |
| Taurus | 5, 12, 24-5; | 6-10; | 3, 15, 27; |
| Gemini | 2, 12, 17, 26, 30; | | 11; |
| Cancer | 12, 17, 23, 26, 30; | 9-15 | 1-4, 15; |
| Leo | 6, 13, 15, 22-3, 28; | 18, 27, 28; | 2, 5, 7, 19; |
| Virgo | 8, 13, 16, 21-2; | | 3, 14, 20; |
| Libra | 1, 7, 20, 30; | | 3, 15, 21; |
| Scorpio | 9-10, 22-3, 27; | 19, 28; | 7, 18, 20; |
| Sagittarius | 7, 12, 15, 24, 27, 30; | 1, 7, 18-19; | 13, 20; |
| Capricorn | 7, 17, 22, 24, 29; | 26-9; | 12-14, 20; |
| Aquarius | 1, 12, 17, 22, 24, 29; | 18-19; | 7, 16-17, 20; |
| Pisces | 4, 9, 24, 27-8; | | 13, 20. |

*4 Further Division of the Ecliptic: The Manilian System*

A system preserved by the poet Manilius (*Astronomicon*, II. 433-52) matches the twelve Olympian deities with the signs of the zodiac, making them 'guardians' of the signs as follows:

| | |
|---|---|
| Aries | Pallas |
| Taurus | Venus |
| Gemini | Apollo |
| Cancer | Mercury |
| Leo | Jupiter |
| Virgo | Ceres |
| Libra | Vulcan |
| Scorpio | Mars |
| Sagittarius | Diana |
| Capricorn | Vesta |
| Aquarius | Juno |
| Pisces | Neptune |

This system was far less commonly employed than its Ptolemaic counterpart.

## II. 17 Accidental Dignities: the Houses

The astrological houses have their own hierarchy. The primary four are:

1 4 7 10    the angles (or, cardins)

followed by:

2  5  8  11    the succedents

and

3  6  9  12    the cadents.

It is worth noting here that the earth's daily rotation takes a planet
directly from a given angle to its neighbouring cadent (say, from the
1st, straight to the 12th). Anomalously, the planet does not first
pass through a 'succedent' house.

The allocation of dignities to a planet for being in a particular
house takes account of the greater importance of the ascendant and the midheaven over the other two angles:

for a planet in    1 or 10 there are 5 dignities
                   4 or  7          4 dignities
               2, 5, or 11          3 dignities
                        9           2 dignities
                        3           1 dignity.

We notice here that the 8th among the succedents and the
6th and 12th among the cadents are missing. This is because
in fact they have a minus value:

for a planet in       12 there are 5 debilities
               8 or  6             3 debilities.

## 1 Properties of Houses

Why this demotion should have taken place will be understood
if we look at the areas of life which the houses were considered to govern:

1 Life
2 Riches
3 Brothers, Sisters
4 Father
5 Children
*6 Sickness
7 Wife (and Open Enemies)
*8 Death

9 Voyages, Religion
10 Trade, Honours
11 Friends
*12 Enemies, Prison.

We might think that (in this secular listing) death would be the worst of the fates. By convention, though, it is the 12th house that is regarded as the worst.

### 2 Special Names of Houses

1 Horoscope
2 Inferna Porta (Hell's Gates)
3 Dea (Goddess)
4 Imum Coelum (Bottom of the Heaven)
5 Bona Fortuna (Good Fortune)
6 Mala Fortuna (Ill Fortune)
7 Occidens (the West)
8 Mors (Death)
9 Deus (God)
10 Medium Coelum (Midheaven)
11 Bonus Genius (Good Spirit)
12 Malus Genius (Evil Spirit)

### 3 Consignificators and Dispositors

Although it is important to keep the distinction between signs and houses in mind, there was a system of pairing the two together with the planets. The planets and the signs were said, in this system, to be 'consignificators' with the houses, whereas the planet whose mansion ('proper sign') lay on the cusp of a given house was said to be the 'dispositor' of that house.

These, we can see, are more minor forms of ownership. They are the equivalent, in the 'accidental' configuration of the houses, to the owning of signs as mansions. The convention is extremely useful to the astrologer, however. If he finds Cancer on the cusp of the 9th house (voyages), then he can argue that the moon, whose mansion Cancer is, has something to say in the matter of the voyage in question.

It will be convenient to tabulate the relationships:

| house | sign | planet |
|---|---|---|
| 1st (life) | Aries | Saturn |
| 2nd (riches) | Taurus | Jupiter |
| 3rd (siblings) | Gemini | Mars |
| 4th (father) | Cancer | sun |
| 5th (children) | Leo | Venus |
| 6th (sickness) | Virgo | Mercury |
| 7th (enemies) | Libra | moon |
| 8th (death) | Scorpio | Saturn |
| 9th (voyages) | Sagittarius | Jupiter |
| 10th (trade) | Capricorn | Mars |
| 11th (friends) | Aquarius | sun |
| 12th (prison) | Pisces | Venus |

It will be observed that the initial posit of this scheme is merely to match the first house with the first sign and the outermost planet. The consequences are considerably less elegant than those thrown up by the distribution employed for the mansions (II. 13). The scheme allows the moon only one house (the 7th), but allows the sun two houses (the 4th and the 11th) and deprives Mercury of a second house. There is little appropriateness, either, in the matching of planets and houses. The 6th (sickness) happens to be paired with Mercury (doctors), the 8th (death) with Saturn (Father Time); but only the love-sick poet would find much appropriateness in the pairing of Venus with the 12th (prison). The 9th (Jupiter–voyages) and the 10th (Mars–trade) are also poor matches. Perhaps for these reasons the system was little used.

## II. 18 Accidental Dignities: Aspect Evaluated

Recognizing dignities and debilities, and identifying dispositors were operations important to the astrologer in his word-spinning, but there is no doubt that the dramatic element for the customer (as today) was how the planets stood in relation to each other on the circle of the zodiac. You need only be told that Saturn is opposing Venus in your horoscope to feel some degree of gloom.

It is plain that a logic of a kind governs the operations of astrology, but it will not be surprising to find that there were circumstances in which its counsels failed. Take a hybrid case: what if there is a benign aspect between the two malevolent planets? Which element should be taken to be the overriding one—the evil nature of the planets or the benign nature of their aspect? Since their natures are 'essential' and their aspects are 'accidental', one might expect their natures to override.

The handbooks tend to side-step the issue, at least as regards its finer details. Haly does lay down one rule of thumb (Pt. I, cap. 6): 'the trine or sestile aspect of the infortunes does not bring advantage (*non prodest*), just as the quartile aspect or opposition of the fortunes does not bring impediment (*non obstat*)', from which one can see that aspect does not overrule nature when the natures are akin. But there is no rule of thumb for more complicated cases (though one would have thought the astrologer would have treasured precisely this kind of extension to his arbitrary system). Few handbooks determine what would be the consequences of finding that Venus (the minor fortune) was in trine (the larger of the benign aspects) with Mars (the minor infortune). The sheer 'logic' of the system, one would think, should have dictated, not the *non prodest* of Haly's judgement, but a positive dominance to Venus.

Perhaps this dereliction at a theoretical level may be explained by its consequences at a practical one. In a given horoscope there is a host of items to be taken into account: and their 'testimonies' (we might say, 'messages), when they were weighed up, would tend to make it unlikely that further reference would be required to such subtle points of doctrine.

## 1 Sinister and Dexter

Aspects were read in both directions: those cast from west to east (as the astrologer says, by ascending order of signs) were called 'sinister' (left-handed) aspects; those cast from east to west (against the order of the signs) were called 'dexter' (right-handed).

We can see the orientation of the model in which these terms make sense. In the northern hemisphere, face south, so that the east horizon is on your left, the west horizon on your right. If Aries rises, the succession of signs will put Taurus to the *left* of Aries and Pisces to the *right*. In this context 'sinister' has no dire implication.

## 2  *Aspect by Sign, not by House*

Aspects are reckoned from sign to sign, *not* from house to house. In other words the position of a planet in the 1st house and of another in the 4th would not necessarily mean that they were in square, since this interval between houses could well be embracing considerably more than three signs (90°). Indeed, in some circumstances a planet in the 1st could be in trine with (120° away from) a planet in the 4th —only three houses distant, but four signs away.

## 3  *Partile and Platic Aspect*

Strict convention required the angular relations of the planets, their aspects, to be read in multiples of 30°. And one might have thought that with seven planets and five kinds of aspect (three of them readable in either direction) the possibilities of permutation were sufficient. But consider: the actual chances of the distance between any two planets being precisely 60°, or precisely 90°, at any given instant are not strong, and the astrologer was obliged to accommodate given instants of time. It is not surprising, therefore, that he sought to increase the flexibility of his system.

When the longitudinal distance of one planet from another was exactly 0°, 60°, 90°, 120°, or 180°, then the two were in 'partile' aspect; but when the planets concerned were not yet, or no longer exactly, in partile aspect, they could none the less (within certain specified limits) be in 'platic' aspect.

The word *'partilis'* means 'divisible' (i.e. evenly by 30°), whereas the Latin *'platicus'* derives from the Greek word meaning 'broad'.

## 4  *Orbs*

To bring this system into operation, each planet was assigned a 'halo' of specific diameter and platic aspect lasted from the time when these haloes first came into contact until they ceased contact. The values given to 'orbs' varied: those widely adopted in the Renaissance were:

| Saturn | 10° |
|---------|------|
| Jupiter | 12° |
| Mars | 7½° |
| sun | 17° |
| Venus | 8° |
| Mercury | 7° |
| moon | 12½° |

Earlier authorities give different values. For example, the 'radii sive orbes' listed by Haly (Pt. I, cap. 6) are:

| Saturn | 9° |
|---------|------|
| Jupiter | 9° |
| Mars | 8° |
| sun | 15° |
| Venus | 7° |
| Mercury | 7° |
| moon | 12°. |

Bonatus (sig. f6ᵛ ff.) gives the same values as Haly, and indicates that the 'radii' (rays) are to be read 'ante & retro' (backwards and forwards). Notwithstanding this, the values given were *diameters* as the worked examples make plain.

For the purposes of calculating whether or not a platic aspect was in operation, simple arithmetic was employed. The aspect continues while the two planets concerned remain within the range of half the sum of their orbs. An example will demonstrate the thinking. Let us suppose that Venus (the faster moving of the two) is approaching a situation in which she will adopt an exact sestile aspect with Saturn, in other words is 'applying to a sestile' with Saturn, after which she will be 'separating from a sestile' with him.

The scheme would appear as follows:

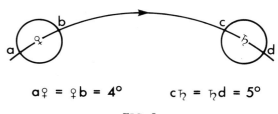

$a♀ = ♀b = 4°$     $c♄ = ♄d = 5°$

FIG. 9

When *bc* equals 60°, the platic phase begins and the planets will be 69° apart. Then they pass through partile (exact) aspect, and when thereafter *ad* equals 60°, the platic aspect ends and the planets will be 51° apart.

## II. 19  Accidental Dignities: Oriental and Occidental

A planet's position to the east or west of the sun when visible (irrespective of the aspect involved) was taken into account by the astrologer in its own right. The conceptual principles were these:

### 1 Superior Planet

A *superior planet* (Saturn, Jupiter, Mars) is oriental when it rises before the sun. This condition applies between the time when the (faster-moving) sun is in conjunction with it and the time when the sun is in opposition to it. For being in this condition a superior planet receives two plus points. The converses apply: to be 'occidental' (to rise after the sun), and therefore to lie between opposition and conjunction, attracts two minus points.

### 2 Inferior Planet

The *inferior planets* (Venus and Mercury) are occidental when they rise after the sun (Venus is then Hesperus, the evening star). For this condition they receive two plus points and the converses apply: if their longitudes are less than the sun's (Venus is then Lucifer, the morning star), they receive two minus points.

### 3 The Moon

The *moon* is occidental when between new and full; she is then waxing, or 'increasing in light'. She then receives two plus points, and the converses apply: if between full and new (passing through her last quarter and 'decreasing in light'), she receives two minus points.

### 4 An Illustration

In order to feel confident about one's ability to say which planet is in which situation at any particular time, one needs to be able to reproduce for oneself the diagram that the particular occasion demands. An example may assist here: for example, place the sun at Aries 0 and Saturn at Sagittarius 24. Is Saturn oriental or occidental? Since the sun moves so much faster than Saturn, it is the sun's future motion that we take into account. And since Saturn's nadir (the opposite point to the one he now occupies and the point close to where the sun will come into opposition with him) is Gemini 24 and lies *ahead* of the sun at Aries 0, we can see that Saturn lies in the phase between conjunction and opposition, and is therefore oriental.

## II. 20 Accidental Conditions: Application

The considerations we have examined so far have all been related to the planets as they stand, momentarily frozen, at the time for which the horoscope is cast. This way of looking at the situation, however, is far from exhausting the astrologer's talents. So far he has pronounced only on what that frozen sky indicates. But anxious parents would wish to know what it was that the planets promised in time to come.

In order to answer questions of this kind he devised ways of bringing their continuing motion into his reckoning. One of these he called 'application'.

It works in three ways. One planet is 'applying' to another (1) when, in a given configuration, both are direct in motion (i.e. increasing in longitude), and one is about to overtake the other; (2) when both planets concerned are retrograde and about to meet; (3) when one is direct and the other retrograde, and they are about to meet.

Since retrogression is itself considered to be bad, conditions 2 and 3 must be malign.

## II. 21 Accidental Conditions: Separation

This is the condition under which one planet leaves a particular configuration with another. It is said (e.g. by Lilly, p. 110) to begin when the two are 6′ distant from each other after (partile) conjunction, and it continues while they are still in platic conjunction.

## II. 22 Application and Separation by Aspect

By natural consequence the concepts of application and separation, which relied initially for their operation on physical proximity between the planets, were extended so as to operate through planetary aspect. The astrologer could therefore talk about Venus 'applying to a sestile' with Mars, or of the moon 'separating from a square' with Jupiter. By this means he found another way of massively extending the permutations open to him.

By the very nature of the operations of application and separation, only a planet with a faster motion than its orbitally superior neighbour could make application to it. Here again, though, is an astronomical fact that can be given metaphoric extension: 'application' is sometimes equated with a subject's approaching his lord and master.

## II. 23 Additional Aspects

In 1647 Lilly (p. 32; cf. p. 512) indicated that 'one Kepler, a learned man', had devised a sophistication that allowed the aspects to come into force at intervals of other than 30 degrees.

Lilly was not a hack: it is curious that he refers to Kepler in such distant terms seventeen years after his death.

Kepler's reworking of the system more than doubled the number of aspects, and if these innovations had been allowed to operate not only as partile, but also as platic aspects, there would hardly have been a position left in the circle of the zodiac in which one aspect or other did not operate. Kepler introduced the following angular relations:

30° semisextile (half of sestile)
36° semiquintile (half of 72°)
45° semiquadrate (half of square)
72° quintile (five to a circle)
108° sesquiquintile (one and half times 72°)
135° sesquiquadrate (one and a half times square)
144° biquintile (twice 72°)
150° quincunx (five times 30).

One can see why traditional astrologers did not accept this sophistication. There is some elegance in it (as will appear below), but to an orthodox and conservative astrologer the quincunx, for instance, would translate as 'five times half a sestile'. Kepler's successors were either unimpressed or left behind; and the innovation, while not wholly neglected in the nineteenth and twentieth centuries, was not enthusiastically received in the seventeenth.

It is worth noting what the skeleton of Kepler's system was. If one takes its axis to be 90°, then it has a precise symmetry:

| | 0° | |
|---|---|---|
| +30 | | 30 |
| +6 | | 36 |
| +9 | | 45 |
| [+15 | | 60] |
| +12 | | 72 |
| [+18 | | 90] |
| | 90° | |
| — | | — |
| +18 | | 108 |
| [+12 | | 120] |
| +15 | | 135 |
| +9 | | 144 |
| +6 | | 150 |
| [+30 | | 180] |
| | 180° | |

## II. 24 Other Conditions of Planetary Motion

*Prohibition* occurs when, as a result of its faster motion, a third planet intercepts (either 'bodily' or by aspect) the relation that two others were about to take up.

*Refrenation* occurs when an imminent relation between two planets is frustrated by the beginning of retrograde motion in one of them.

*Void of Course* is a condition in which a planet, having separated from another in a given sign, does not, while in that sign, take on another aspect with another planet.

*Frustration* is a more narrow version of prohibition, in which a swifter planet is about to join with a slower one, but before the relation is established, the slower one joins instead with another.

*Haiz* occurs when a masculine planet is above the horizon during the day and is also in a masculine sign; or when a feminine planet is below the horizon at night and in a feminine sign.

*Beseiged.* A planet is so when flanked by the two malevolent planets, they all being in the same sign.

*Elevated.* One planet is said to be elevated above another in a variety of ways. It may be (i) at a greater latitude, (ii) further above the horizon, (iii) exerting a greater influence in a particular configuration. The pole, on the other hand, is 'elevated' above the appropriate horizon by the number of degrees that corresponds to the latitude of the place (I. 11).

*Swift of course.* This is the condition in which a planet is moving faster than its mean daily motion (I. 20. 2). It is regarded as propitious.

*Peregrine.* The condition of a planet when in a degree which affords it no essential dignities.

## II. 25  Relations with the Sun: combust, under the sun's beams, *in cazimi*

We have already seen (II. 18. 4) that the diameter of the sun's orb extends for $17°$ (or in some authors, for $15°$). A planet is 'combust' when within half the sun's orb. Lilly (p. 113) and Ball (p. 51) appear to specify, further, that the two should be in the same sign; but this is not insisted upon by others. Lilly says: 'A Planet is said to be *Combust* when being in the same sign where the sun is in, he is not distant from the sun eight degrees and thirty minutes, either before or after the sun.' But this limitation is probably adopted merely for the sake of making the calculation in his example easier to follow. It is to be doubted that if the sun was at Aries 28 and Mars at Taurus 5, for instance, that Mars would not then be combust.

Until elongated from the sun by twice the radius of the sun's orb a planet is 'under the sun's beams', which is a debility; but when only $17'$ away from the sun it is 'in cazimi', and this is a dignity.

## II. 26 Summary

(a) *Dignities (fortitudes)*

|                                                         | plus value |
|---------------------------------------------------------|------------|
| in mansion, or reception by mansion                     | 5          |
| in exaltation, or reception by exaltation               | 4          |
| in triplicity, or reception by triplicity               | 3          |
| in term                                                 | 2          |
| in face                                                 | 1          |
| in 10th or 1st house                                    | 5          |
| in 11th, or 7th, or 4th                                 | 4          |
| in 5th, or 2nd                                          | 3          |
| in 9th                                                  | 2          |
| in 3rd                                                  | 1          |
| in conjunction with Jupiter or Venus                    | 5          |
| the Dragon's Head                                       | 4          |
| Regulus (in Leo)                                        | 6          |
| Spica (in Virgo)                                        | 5          |
| in trine with Jupiter or Venus                          | 4          |
| in sestile with Jupiter or Venus                        | 3          |
| direct in motion (excludes sun and moon)                | 4          |
| outer planet oriental                                   | 2          |
| inner planet occidental                                 | 2          |
| moon occidental (waxing)                                | 2          |
| separating from Jupiter or Venus:                       |            |
| by conjunction                                          | 5          |
| by trine                                                | 4          |
| by sestile                                              | 3          |
| applying to Jupiter or Venus:                           |            |
| by trine                                                | 4          |
| by sestile                                              | 3          |
| not combust                                             | 5          |
| in cazimi                                               | 5          |

(b) *Debilities:*

|                                        | minus value |
|----------------------------------------|-------------|
| in detriment                           | 5           |
| in fall                                | 4           |
| peregrine (no essential dignities)     | 5           |
| in 12th house                          | 5           |
| in 8th or 6th                          | 3           |

|                                   | minus value |
|-----------------------------------|:-:|
| in conjunction with Saturn or Mars | 4 |
| in opposition to Saturn or Mars   | 5 |
| in conjunction with:              |   |
| Caput Algol                       | 5 |
| Dragon's Tail                     | 4 |
| in square with Saturn or Mars     | 4 |
| retrograde                        | 5 |
| outer planet occidental           | 2 |
| inner planet oriental             | 2 |
| moon oriental (waning)            | 2 |
| separating from Saturn or Mars    | 5 |
| applying to Saturn or Mars        | 5 |
| combust                           | 5 |
| under the sun's beams             | 4 |

We notice that the majority of the dignities have an answering debility, giving the two tables a balance. To be retrograde, though, has more negative value than being direct in motion has positive value; and the effect of relation with the sun changes dramatically: to be 17° away (under the sun's beams) is bad, to be 8½° away (combust) is worse; but to be only 17′ away (in cazimi) is good. Having no essential dignities at all (to be peregrine) is also heavily penalized.

## II. 27  A Worked Example

Now that the main heads under which an astrologer would begin analysing a horoscope have been outlined, we may apply their principles to Burton's nativity (Fig. 6), using a tabular form.

The table sets out, in the horizontal axis, the planets in descending Ptolemaic order. In the vertical axis are the essential and accidental dignities, followed by the essential and accidental debilities. Since Burton has Saturn in Capricorn, one of its mansions, we record five plus points at this place of intersection—and so on:

|           | Saturn | Jupiter | Mars | sun | Venus | Mercury | moon |   |
|-----------|:-:|:-:|:-:|:-:|:-:|:-:|:-:|:-:|
| Mansion   | 5 |  | 5 |  |  |  |  | 5 |
| Exaltation |  |  |  |  |  |  |  | 4 |
| Triplicity |  |  |  |  |  | (3) |  | 3 |
| Term      |  |  |  |  |  |  |  | 2 |
| Face      |  |  |  |  |  |  |  | 1 |

| in Houses: | Saturn | Jupiter | Mars | sun | Venus | Mercury | moon |
|---|---|---|---|---|---|---|---|
| 1 or 10 | 5 |  | 5 |  |  |  | 5 |
| 4 or 7 |  |  |  |  | 4 |  | 4 |
| 2, 5, or 11 |  |  |  |  |  |  | 3 |
| 9 |  |  |  |  |  |  | 2 |
| 3 |  |  |  |  |  |  | 1 |
| Direct | 2 |  |  |  | 2 | 2 | 2 |
| Ven./Mer. occidental |  |  |  |  | 2 | (2) | 2 |
| Sat./Jup./Mars oriental | 2 | 2 |  |  |  |  | 2 |
| Moon waxing |  |  |  |  |  |  | 2 |
| in Cazimi |  |  |  |  |  |  | 5 |
| conjunct with Jup./Ven. |  |  |  |  |  |  | 5 |
| conjunct with Dragon's Head |  |  |  |  |  |  | 4 |
| sest./trine with Jup./Ven. | 4 |  |  |  |  | 3 | 3/4 |
| plus points: | 18 | 2 | 10 | 0 | 4 | 2 | 7 |

| | Saturn | Jupiter | Mars | sun | Venus | Mercury | moon |
|---|---|---|---|---|---|---|---|
| Detriment |  | −5 |  | −5 | −5 | (−5) | −5 |
| Fall |  |  |  |  |  | (−4) | −4 |
| Peregrine |  | −5 |  | −5 | −5 | −5 | −5 |
| in 12th |  |  |  | −5 |  | −5 | −5 |
| in 8 or 6 |  | −3 |  |  |  |  | −3 |
| Retrograde |  | −5 |  |  |  |  | −5 |
| Ven./Mer. oriental |  |  |  |  |  | −2 | −2 |
| Sat./Jup./Mars occidental |  |  | −2 |  |  |  | −2 |
| moon waning |  |  |  |  |  | −2 | −2 |
| combust |  |  |  |  | −5 |  | −5 |
| conjunct with Sat./Mars |  |  |  |  | −5 |  | −5 |
| conjunct with Dragon's Tail |  |  |  |  |  |  | −4 |
| opp./square to Sat./Mars |  |  |  |  |  |  | −4 |
| minus points: | 0 | −18 | −2 | −15 | −15 | −26 | −11 |
| balance: | 18 | −16 | 8 | −15 | −11 | −24 | −4 |

The most startling thing about this result is the massive dominance of Saturn over the author of *The Anatomy of Melancholy*. Saturn leads by ten points, while Jupiter, the sun, Venus, and Mercury make a dismal showing. Mercury's score, on the other hand—which may at first appear to have been inconsistently tallied here—is materially affected by its having been placed by Burton in Pisces. Had it been positioned in Aquarius (which is where it was), it would have scored minus 10, not minus 24.

All this labour is only the beginning, however: it is now our task to pursue the analysis in the direction of its more technical procedures. With the figure erected and the preliminary assessment of dignity and debility complete, the astrologer can proceed at last to his conclusions. He will wish to determine the general characteristics of the native—his manners, his length of life; and if he has been given no more than an approximate time of birth, he will wish to 'rectify' the figure in order to obtain a more precise time. He will also (rather late in the piece, one would have thought) wish to determine whether the figure can properly be consulted at all.

## THE HIGHER REACHES

### II. 28 Lord of the Geniture (Almuten)

Which planet governs the horoscope overall is established by adding up the dignities and debilities, as we have just done. In Burton's case it is very plainly Saturn, as he himself observed in 'Democritus to the Reader': '*Saturn* was Lord of my geniture, culminating &c . . .'

> 'Culminating' (alternatively, 'southing') means 'lying on the meridian', as Saturn is doing to within less than a degree and a quarter. If we remember the five-degree rule (II. 4. 2), we will accept Burton's statement all the more readily.

If he chose, the astrologer could now reach for his handbook, to find out what Saturn in Capricorn bodes for the native. Middleton's comments are representative. Saturn in Capricorn represents: 'one of a middle Stature, not very tall, a lean

The Higher Reaches 89

spare person, long Visage, little Eyes, sad brown or black Hair, a duskish Complexion; he is covetous of worldly goods, a melancholy person using but few words; he is peevish, and will retain anger a long time'. (p. 33.) No competent astrologer, though, would commit himself to the description of a person on the evidence of one planet in one sign—the scheme has to be examined overall.

Chaucer's characters, however, have suffered at the hands of literary critics in just this way. Such generalizing statements as Middleton's have been presented as the sum of what astrology would have to say about the make-up of an individual. All too often their 'horoscopes' are not properly such at all; they are merely schematizations based on the little evidence available. All that can legitimately be inferred about the Wife of Bath, for instance, is that she had Mars in Taurus and in the ascendant. This, of course, is sufficient for Chaucer's purpose, but not sufficient for an entire character profile.

It will be plain that a respectable handbook of astrology would contain eighty-four character profiles such as the one we have just quoted from Middleton—one for each of the seven planets in each of the twelve signs. What title, then, do we have to dismiss these as of no account to a conscientious astrologer? The answer is that they are very much in the way of preliminaries, and they tell us something about the psychology of the subject. If the thumb-nail sketch proves right in all its details and suggestions, there is no impulse to look further. If, on the other hand, it is plainly contradicted by the facts, there are two alternatives—dismiss the operation as a fraud, or delve more deeply. And the inclination to dismiss is not going to be strong in those who dabble in astrology—their need to be satisfied may even be sharpened by an initial failure.

The point, then, is that for Burton the position of Saturn in his horoscope undeniably makes that planet Lord of his Geniture—but what of the remarkable weakness of all the other planets? They too must have some bearing, even if it looks gloomily negative. On the question of the native's 'manners' (personality), the astrologer will turn to another place and to another primary influence in the scheme.

## II. 29  Lord of the Ascendant

The planet that controls the ascendant is given the function of being the 'Significator of Manners'. In Burton's case the ascendant is defined by Aries, which automatically creates Mars Lord of the ascendant.

The *OED* (s.v. 'Ascendant', B.I. 1) suggests that the Lord must actually be physically present in the 1st house. A moment's reflection, though, will show that this cannot be the case. There are twelve signs, but only seven planets. For a great part of the time, therefore, the first house will not be occupied by a planet. This, however, does not mean that there will be no lord of the ascendant at such times; on the contrary, the lordship is determined merely by establishing whose mansion it is that is rising. If Cancer is rising, then the moon will automatically be Lady of the ascendant.

In Burton's case it happens, not only that Aries is rising, but also that Mars is physically (the astrologers say 'bodily') present in that house. This, of course, will reinforce his title. Burton comments on this particular in 'Democritus to the Reader: '*Saturn* was Lord of my geniture . . . and *Mars* principal *significator* of manners, in partile conjunction with mine *Ascendant*; both fortunate in their houses, &c'.

Mars was indeed 'partile' (II. 18. 3) to within a degree, and our table of his dignities and debilities shows that both planets were indeed 'fortunate' (i.e. dignified) both in their houses and in their signs. This raises the question whether Burton, by 'houses' really means 'signs'—a common and tiresome confusion. On balance I would argue that he does mean 'sign' by house. To one who recognises that 'culminating' relates to the 10th house and that the 'Ascendant' is of course the first house, it will be *self-evident* that Saturn and Mars are fortunate in their astrological houses. But it will not be self-evident that both planets were also well disposed as to their zodiacal signs: 'both fortunate . . .', then, may be read as additional information relating to the signs, rather than as tautological confirmation of what has been said about the astrological houses.

Predictably, when Mars is 'well dignified', as he is in Burton's case, (he is the only other planet with a plus score!) he produces 'Generous men, valiant, full of courage, irefull, fierce, violent' (Lilly, p. 535).

## 1 Lord of the House (Dispositor)

The Lord of a given house will be whichever planet it is whose sign lies on the cusp of the house—i.e. the principle relating to the lord of the ascendant is extended to the other houses.

This being the case, the lord of the house is not in fact its 'Consignificator' (II. 17. 3). The systems of distribution are such that only Mercury (in relation to Virgo) and Jupiter (in relation to Sagittarius) could simultaneously be both Lord of the House and its Consignificator. And this condition could, even then, only come about when Virgo lay on the cusp of the 6th in the one case, or Sagittarius lay on the cusp of the 9th in the other.

The lordship of a house is of particular concern in judicial astrology. If the querent (the one who does the asking and the paying) comes with the question, 'Will I get riches?', it will have a material influence on the answer if in the horoscope drawn up for this occasion it is found, for instance, that Mercury is dispositor of the 2nd house. There will then be a match between the god of merchants and the house of riches.

## II. 30 Lord of Life (Hyleg)

Besides determining the native's general characteristics and his manners, the astrologer may be required to say how long he will live. In this area patience and perseverance are required —not to speak of a clear head.

The procedure eventually leads to a simple numerical calculation. There is a set of rules to determine the order in which the inspection is conducted—if one planet fails to satisfy the constraints imposed, pass on to another. A further complication is that if the actual positions of the planets in the horoscope will not yield up answers, the astrologer may proceed by looking at the state of the heavens before the time of birth.

The rules are complex (and give one the feeling of being endless), but the essential outline is all we need for an understanding of the principles.

Lilly (pp. 527–8), for instance, declares that the place occupied by the sun should be hyleg if the geniture is diurnal, and that occupied by the moon should be hyleg if the geniture is nocturnal—provided that they are above the horizon and do not lie in either the 8th (death) or the 12th (prison). If these conditions are not satisfied, examine the period leading up to the birth. If the geniture is diurnal, look to find where the sun was in the zodiac at the time of the new moon next before the birth. Then determine (by the dignities/debilities table) which planet, if any, has three essential dignities in that degree. This planet (if there is one) will be hyleg.

If on the other hand the geniture was nocturnal, look elsewhere, and at three other elements: where the moon was at the time of the birth, where *pars fortunae* lies in the horoscope, and where the sun was at the full moon next before the birth. Now determine which planet has most essential dignity in the combination of all these three places. The initial constraints still apply—if the planet that survives this ordeal is in any but houses 7, 9, 10, or 11, it will still not qualify. In the last resort, revert to the degree ascending—i.e. make the ascendant hyleg.

## 1 An Example

The reader will, perhaps, be relieved to learn that this is about as complex as our subject will become. With perseverance, though, the principle can be mastered. Let us see how it applies to Burton.

In his nativity, which is diurnal, the sun is in the 12th house, and so cannot be hyleg, at least at this stage. This failure requires us to look at the preceding new moon. At the time of its occurrence the sun, we find, was at Aquarius 9 (Goldstine, p. 215, under 19 January 1577). This degree now has to be classified, according to the dignities it allocates. It is

> *in Saturn's mansion
> nobody's exaltation
> *in Saturn's triplicity by day
> in Mercury's terms
> in Venus's face.

Here we see that no planet (though Saturn came close) has

three essential dignities in this degree. We must therefore revert to the ascendant to determine hyleg.

We may note here that it is not a question of finding a planet that will score three plus points, since Saturn would have scored 5 merely for having Aquarius as its mansion. Instead, the planet must own at least three of the five essential dignities—a considerable constraint.

## II. 31 The Giver of Years (Alchocoden)

Having found where the hyleg is, we may now proceed to compute the native's life expectancy. The initial rule is that the planet which (a) has most essential dignity (singular, not plural) in the place of hyleg and which (b) bears some aspect to that place is constituted alchocoden.

In Burton's case the hyleg (the ascendant) is Aries 28. This degree is:

> In Mars's mansion (5 points)
> *in the sign of the sun's exaltation (4 points)
> *in the sun's triplicity by day (3 points)
> in Saturn's terms (2 points)
> *in the sun's face (1 point)

The sun, then, has a strong title here. But we must be on our guard. Mars scores 5 points, and the sun scores 8—but it is Mars that is also in the strongest aspect with the hyleg, in fact being effectively in conjunction with it. So it is Mars who becomes alchocoden.

We pass to the next step, which is to make the numerical calculation that will tell us how long the native will live. This will partly depend on whether, as alchocoden, the given planet occupies an angle, a succedent, or a cadent (II. 17). If in an angle, it contributes its 'greater' years; if in a succedent, it contributes its 'mean' years; if in a cadent, it contributes its 'lesser' years.

Bonatus (sig. c5ᵛ) indicates that the greater years of the planets are determined by the number of degrees a planet has as its terms on Ptolemy's reckoning (II. 16); that the lesser years are determined by various factors—revolution period, period of epicycle, etc.; and that the mean years are half the sum of the greater and the lesser. These last are often rounded down.

The allocations are as follows:

|        | greater | mean | lesser |
|--------|---------|------|--------|
| Saturn | 57      | 43.5 | 30     |
| Jupiter| 79      | 45.5 | 12     |
| Mars   | 66      | 40.5 | 15     |
| sun    | 120     | 69.5 | 19     |
| Venus  | 82      | 45   | 8      |
| Mercury| 76      | 48   | 20     |
| moon   | 108     | 66.5 | 25     |

Now, in Burton's case, Mars is in an angle: he therefore yields his greater years: 66. This is not the end of it, however, since the alchocoden may itself be aspected. If it is, then further adjustment is necessary—on the following principles:

|          | sestile/trine | square/opposition |
|----------|---------------|-------------------|
| Saturn   | no effect     | − lesser          |
| Mars     |               |                   |
| Jupiter  | + lesser      | + lesser          |
| Venus    |               |                   |
| sun      |               |                   |
| Mercury  | + lesser      | − lesser          |
| moon     |               |                   |

The aspects to Mars in Burton's figure (both of them platic) are a sestile from Mercury and a sestile from the sun. On this account it will follow that the sun and Mercury also contribute their lesser years to the computation: 66 (Mars's greater) plus 20 (Mercury's lesser) plus 19 (sun's lesser) = 105 years—a ripe old age.

## II. 32  Hyleg: an Alternative Method

Lilly's, the method of determining hyleg which we outlined earlier, was not the only one. If, therefore, one encounters an instance in which the conclusions arrived at appear to be odd, one should check to see whether the alternative mode yields the required result.

According to this variant method, either the sun or moon may be hyleg either by day or by night—provided always they lie in certain specified houses (some of them being constrained as to gender). Thus the sun may be hyleg in houses:

> 1 10 11, or in 7 9 (if its cusp is male), in daytime births
> 4 5 7, or in 1 2 (if its cusp is male), in night births;

the moon may be hyleg in houses:

> 1 2 3 7, or in 4 5 10 11 (if its cusp is female), in night births
> 1 2 3, or in 4 5 10 (if its cusp is female), in daytime births.

If the sun or the moon do not qualify, look to the previous new or full moon, whichever was more recent. If it was a new moon, take the sun's place; if it was a full moon, take the moon's place. If the degree selected falls either in an angle or a succedent in your figure, then that is hyleg. If all else fails, take the ascendant as it stands.

In Burton's case, the full moon was the more recent (3 Feb. 1577) and the moon's longitude was Leo 24° 18'. This falls (narrowly) into a cadent—the 6th house—and so takes us back again to the ascendant.

## II. 33 Rectifying a Figure, and Rules before Judgement

The authorities have it that a figure is fit to be judged when it is 'radical'. It is so when the Lord of the Planetary Hour and the Lord of the Ascendant are:

> in the same triplicity (II. 15), or
> one and the same, or
> of the same nature (II. 15. 1).

### 1 Lord of the Planetary Hour

A planetary, or 'unequal', hour is one twelfth of the time between sunrise and sunset in the case of day hours, or one twelfth of the time between sunset and sunrise in the case of night hours.

These 'hours' are assigned to the planets on the following principle: take the planets in descending Ptolemaic order and let them govern successive hours by rotation. If we begin with the first hour of Sunday, we obtain the following pattern.

| Saturn | 5 | | | | 23 | | |
|---|---|---|---|---|---|---|---|
| Jupiter | 6 | | | | 24 | | |
| Mars | 7 | | | | 1 | 8 | ... |
| sun | 1 | 8 | 15 | 22 | | | |
| Venus | 2 | | | | 23 | | |
| Mercury | 3 | | | | 24 | | |
| moon | 4 | | | | 1 | 8 | 15 | 22 |

Thus, if the sun governs hour one of day one, by strict rotation the moon will govern hour one of day two, Mars will govern hour one of day three, and so on. The hours of the entire week can therefore be expressed in a more compact table:

| | Day | | | | | | | Night | | | | | | |
|---|---|---|---|---|---|---|---|---|---|---|---|---|---|---|
| | Su | Mo | Tu | We | Th | Fr | Sa | Su | Mo | Tu | We | Th | Fr | Sa |
| sun | 1 | 12 | 9 | 0 | 10 | 0 | 11 | 3 | 0 | 11 | 1 | 12 | 2 | 0 |
| Ven. | 2 | 0 | 10 | 0 | 11 | 1 | 12 | 4 | 1 | 12 | 2 | 0 | 3 | 0 |
| Mer. | 3 | 0 | 11 | 1 | 12 | 2 | 0 | 5 | 2 | 0 | 3 | 0 | 4 | 1 |
| moon | 4 | 1 | 12 | 2 | 0 | 3 | 0 | 6 | 3 | 0 | 4 | 1 | 5 | 2 |
| Sat. | 5 | 2 | 0 | 3 | 0 | 4 | 1 | 7 | 4 | 1 | 5 | 2 | 6 | 3 |
| Jup. | 6 | 3 | 0 | 4 | 1 | 5 | 2 | 8 | 5 | 2 | 6 | 3 | 7 | 4 |
| Mars | 7 | 4 | 1 | 5 | 2 | 6 | 3 | 9 | 6 | 3 | 7 | 4 | 8 | 5 |
| sun | 8 | 5 | 2 | 6 | 3 | 7 | 4 | 10 | 7 | 4 | 8 | 5 | 9 | 6 |
| Ven. | 9 | 6 | 3 | 7 | 4 | 8 | 5 | 11 | 8 | 5 | 9 | 6 | 10 | 7 |
| Mer. | 10 | 7 | 4 | 8 | 5 | 9 | 6 | 12 | 9 | 6 | 10 | 7 | 11 | 8 |
| moon | 11 | 8 | 5 | 9 | 6 | 10 | 7 | 0 | 10 | 7 | 11 | 8 | 12 | 9 |
| Sat. | 12 | 9 | 6 | 10 | 7 | 11 | 8 | 0 | 11 | 8 | 12 | 9 | 0 | 10 |
| Jup. | 0 | 10 | 7 | 11 | 8 | 12 | 9 | 1 | 12 | 9 | 0 | 10 | 0 | 11 |
| Mars | 0 | 11 | 8 | 12 | 9 | 0 | 10 | 2 | 0 | 10 | 0 | 11 | 1 | 12 |

From this table it emerges, for example, that the 5th planetary hour of day on a Friday is governed by Jupiter.

In order to find Burton's Lord of the planetary hour we need to know, first, what day of the week 8 February 1577 was, and, second, to know the interval between sunrise and sunset on that day.

To establish the day of the week we may discover its Julian Day number (I. 28). It is 2,297,096, which, divided by 7, leaves 4, i.e. a Friday. We can also say that with the sun at

Aquarius 28° 46' (at lat. 52° 20' and with an obliquity of 23° 28' 30") the day will be 9 hrs. 52 mins. long.

See Mathematical Formulas 2-3 for the procedure.

This in turn tells us that sunrise was at 7.04 a.m., the 2nd planetary hour began at 7.53 a.m., . . . and the 4th began at 9.32 a.m. Burton's birth at 8.44 thus falls in the 3rd planetary hour of day on a Friday—which we find is governed by the moon. We may note here that even if Burton had stayed with 9 a.m. and not corrected it by 'Animodar' (next section), his birth would still have fallen in the 3rd hour, which ended at 9.31 a.m.

We now recall the requirements for determining whether a figure is 'radical', and consider Mars in Aries (as Lord of the Ascendant) and the moon in Scorpio (as Lord of the Planetary Hour). They are not

> located in the same triplicity (II. 15)
> not one and the same
> not of the same nature (II. 15. 1).

On this count, then, the horoscope, in strict terms is 'not fit to be judged'. We note, though, how late in the piece such a conclusion surfaces—the astrologer has to do a great deal of work before he can see this to be the case. We note, too, that the odds in favour of any one of this set of criteria being met are not very high—a great many horoscopes would turn out not to be radical. This suggests that the constraint was rather in the nature of an escape route for the astrologer, should he require one.

## 2 Animodar

What if the astrologer is not given a precise time of birth? How does he then 'rectify' the nativity? The process, deriving in broad terms from Ptolemy, is known as 'animodar', and has features similar to those employed in the discovery of the hyleg.

Proceed as follows: determine an approximate time of birth and observe whether it was a new moon or a full moon that occurred the more recently. If it was a *full* moon, select either the sun or the moon, depending on which was then visible. If it was a *new* moon, select the moon.

Now take the celestial longitude of the sun or the moon (as appropriate) at that time, and see which of the planets has most essential dignity at that longitude. Having identified that planet, enter the horoscope and find its longitude there. Finally, transfer its longitude in the horoscope either to the ascendant or to the meridian, depending on which is numerically the closer. With either the meridian or the ascendant thus newly defined, a 'precise' time of birth can be calculated.

If we thought it would be extreme to impose this procedure on Burton's horoscope, then we would be in for a surprise, since this is exactly what he did do. Various hints in the diagram suggest it, and even if they did not, the centre square carries the annotation: 'Correct. ex . . . Animodar'.

Let us trace Burton's steps, then. As we have seen (II. 32), the full moon was the event that occurred the closer to his birth. When it took place, at 4.16 a.m. on 3 February, it was (obviously) the moon that was visible. It was then at Leo 24. This degree is:

*in the sun's mansion
in no one's exaltation
in Jupiter's triplicity by night
in Venus's terms
in Mars's face.

The sun therefore has most essential dignity, his longitude in the figure is Aquarius 28° 46′, and this is why Aries 28° 46′ appears in the ascendant.

Elsewhere in the Diary, Burton notes (in Latin) that his birth took place 'about nine in the morning'. This would have placed Taurus 5, or so, in the ascendant, had the horoscope not been 'corrected'.

Armed with this new value Burton calculated and recorded what the oblique ascension of the ascendant was—'12.5'. This made the right ascension of the meridian '282.5'. The sun's right ascension, however, was 330° 55′—an interval of 48° 50′ from the meridian. Converted to time, and rounded up, this interval answers to 3 hrs. 16 mins., recorded as 'horis .3. scrup. 16' in the centre of the diagram.

## 3 *The Trutine of Hermes*

Burton indicates that his horoscope has also been 'corrected' by this method. It is a procedure that purports to reveal the period of the infant's gestation, and so is closely connected with the moon.

Observe the moon's position in the horoscope. If she is 'above the earth' (in houses 7–12), take her distance from the cusp of the 7th house. If she is 'below the earth' (in houses 1–6) take her distance from the ascendant.

When you have a value, in signs and degrees, for the moon's distance from the appropriate 'angle', enter the following table. Find the nearest point of agreement, and read off the value in the appropriate column:

| Distance from 1/7 sign/degree | | moon in 7–12 days | moon in 1–6 days |
|---|---|---|---|
| 0 | 00 | 258 | 273 |
| 0 | 12 | 259 | 274 |
| 0 | 24 | 260 | 275 |
| 1 | 06 | 261 | 276 |
| 1 | 18 | 262 | 277 |
| 2 | 00 | 263 | 278 |
| 2 | 12 | 264 | 279 |
| 2 | 24 | 265 | 280 |
| 3 | 06 | 266 | 281 |
| 3 | 18 | 267 | 282 |
| 4 | 00 | 268 | 283 |
| 4 | 12 | 269 | 284 |
| 4 | 24 | 270 | 285 |
| 5 | 06 | 271 | 286 |
| 5 | 18 | 272 | 287 |
| 6 | 00 | 273 | 288 |

The value you obtain tells you, in days, how long the gestation was.

Applying these rules to Burton, we can recover the time at which he will have thought he was conceived (he does not record it in his diagram). It is clear, though, that the table is a pretty crude one, making an even 12° represent one day in the moon's motion, rather than the 13° which was the usual round figure (I. 20. 2).

Inspecting Burton's chart, we discover that the moon is 13° 29′ removed from the cusp of the 7th house. The gestation period was therefore 259 days, one more than the minimum the table allows. Now we have already seen (II. 33. 1) that Burton's day of birth was Julian Day 2,297,096. The day of conception was 259 days earlier, which leads to 25 May 1576.

Further perseverance presents the Shandeian prospect of yielding up a time. At noon on 25 May 1576, the moon was at Taurus 9° 10′ (Tuckerman, p. 806, by interpolation). This is 10° 24′ removed from the degree of the ascendant in the diagram, and since the moon's daily motion at this time was 13° 47′, she must have lain in the degree now occupied by the ascendant in the horoscope some 18 hrs. 07 mins. earlier —at 5.53 p.m. on 24 May 1576.

## LONG-TERM PREDICTION

### II. 34 The Radix

This term can mean, simply, the point of departure in a calculation. Some tables of mean planetary motion, for instance, are headed 'epochae seu radices' and begin with 'epocha Christi' (i.e. AD 1). In astrological contexts, however, 'radix' tends to refer to the original horoscope, in circumstances where certain elements in it are projected forward in order to create new aspects that will forecast events in the native's later life. These elements are the 'hylegiacal places'—i.e. those important in the matter of taking the hyleg (II. 30). The projections take two main forms—the 'art' of *directions* and that of *profections*.

### II. 35 Directions

The parent or the querent will often want to know in some detail when the key events in later life will occur. 'Directions' provide this service. The planets and the five 'hylegiacal places' now take on a role as 'Significators', and are brought into conjunction with other places in the horoscope—even with their own essential or accidental dignities or debilities. This, perhaps, needs some explanation. For instance, let us suppose that Mars happens to be located at 19 Aries in a particular figure; now, 22 Aries happens to be one of the terms of Mars (II. 16). The astrologer may therefore say that in a relatively short time after the birth 'Mars will come to the terms of Mars'. The problem, then, is to say in how long a time after the birth this 'event' will take place: in what sense does Mars 'come' to his terms? The point to be firmly grasped in this context is that the supposed motion has no existence in real time—the system of directions relies upon certain mathematical calculations based solely on the actual configurations in the original horoscope. It will therefore be most convenient to proceed from here by an example based on Burton's nativity.

*1 An Example*

As the Significator let us choose the moon, and as the Promittor let us choose the 8th house. The question to determine is at what time in Burton's life will the moon 'come' (in this artificial sense) to the 8th house, the house of death?

The details of this calculation are given in Mathematical Formulas 9 (Appendix). Here I will say a word about the procedure in general terms. The problem may be expressed as follows: in the given horoscope the plane of the horizon may be notionally rotated, such that it comes to intersect with a given degree of the ecliptic.

When repositioned in this way the horizon is renamed 'the circle of position'. This circle of position is always brought to the longitude of the Significator, and the longitude of the Promittor is then itself brought to the circle of position.

The first question, then, is as follows: when the plane of the horizon is brought to a point where it intersects with Scorpio 12° 15′, with what degree of the celestial equator will it then also intersect? The answer (198° 45′) defines the oblique descension of the moon in this instance.

Keeping the circle of position fixed at the point where it intersected with the Significator, one now notionally rotates the heavens until the longitude of the Promittor (Sagittarius 10° 50′ for the 8th house) comes to intersect with it. The degree of the celestial equator that then also lies on the circle of position (217° 36') gives us the oblique descension of the Promittor.

> They are 'descensions' in the western quadrants and 'ascensions' in the eastern quadrants. When the mid-heaven (which lies between them) is used as Significator, right ascensions are employed.

At last we have an interval—18° 51'. The next step is to convert this interval into time. By Ptolemy's method (so called), one degree comes to stand for one year and one minute of arc to stand for six days. 18° 51' therefore converts to 18 years 306 days.

Now, Burton's birthdate is 8 February 1576/7 (not a leap year). We now have a sum:

$$
\begin{array}{r}
1576 \text{ yrs.} \quad 39 \text{ days} \\
+ \quad 18 \qquad 306 \\
\hline
1594 \text{ yrs.} \quad 345 \text{ days.}
\end{array}
$$

This converts to 11 December 1595.

## II. 36 Profections

These are similar to directions, but make more general predictions, chiefly on a monthly or an annual basis. In *annual* profections, the degree that lay in the ascendant at birth was moved on one whole sign for each year (giving, of course, a twelve-year cycle). In *monthly* profections, on the contrary, one sign was allowed to stand for one month.

In order to predict what fortune people might have in their fourteenth year (then, of course, at the age of 13), if they had Taurus 10 rising in their nativity, one would merely need to set Gemini 10 in the ascendant of the horoscope for that year—and the whole game would be ready to be played again.

## II. 37 Lord of the Year

This office was determined both for individuals and, in more general terms, for nations, cities, etc. It was therefore a popular ingredient in the almanacs. The rules are of a bewildering complexity—even for astrology. Bonatus (sig. F3$^r$), for instance, lists fifty-four separate items to be considered in choosing the lord of the year. For those whom this complexity defeated, the simple procedure was to cast a figure for the exact time of the vernal equinox and read the result like a conventional nativity. Astrology, though, was nothing if not wilfully complicated, and it is almost always dangerous, on the evidence available, to attempt to reconstruct how the lord of the year 'would have' been determined.

Here we may leave the subject, with the sense that it is a game playable *ad infinitum*. There seems to me, indeed, at one extreme, to be a parallel with the paradox of the stream-of-consciousness novel: an individual could spend so much time calculating his marriage, children, honours, fortune, that he left himself no time to acquire any. One need only look at the Diaries of such men of attainment as Philip Henslowe or Elias Ashmole, however, or many a comment in John Aubrey's *Brief Lives*, to see that astrology, if not a consuming passion, was at least a matter of serious engagement in their lives.

# Part III: Literary Texts

## INTRODUCTION

In the analyses that follow I have chosen a number of passages that contain astronomical or astrological reference, usually of some degree of complexity. Sometimes I have two objectives: one is always to explain their language when they venture into what is to us a remote territory; occasionally the other (the old debate about the intentionalist fallacy notwithstanding) is to try and assess the extent to which the reader/audience might have assimilated what was said.

I have divided my examples into three periods—the fourteenth and fifteenth centuries; the sixteenth; and the seventeenth and eighteenth. This division has been made only after considerable hesitation, since I do not wish to imply that there was a conscious or continuous development in the use of astrological allusion in English literature. I see no tradition handed down from one writer to another; indeed, the only 'borrowings' (that word beloved of literary historians) which I have detected are one in which Blind Hary seems (I put it no more strongly) to have taken, and misunderstood, a phrase from Chaucer and one in which Douglas (Prologue to *Aeneid*, Bk. XII) seems to take a hint from the same author's poem, *The Complaint of Mars*.

Instead of a continuity or an inherited tradition in the use of astrological reference, I see a marked change in its application. Astrological allusion in Chaucer, Lydgate, or Skelton is often couched in terms which suggest that both the author and his audience understood the subject. If the mode of presentation was not always serious-minded (as in the case of Chaucer's precocious cockerel, or of his blustering Host), the subject was not itself the preserve of a lunatic fringe. By Massinger's day, on the other hand, the subject was amenable only to satirical treatment, even if the language of the subject was itself not always superficially employed. My two selections from the eighteenth century—Hogarth and Sterne (who takes his own eccentric course)—suggest that by then there could no longer be any serious engagement with the subject.

I am far from wishing to argue that when employing an astrological allusion the author was obliged to 'get it right'. He was, of course, at liberty to employ whatever fictions he chose, and if dabbling in astrology he could employ its terms at any level—from superficial blundering to the highest expertise.

How he presents his allusion, though, will be of interest. Our difficulty is to assess that presentation. Being no longer familiar with the complexities of the subject, how are we to tell whether the author knew it well enough to handle it without mistakes? Our consolation is that the subject is so well established in its essential grammar—one universally agreed upon—that when we know that grammar we can usually construe a text with confidence, or else conclude with confidence that (for whatever reason) it is nonsense.

There are occasions, too, on which what at first appeared to be the straightforward meaning of a passage will have to be taken differently when we see its implications. Bellenden, for example, portrays the constellation Boötes as striving to set 'his visage' in the 'grit Eist'—which we would reasonably take to mean that it was rising due east. When we examine where Boötes rises at Bellenden's Scottish latitude, however, we find his 'visage' rises 40° north of east—was Bellenden simply not aware of this? Or is there another explanation, one we should be prepared to consider before we judge that he was ignorant or careless?

We have some powerful tools at our disposal in checking such assertions as Bellenden's. The most important of them is the principle of simultaneous constraint. If an author places the sun in Aries and the moon in Cancer, and then claims that the moon is full, something must be wrong somewhere —Cancer is only 90° removed from Aries, and the moon cannot be full until 180° removed from the sun.

Those who are expecting Shakespeare to figure large here

will be disappointed. His allusions are almost entirely straight-forward. That 'The fault, dear Brutus, is not in our stars, / But in ourselves that we are underlings' (*Julius Caesar*, I. ii. 138–9), or that 'My father compounded with my mother under the dragon's tail' (*King Lear*, I. ii. 125–6), is not open to the kind of analysis which is our business here. There is nothing in the way of the verifiable or the problematic.

Bracketed references attached to the technical terminology in Part III refer the reader to the appropriate sections of Parts I and II. When no reference is given, the Index of Terms may be used.

It will be helpful, I believe, to begin this section with an example. I choose a passage from Chaucer's *Troilus and Criseyde*:

> The bente moone with hire hornes pale,
> Saturne, and Jove, in Cancro joyned were . . .
> (III. 624–5)

Our first question must be whether this grouping of Saturn, Jupiter, and the moon is astronomical in significance, in the sense that it leads to a date. The significance of such a date (if one can be determined) will have to be determined separately.

We should note, too, that conjunctions of Saturn and Jupiter are necessarily of rare occurrence (they being the two slowest-moving planets), and in astrological terms the conjunction of the 'major infortune' and the 'major fortune' is momentous.

Later writers continued the intense interest of the Arabs in this topic. See, for instance, John Holwell, *Catastrophe Mundi* (London, 1682), which includes a 'Table of the Conjunctions of *Saturn* and *Jupiter*, in each of the Triplicities for *3958* Years before the coming of Christ; and the Table continued from Christ to *1702*'.

Here, then, is an event which in astrological terms is highly charged. In its context, however, the issue is not a *catastrophe mundi*, but a deal of rain:

> The bente moone . . .
> Saturne, and Jove, in Cancro joyned were,
> That swych a reyn from heven gan avale,
> That every maner womman that was there
> Hadde of that smoky reyn a verray feere . . .

Astrologers who dealt with conjunctions of Saturn and Jupiter analysed them in terms of the triplicity (II. 15) in which they fell. A conjunction that fell in either Cancer (as here), Scorpio, or Pisces would have similar effects, since these three signs comprise the 'watery' triplicity. Perhaps, then, there is a connection between the Cancer conjunction and Chaucer's 'smoky reyn'.

Before investigating the datability of the configuration, we must determine precisely what is being said. How much significance, for instance, do we attach to 'hornes pale'? Is the moon here merely given one of her familiar periodic attributes, or does Chaucer mean more precisely that she is close to new? Then, too, we should examine how strictly we should apply the phrase 'in Cancro joyned'. Does this mean 'all lying in the sign Cancer at the same time'? Or does it mean, more narrowly, 'all at the same longitude in Cancer'?

As soon as one begins to ask the questions in these terms one sees that a problem of circularity is involved. If, for instance, we considered that a date in the region of 1385 would be acceptable on grounds other than astronomical ones, and if we found Saturn, Jupiter, and the moon sprawled across Cancer, we would be likely to read 'joyned' in a different sense from the one that would be prompted by finding them all three locked together in the same degree. We must proceed cautiously.

With any configuration such as this, the principle is to begin with the slowest-moving planet as being the one that will satisfy the constraints the least often. The longitude of the sign Cancer is 90°–119°, and in Chaucer's lifetime Saturn came within this segment of the zodiac twice only: once in 1355–7 and again in 1385–6 (see table). On the first occasion Jupiter was a long way from Cancer, whereas on the second occasion there were two periods in which Jupiter also lay within Cancer, and ten times when the moon (moving much faster) encountered them there. If, however, we were to require them all to be located in the *same* degree of longitude, there would be none (you can see, by inspection, that in May 1385 Jupiter was already ahead of Saturn when the latter reached Cancer). Perhaps, then, we should accept those conjunctions that were 'platic' (II. 18. 3, 4). This would mean

| | Saturn | Jupiter | moon | |
|---|---|---|---|---|
| 18 July 1355 | 90.56° | 253.74° | — | (Saturn in; Jupiter out) |
| 26 Aug. 1357 | 120.02° | 325.39° | — | |
| 21 May 1385 | 90.52° | 94.08° | 202.0° | (Saturn in) |
| 10 June | 93.07° | 98.46° | 110.8° | (new moon, in on 8th) |
| 10 July | 96.95° | 105.16° | 143.6° | (old moon, in on 6th) |
| 30 July | 99.36° | 109.52° | 57.1° | (moon in on 2 Aug.) |
| 29 Aug. | 102.36° | 115.46° | 89.4° | (moon in on 30th) |
| 28 Sept. | 104.19° | 120.10° | 121.0° | (Jupiter going out) |
| 27 Dec. | 100.79° | 119.65° | — | (Jupiter back in) |
| 16 Jan. 1386 | 99.24° | 117.02° | 130.3° | (moon in on 13th) |
| 15 Feb. | 97.77° | 113.79° | 163.0° | (moon in on 9th) |
| 7 Mar. | 97.64° | 112.93° | 76.0° | (moon in on 9th) |
| 6 Apr. | 98.80° | 113.99° | 108.2° | (moon in on 5th) |
| 6 May | 101.32° | 117.45° | 139.7° | (moon in on 2nd) |
| 26 May | 103.52° | 120.73° | — | (Jupiter out) |

from Tuckerman, pp. 695–6, 710–11

that provided Saturn and Jupiter were less than 9° distant from each other, they could be regarded as being in conjunction. (I argue in my commentary on *The Complaint of Mars* that Chaucer made use of this astrological convention.) This slackening of the constraints would admit the first two of the occasions on which the moon was also in the right position, but would still exclude the other eight.

What of these two? Considering more closely, we find that the narrative allows us to distinguish. In June 1385, when the moon reached 90° it was new; whereas in July of that year (the other occasion that matches) it was old. One might argue it was 'horned' on both occasions; but in the sequence of the narrative the lines we are considering come at a time when it is 'after soper' (III. 610). This makes it plain that a new moon at sunset (June) is intended, not an old one at sunrise (July).

As North indicates (p. 144), there is a still earlier reference to 'the chaungynge of the moone / Whan lightles is the world a nvyght or tweyne' (III. 549–50).

The evidence, then, points rather distinctly to a precise date —all the more distinctly when we recognize that it had been more than 600 years since the last conjunction of Saturn and Jupiter in Cancer. And though we were rather conveniently at liberty to take 'joyned' in any one of three senses, we can at least say the sense we chose (platic conjunction) is entirely legitimate and was known to Chaucer.

We have a title to demand rigorous, firm, and strongly sequential argument in such cases as this: in particular we should be on the alert to see that such hints as 'hornes' and 'joyned' in this example can be fully and comfortably accommodated. When they can, we may repose some confidence in our findings, the odds against coincidental agreement usually being very considerable.

# Fourteenth and Fifteenth Centuries

*c.* 1385

**III. 1 Geoffrey Chaucer, *The Complaint of Mars* ('The Story'), in *Works*, ed. F. N. Robinson, 2nd edn., London, 1957, pp. 530 ff.**

The narrative section of the *Complaint* is astronomical in structure. There are several stages in it, and it will be convenient to list them briefly in their order:

1. Venus and Mars are in aspect in some unspecified part of the zodiac: 'Thus be they knyt, and regnen as in hevene / Be lokyng moost' (50-1);
2. Mars moves on to Venus's 'nexte paleys' (54);
3. Venus later catches up with Mars: 'she sped her as faste in her weye / Almost in oo day as he dyde in tweye' (69-70);
4. The sun approaches: 'Phebus, that was comen hastely / Within the paleys yates sturdely' (81-2);
5. Venus flees to 'Cilenios tour' (113)
6. Mars dates his misadventure to 12 April (139);
7. Venus is comforted by Mercury, who is in her 'valaunse' (= detriment), she being in his 'paleys' (145).

This scheme is interconnected in so many ways that it does not matter in the least that Chaucer never calls any of the zodiacal signs directly by its name. The most convenient way to begin is with the expressed date. At this epoch 12 April is the date of the sun's entry into Taurus (which explains the 'white boles grete' of line 86). Now, since the date places the sun in Taurus, it simultaneously identifies the sign in item 2 as Taurus, and not Libra (the other possibility); the sign in item 5 as Gemini, not Virgo; and the 'valaunse' in item 7 as Aries, not Scorpio.

With the topography of the zodiac thus established, we may examine in general terms the further constraints that an astronomical date for the poem would have to satisfy:

1. At the beginning of the narrative Venus and Mars are 'kynt . . . / Be lokyng' (50-1). Taken on its own, 'knyt' would suggest conjunction; but 'lokyng' means 'aspect', and given the relative motions of the two planets and their subsequent meeting in Taurus, it would make sense of this preamble, with its 'stevene' (appointment) to meet in Venus's 'nexte paleys', if the aspect was sestile—Mars being in Aries and Venus some way behind him in Aquarius.

> Conjunction is precluded by 'lokying'; square aspect is precluded by being malevolent; and trine aspect by the distance Venus would have to travel to catch Mars up. Our requirement here is merely to satisfy the constraints of the text by a possible configuration.

2. Mars is already in Taurus when Venus and the sun arrive there. It will be easy enough to narrow the options here. Mars will be in Taurus once every two years or so, but the sun will only rarely be simultaneously present there. Furthermore, the configuration Mercury–sun–Venus is only one of six possible configurations that the three of them might have when the sun joins Mars in the Bull.

As a check on the frequency of the occurrence, we may scan the entire fourteenth century without much trouble. We may reduce the possibilities rapidly by selecting only those years in which Mars is in Taurus at the same time as the sun (fifteen occasions); those in which Venus is then ahead of the sun (seven of the fifteen); then those in which Mercury is also behind the sun (five of the seven): 1321, 1323, 1353, 1383, 1385.

Now we proceed more narrowly. On Tuckerman's evidence, 1321 and 1323 would fail to be acceptable years, since Venus then reaches Taurus ahead of Mars; 1383 would fail because Venus is much too close to the sun; and 1385 would fail because Mercury was in Taurus, not Aries, at the critical time; while, finally, 1353 would fail because Venus had moved into Gemini by the time the sun had reached Taurus.

At this point we might want to conclude that we should accept some greater tolerance than modern tables will allow, if only because contemporary ones might have been so much less accurate as to coincide with Chaucer's implied configuration. Other considerations, however, suggest a different tactic: we have not yet acquainted ourselves with all the constraints Chaucer lays down, and they will suggest a different course.

When the sun arrives in Taurus (78 ff.), Mars is in danger of being burnt up, Venus is told to flee, and then flies. Between the bidding and the flight Chaucer tells Mars that

> . . . she that hath thyn herte in governaunce
> Is passed half the stremes of thin yen.
>
> (110-11)

Skeat (*Works*, 2nd edn., I. 498) recognized that 'stremes' here means 'beams', 'rays', and he glossed line 111 by remarking that 'Venus is already half past the distance to which Mars's beams extend'. He found the phrase 'obscure and fanciful'. But it is neither, if we recognize that Chaucer is here alluding to the convention of the planetary 'orbs' (II. 18. 4). The point is that for as long as Mars and Venus were still not separated by more than half the sum of their orbs they were in platic conjunction (II. 18. 3). This time, however, has now come, and the indication that it has is of the utmost importance to an understanding of how the narrative is arranged.

In Chaucer's day the orbs of Mars and of Venus were thought to extend for 8° and 7° respectively (these are diameters). But if Venus was only 4° distant from Mars (Skeat's 'half past the distance . . .') then her halo would still be in contact with his—it would merely be that she, in the middle of her halo, lay on the boundary of his (Fig. 10. 1). Her own 'orb' therefore must also be taken into account.

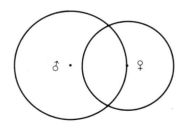

1: Venus bodily
past Mars's orb

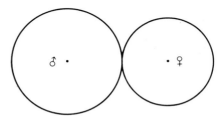

2: Venus's orb
past Mars's orb

FIG. 10

Clearly it is the condition of Fig. 10. 2 that is lamentable
(wel maist thou wepe', 112), since it is at this point that the
contact between them is finally broken.

This consideration becomes of great importance when we
consider the sequence of Chaucer's narrative. He makes it
plain that Venus passes out of contact with Mars *before* she
reaches 'Cilenios tour' (Gemini). He is also particular about
their relative motions and about the sun's behaviour. When
the sun arrives 'Within the paleys yates' of Taurus (82), Mars
is 'amyd the paleys' (79) and Venus embraces Mars in her
distress at the sun's arrival (90). This may be taken to imply
that they are indeed still in 'bodily' conjunction, as the astrologers would say.

Later Chaucer indicates that Mars's speed is only half a
degree a day ('o steyre in dayes two'; 129), and he may even
be indicating that Mars is not retrograde when he says: 'But

nathelesse, for al his hevy armure, / He foloweth her that is
his lyves cure' (130-1). Now, when Venus is ahead of the sun
and still working her way towards maximum elongation, as
here, she will have a slight acceleration on the sun. We can
readily see, then, that Venus will recede from the striken
Mars at a slightly faster rate than the sun will approach him.
We already know, however, that she must be out of contact
with Mars while still in Taurus, since she does not reach the
tower until after she is past 'half the stremes . . .' From this
it follows, that if she must put 7½° (half the sum of their
orbs) between them while still in the same sign, and if she
gains half a degree a day, the closest she can be to the end
of the sign before she commences her flight is fifteen degrees
away. It is no wonder, then, that Chaucer places Venus's
chamber 'amyd' (in the middle of) the palace (sign).

> Those who have argued that the first term (II. 16) of Taurus belongs
> to Venus and that therefore this is the 'chambre' (79), place Mars
> and Venus far too close to the beginning of the sign to give any
> plausibility to the subsequent events of the narrative.

What of the sun in all this? In schematic terms, in the time it
takes Venus to move the 15° from the middle of the sign to
the end, the sun will of course also advance 15° into the sign.
Now, in astrological parlance a planet is 'under the sun's
beams' (II. 25) when its distance from the sun is less than
twice the radius of the sun's orb—in Chaucer's day reckoned
to be 15°.

> The radius of the 'afflicted' planet's orb is not conventionally taken
> into account in this reckoning.

We now see how the pattern works. Mars is in danger ('under
the sun's beams') from the moment the sun arrives; but he is
not actually combust until the time the sun puts only 7½°
between them. And at this very time Venus, moving at the
same rate (or in fact slightly faster), has been able to slip into
Gemini.

We can now see why the sun, despite arriving sturdily, 'On
Venus chambre knokkeden ful lyghte' (84). As with Mars's
tears, an astrological technicality is here given a fine poetic
touch. And there is at least one other: Mars does not want

the sun to 'espye' Venus, which means, in astrological terms, that they must not come into aspect with each other. This is indeed what happens: her journey is made 'With voide cours' (114)—she comes into aspect with no other planet while still in Taurus (II. 24), and it is only when arrived in Gemini that Mercury greets her.

Chaucer's greater familiarity with the subject put him beyond making a plodding count on his fingers. We, on the other hand, by laboriously working out what the text implies, can see that, ultimately, its structure has a disarming simplicity —one visible only when one sees what astrological application the language of the narrative bears. Dates in real time are irrelevant here.

**1390s**

**III. 2 Geoffrey Chaucer, Prologue to *The Canterbury Tales*, 1-2, 7-8 (ed. Robinson, p. 17):**

> Whan that Aprill with his shoures soote
> The droghte of March hath perced to the roote
> . . . and the yonge sonne
> Hath in the Ram his halve cours yronne . . .

In his fine ceremonial opening to the Tales, Chaucer says that when it comes to *this* time of year the pilgrims go to Canterbury. His modern readers can see that April has made inroads upon March—its drought being pierced 'to the roote'—but how much more precisely can the time be narrowed down?

This example at once shows the economy of expression the poet could employ (a paraphrase requires considerable expansion of the lines) and the need for caution (in that some knowledge of the sun's motion is essential, if one is to arrive at the intended date).

We notice that the sun has run 'his halve cours', *not* 'half his course'. Were it the latter, the 'half' would have to be the first half. The inversion is necessary because the half intended is the *second* half. In Chaucer's day the sun entered Taurus (completed his course in Aries) on or about 12 April. From this it follows that on 1 April (having entered Aries on or about 12 March) the sun has 'half a course' in Aries still to run during that month.

Chaucer's allusion is not cast in such a way as to imply a date to the very instant; but it does operate in a way that argues an ability in his audience to see, in general terms, what is implied and to deduce what part of the month it was in which the pilgrimage began.

### III. 3 Geoffrey Chaucer, *The Franklin's Tale*, 1245-9 (ed. Robinson, p. 140):

> Phebus wax old, and hewed lyk laton,
> That in his hoote declynacion
> Shoon as the burned gold with stremes brighte;
> But now in Capricorn adoun he lighte,
> Where as he shoon ful pale, I dar wel seyn.

This is a fine representation of the changes in the sun's appearance from mid-summer to mid-winter. In the latitude of London (52°N) the sun's altitude at noon on mid-summer's day will be 61° 30', and its altitude at noon on mid-winter's day will be a mere 14° 30' (I. 12. 2). Its nearness to the horizon at the winter solstice is indeed likely to give it a coppery colour. (Its 'hoote declynacion' is its declination—northern distance from the equator—in mid-summer.)

Chaucer casts his description in terms that suggest it would be readily understood. Otherwise the circularity in 'laton'-'gold'-'pale', reflecting the periodicity of the seasons, and the connection between 'wax old' and 'now in Capricorn' would simply be lost.

### III. 4 Geoffrey Chaucer, *The Franklin's Tale*, 1273-93 (ed. Robinson, p. 141).

This section, in which the 'subtil clerk' of Orleans begins by producing his Toledo Tables and ends by making the rocks of Brittany disappear, has traditionally been taken to be vexatious, to say the least. I wish to argue differently, and to show that a person with some understanding of the procedures the Clerk employs will find these lines to be orderly and comprehensible.

First for the circumstances: Aurelius has been languishing

for two years, and his brother decides that he will look for some remedy. He remembers that while he was a student at Orleans he saw a book that 'spak muchel of the operaciouns / Touchynge the eighte and twenty mansiouns / That longen to the moone' (1129-31). The memory of the book gives the brother the idea of finding an old friend ('som oold felawe') 'That hadde thise moones mansions in mynde' (1154). By this means the rocks of Brittany might be removed, and his brother thereby achieve the task that would allow him to 'han his love'. The relation of the moon to tides is obvious in this—drowning the rocks for long enough for Aurelius to achieve his aim would answer the demands of the situation, and would be less implausible in the narrative of the Tale than the implication that they had been somehow physically removed.

The man with the requisite knowledge is duly found and brought back to the scene of operations. Chaucer then describes, in a detailed passage, what it is that he does. Our problem is now to follow his operations. The first thing he does is to consult his 'tables Tolletanes'. It is not certain whether Chaucer here means the Tables compiled for Alphonso the Wise or those compiled earlier in Toledo by Arzachel. But even if we knew, we would not be much the wiser, in the sense that there is nothing in the Clerk's operations that requires us to recover figures from astronomical tables. Instead we are concerned with the principles of the operation—or rather with comprehending the language the Franklin uses. As will appear, however, it is the common parlance of medieval astronomy.

The point is easily established. The Clerk's tables provide him with

> . . . his centris and his argumentz
> And his proporcioneles convenientz
> For his equacions in every thyng.
>                                    (1277-9)

Each of these terms may be found in the explanations given by the ABC of planetary motion, the *Theorica Planetarum*.

See, e.g. *A Source Book in Medieval Science*, ed. E. Grant, Cambridge, Mass., 1974, pp. 453-5.

'Centres, arguments, and proportionals', then, would be familiar to anyone with a basic grounding in medieval astronomy. Moreover, there are no such things as 'proporcioneles convenientz' to be found in this theory—they are the invention of commentators relying on the syntax of the passage. Instead, the 'proportionals' are 'convenient for his equations'.

We should now concentrate our attention on the Clerk's procedures in their sequence, the sequence being advertised by the verbs 'know' and 'find'. (The reader is at liberty to check that no distortions result from the compression.) The phases of the operation are indicated by numerals:

(1) His tables Tolletanes forth he brought,
   . . . ne ther lakked nought . . .
For his equacions in every thyng.

(2) And by his eighte speere in his wirkyng
He knew ful wel how fer Alnath was shove
Fro the heed of thilke fixe Aries above . . .
Ful subtilly he kalkuled al this.

(3) Whan he hadde *founde* his firste mansioun,
He *knew* the remenaunt by proporcioun,
*And knew* the arisyng of his moone weel . . .
*And knew* ful weel the moones mansioun . . .
*And knew also* his othere observaunces
For swiche illusiouns . . .

Even if you do not agree entirely with my selection of what portions of the text should be preserved in the compression, you will recognize that the sequence of the verb 'know' is somewhat deliberate here. What we need to discover is whether there is an answering sequence in the argument.

There seems to be no interpretation of this passage that does not rely on Skeats's contention that by finding out where 'Alnath' was, the Clerk was discovering the extent of the precession of the equinoxes.

W. W. Skeat (ed.), Chaucer's *Treatise on the Astrolabe* (EETS ES XVI, London, 1872), p. lx.

But since the extent of precession would merely have told the Clerk what longitude the star Alnath now had, how are we to jump from phase (2) of his operation to phase (3), which tells him about his 'firste mansioun'? The Ellesmere MS points the way—though its pointer has not always been recognized. It notes here that 'Alnath dicitur prima mansio lune'—'Alnath is called the moon's first mansion'. This gloss could mean, among other things, (1) Chaucer makes Alnath the first mansion; (2) Alnath is commonly known as the first mansion. But whichever way it is read, the connection is made. And it is a connection that Chaucer's own syntax reinforces:

> He knew . . . how fer Alnath was shove . . .
> Whan he hadde founde his firste mansioun . . .

It may be added, too, that those commentators who have followed Skeat in supposing the Clerk was involved with determining the extent of precession have never shown *why* its amount is material to the Clerk's operations. As we pursue them, we shall see that it does indeed make sense to regard 'Alnath', not as the star of that name in the constellation Aries, but as the moon's first mansion.

The third phase of the passage describes the Clerk, after he knows the moon's first mansion, (1) as knowing the 'remenaunt'; (2) as knowing the moon's rising; (3) as knowing the moon's mansion; (4) and as also knowing his 'othere observaunces'.

Is there any rationality in this sequence? If we accept that the Ellesmere is right, and that Alnath is here the moon's first mansion, then we can proceed. Systems of determining the mansions of the moon had to cope with the awkwardness that the 28 mansions do not match very readiy with the 360° of a circle. One common expedient was to distribute 7 mansions to each quadrant and to say that 6 times 13 equals 78, plus 12 is 90—one of the seven houses in a quadrant has to be of only 12° in extent; the others can all be of 13°. With the first quadrant established, the remaining quadrants repeat the pattern: if the 2nd house happened to fall at Taurus 20 (50°), the 9th house would fall at Leo 20 (140°), and so on. This is the reason why Chaucer can say that the Clerk knew the remnant (his remaining mansions) 'by proporcioun'—you need only define where it is that you break into the circle (the motive for determining where Alnath is), and the rest follows.

The Clerk could have found from the Toledo tables what the longitude of the moon was at his time of operation ('knew the arisyng of his moone'); from calculating the moon's mansions, he will also know in which one it is located at the present ('knew ful weel the moones mansioun'). This sequence may sound tautologous until we see what it implies. The moon will have a longitude independent of how the mansions are disposed, so the lunar longitude and the longitudes of the mansions have to be determined separately, just as the planetary longitudes and the longitudes of the houses have to be determined separately in the drawing up of a horoscope. The phraseology, in other words, so far from being lame, matches the steps in the procedure.

We come now to the last stage. The final ingredient of the sequence is that the Clerk knew 'his othere observaunces / For swiche illusiouns and swiche meschaunces / As hethen folk useden in thilke dayes'. Here, for the first time, Chaucer is unspecific—and he needs to be. What has preceded has been orderly, everyday, astronomical calculation—the determining of which of its mansions the moon occupies. The conventional astrologer (e.g. Searle) would tell you that if the moon was in its first mansion you may 'Take thy voyage'; with the moon in its third mansion: 'enterprise not navigation'.

No astrologer with paying clients, however, would describe such and such a mansion as 'good to drown rocks'. Here Chaucer—as he is obliged to be—is suitably vague: any contemporary who was moderately acquainted with astrology would know that what he had been told of the Clerk's manipulations was workaday. Dabbling in the Toledo Tables or making rocks disappear and the moon stand still are widely differing occupations. Hence the 'othere [unspecified] observaunces' that the Clerk needs to close the credibility gap.

Chaucer, I feel, had it both ways here. The rank layman would be nonplussed by the jargon. The possible objections of the expert, on the other hand, are forestalled by the mumbo-jumbo implied in the 'othere observances'—employed, moreover, by *'heathens'* *'in those days'*. Chaucer thoroughly distances himself from the end result of the Clerk's manipulations.

**III. 5  Geoffrey Chaucer, *The Knight's Tale*, 2209-369 (ed. Robinson, pp. 38-40:**

2209  The Sonday nyght, er day bigan to sprynge,
Whan Palamon the larke herde synge,
(Although it nere nat day by houres two,
Yet song the larke) and Palamon right tho
With hooly herte and with an heigh corage,
He roos to wenden on his pilgrymage
Unto the blisful Citherea benigne . . .

2271  The thridde houre inequal that Palamon
Bigan to Venus temple for to gon,
Up roos the sonne, and up roos Emelye,
And to the temple of Dyane gan hye . . .

2367  The nexte houre of Mars folwynge this,
Arcite unto the temple walked is
Of fierse Mars, to doon his sacrifise . . .

Earlier in the Tale Theseus has caused three shrines to be built on the tournament ground on which Palamon and Arcite will fight: one to Venus in the East, one to Mars in the West, and one to the moon in the North (1903 ff.). The three principals in the action now make their way to the appropriate shrine at the appropriate planetary hour (II. 33. 1). The pattern may be seen from the following table:

|  |  | planetary hour | event |
|---|---|---|---|
| Sunday night |  |  |  |
|  | 11th: | *Venus* | Palamon rises |
|  | 12th: | Mercury |  |
| Monday morning |  |  | sunrise |
|  | 1st: | *moon* | Emelye rises |
|  | 2nd: | Saturn |  |
|  | 3rd: | Jupiter |  |
|  | 4th: | *Mars* | Arcite rises. |

The scheme is not one that requires great ingenuity or expertise to detect, since its presence is made explicit by the references to 'the thridde houre inequal' and 'the nexte houre of Mars'.

We notice that there is a triple set of correlations at work here:

```
                North
                moon
                Emelye
    West                    East
    Mars                    Venus
    Arcite                  Palamon
                South
                  ?
```

It is plain enough that this scheme is deliberate: its formality and Chaucer's expression declare as much. Indeed, it is achieved at some cost, in the sense that if the planetary hours are converted to clock time (as they easily may be), it appears that Arcite is obliged to rise more than five hours later than Palamon, in order to make his appearance at the appropriate hour. The existence of this express scheme, however, raises an intriguing question in relation to the events of the following day, the day of the tournament itself. The arrival at the tournament ground is highly ceremonious:

> . . . westward, thurgh the gates under Marte,
> Arcite, and eek the hondred of his parte,
> With baner reed is entred . . .
> And in that selve moment Palamon
> Is under Venus, estward in the place.
>                                (2581–5)

It could be argued that 'under Venus' is fully accounted for by the fact that we already know where her temple was built and that Palamon visited it the previous day. But there may be more: it being early in May, it follows (without tedious calculation) that the sun lies somewhere past the middle of Taurus. Rule of thumb demonstrates as much:

| | |
|---|---|
| sun enters Aries | mid-March |
| enters Taurus | mid-April |
| in mid-Taurus | beginning of May. |

It is (explicitly) close to dawn when the company gathers— therefore Taurus will itself be in the ascendant. From this it follows directly that Scorpio must be in the 7th house. Now, there is a very common correlation (one that Chaucer recognized) between the 1st astrological house and the eastern horizon, and between the 7th astrological house and the western horizon. By direct inference, therefore, we can generate a further set of correlations:

| West | East |
|------|------|
| Scorpio | Taurus |
| (Mars's mansion) | (Venus's mansion) |
| 7th house | 1st house |
| Arcite | Palamon |
| Mars's shrine | Venus's shrine |

This much may be concluded by direct inference—by those, at least, who are able to deduce from the May date where the sun will be. The further correlation between north, Cancer, the 4th house, and Emelye, on the other hand, is readily deducible. The relation between Emelye, north, and the moon is already patent, and since the moon's sole mansion is Cancer the scheme would itself require the 4th house (in the north) to be occupied by Cancer. From which it follows, by rote, that the 10th house should be occupied by Capricorn. No special reference to tables of houses is required in this case to establish the configuration, though it may readily be confirmed by consulting Nicholas of Lynn's *Kalendarium* (ed. Eisner, p. 165).

If we allow the tournament to occur at any time within the first week of May—an acceptable margin—then (in Chaucer's day) the sun will lie between Taurus 19 and Taurus 24. In this period the configuration of the zodiac at sunrise will range as follows:

    10 Capricorn 23-5
     1 Taurus 19-24
     4 Cancer 23-5
     7 Scorpio 19-24.

There is some incentive, indeed, for placing an emphasis on the configuration. It will have been noted that there is no southern temple (and no fourth party to visit it). The configuration, however, entails the presence of Capricorn on the meridian—astride the heavens, as it were; and there is a ready appropriateness in this. Capricorn is Saturn's mansion, and it is Saturn who will determine the outcome of the contest.

### III. 6 Geoffrey Chaucer, Introduction to *The Man of Law's Tale*, 1-14 (ed. Robinson, p. 62):

Oure hooste saugh wel that the brighte sonne
The ark of his artificial day hath ronne
The ferthe part, and half an houre and moore,
And though he were nat depe ystert in loore,
He wiste it was the eightetethe day
Of Aprill, that is messager to May;
And saugh wel that the shadwe of every tree
Was as in lengthe the same quantitee
That was the body erect that caused it.
And therfore by the shadwe he took his wit
That Phebus, which that shoon so clere and brighte,
Degrees was fyve and fourty clombe on highte;
And for that day, as in that latitude,
It was ten of the clokke, he gan conclude . . .

First for the tone of this passage. The Host, not deeply versed in these matters, makes a deal of calculation that brings him in the end to the round conclusion that it is 10 o'clock. The comment that he is not expert is also followed immediately by his knowing, forsooth, what day of the month it is. What, then of the rest? This requires rather patient analysis.

The 'artificial' day is the time between sunrise and sunset, and since we are given a calendar date, we can compute what that time must have been. If in possession of an astrolabe, we can even use the method outlined by Chaucer in his *Treatise*, II. 7. The date 18 April places the sun in Taurus 6, from which we may determine that half of the arc of its travel between sunrise and sunset is 109°.

> This is to say that the amount of the celestial equator that must turn to bring the sun from rising to the meridian is 109°.

The Host, however, sees that the sun has travelled half of this half. Here we need to be aware of what is implied. It means that while on the move he supposedly knows where due south is (to project the sun to its midday position); where the sun rose; and what track it is taking between the two points. Having found the mid-point between sunrise and midday, he is also able to estimate that the sun's present position is about 7½° ('half an houre and moore') beyond it. All this, and more, to come to the conclusion that it is ten o'clock— not 9.40 or 10.15. If we make analogy with a scout using the dial of his wrist-watch to find where north is, then perhaps the Host's expertise is not wholly implausible.

What about the result he arrives at? As already indicated, the method he supposedly takes is readily reproducible. But when it is implemented, the result is surprising. We have already stated that the interval between sunrise and midday on the date specified is 109°. Half of this is 54° 30'. Divide this latter figure by fifteen, to obtain an elapsed time since sunrise—3 hrs. 38 mins. Add this elapsed time to the time of sunrise (4.44 a.m.), to obtain 8.22 a.m. We have completed the calculation, but are still considerably more than 30 mins. away from 10 o'clock.

> The time of sunrise is easily found: 109° converts to 7 hrs. 16 mins., which subtracted from noon gives 4.44 a.m.

What has happened? It seems to me implausible to imagine that the Host's calculation is made in such a way that either we or the original and more expert audience are intended to see an error in it. The conclusion necessarily follows that Chaucer himself has slipped up. The question then becomes one of attempting to rework the calculation in such a way that the result the Host arrives at is reproduced.

Here again the astrolabe plays its part. Imagine, for a moment, the sun rising at a particular point on the horizon and making its orderly way towards the meridian. Its path can be measured in two ways—either along the track of the ecliptic, or by relation to the position it occupies above the horizon. The first method uses the 'artificial' arc, the latter uses the 'azimuthal' arc. Let us test, therefore, whether the Host's conclusion can be reached if we use the azimuthal arc as our reference point.

If the sun lies at Taurus 6, it will (at Chaucer's latitude) rise roughly 113° away from the south line.

> Mathematical Formulas 7 comes into play here.

Half of this interval is 56° 30', and the sun will not stand above this point of the horizon until about 9.20 a.m. If, then, we allow 'and moore' to represent 10 minutes of time, 'half an houre and moore' will bring us to 10 o'clock, as required.

It does not follow from this argument that Chaucer did not know what the 'artificial arc' was—there is abundant evidence that he did know. The point, instead, is that when devising the elaborate manipulations foisted on the Host he momentarily confused the two arcs.

Having used an astrolabe intermittently for a decade or so, I can testify to the ease with which such confusions can occur.

So much for the sun's arc. The Host also employs some trigonometry: he finds that the shadow the sun casts is equal in length to the height of the body that casts the shadow. It is no wonder, then, that he recognizes that the sun is elevated 45°. What is remarkable, however, is that the Host also has the capacity to make, unaided, the other necessary adjustments. The sun may well be elevated 45°—but at what latitude and at what time of year? Until both are known the Host is no wiser, has no means of proceeding from shadow length to time of day. And where is our warrant for imagining that he is equipped with the handy tables that would give him his answer? There is none.

As it happens, however, Nicholas's *Kalendarium* does include a set of tables that equates shadow length with the sun's altitude for each daylight hour throughout the year and for the latitude of Oxford. And it so happens that the round figure 45° may be read at the intersection of 10 a.m./2 p.m. (the values being symmetric about the axis of midday) and 18 April. How could the inference be plainer? What the Host calculates so elaborately, Chaucer recovered from Nicholas's table. He knew, too, that modification for latitude and time of year was required in such calculations, and presents the Host as duly taking these elements into account—though empty-handed and not 'depe ystert in loore'.

There is a distinct element of parade in all this—one designed to match with the Host's blustering personality. But part of the sport in observing his gesticulations would be lost on those who did not recognize that he uses two independent methods—either of which (given the necessary equipment) would lead to the desired answer, but neither of which would lead anywhere without that equipment.

### III. 7 Geoffrey Chaucer, *The Man of Law's Tale*, 295-308 (ed. Robinson, p. 65):

> O firste moevyng! crueel firmament,
> With thy diurnal sweigh that crowdest ay
> And hurlest al from est til occident
> That naturelly wolde holde another way,
> Thy crowdyng set the hevene in swich array
> At the bigynnyng of this fiers viage,
> That crueel Mars hath slayn this mariage.
>
> Infortunat ascendent tortuous,
> Of which the lord is helplees falle, allas,
> Out of his angle into the derkeste hous!
> O Mars, o atazir, as in this cas!
> O fieble moone, unhappy been thy paas!
> Thou knyttest thee ther thou art nat receyved;
> Ther thou were weel, fro thennes artow weyved.

At first sight this passage appears fiercely difficult. It will assist in the unravelling of it, if we divide it into three sections (guided by the syntax) and if we also link it with what follows. Chaucer goes on to lament the imprudence of Constance's father in permitting the voyage:

> Was ther no philosophre in al thy toun?
> Is no tyme bet than oother in swich cas?
> Of viage is ther noon eleccioun,
> Namely to folk of heigh condicioun?
> Noght when a roote is of a burthe yknowe?
> Allas, we been to lewed or to slowe!
>
> (310-15)

These later lines merit some attention, since they continue in the spirit of the more difficult lines that precede them. Gaining the drift of the later passage may materially assist in our understanding of the earlier one.

Chaucer's 'philosophre' is clearly someone with the ability to make 'eleccioun', this being a subsidiary branch of astrology with its own rules and criteria. One of the major compendia,

Haly's *De iudiciis astrorum*, has an interesting chapter, 'Amphorismi in discordantiis sapientium', which contains a section on the learned differences of opinion 'in questionibus & electionibus'. It includes the following (my translation): 'he who has it in his nativity or his annual revolution that voyaging or marriage will not be good for him and takes on either of them by election or question will not be in good case (*bonum*), because neither election nor question is able to negate what the nativity or the annual revolution predicted (*demonstravit*)'. (1485, fol. 72.) The lament for Constance implies an acceptance of elections as a form of astrological inquiry, and it is clear from Haly's remarks that marriage and voyages were part of its concerns. Prima facie, then, Chaucer knows what he is talking about (the alternative conclusion is that he was simply speaking more wisely than he knew when he made the connection between elections and voyage/ marriage).

The vital point to note in Chaucer's upbraiding of Constance's father, however, is not that the voyage was undertaken at all, but that the right moment for it was let slip. This is the thrust of the earlier passage, to which we may now turn.

Its lament begins with an exclamation against the heavens entire, the 'crueel firmament'. There is a cosmic violence, a continual struggle in the outer spheres. The heavens (in this case the planets) would 'naturelly' move in one direction (from west to east); but the 'firste moevyng' (the *primum mobile*, or outermost sphere) hurls everything in the opposite direction (from east to west). All this sounds dramatic enough; but that it is not mere poetical frenzy can be demonstrated from the sober pages of Sacrobosco, where we read (my translation): 'the first mover, by its impetus, hurls (*rapit*) all the other spheres around the earth once within a day and a night; they, however, struggling against it (*contra nitentibus*)'. (*Tractatus de Sphaera*, cap. 1.) Chaucer's outburst reads like a translation of Sacrobosco. With such mighty struggles going on, it is inevitable that disastrous configurations will arise (in another mood Chaucer might have pointed to the orderly and harmonious motion of the universe: here, however, things must be drastic).

We are not told where Mars is, how the motion 'from est

til occident' has blighted the marriage, or why the configuration is so dire—all of that lies concealed under 'swich array'. Chaucer knows his business: we do not need detailed demonstration; we merely need to give assent (as we freely may) to the proposition that in certain circumstances the position of Mars could be ruinously strong.

Having given this assent, we find ourselves confronted by yet more strong language:

> Infortunat ascendent tortuous,
> Of which the lord is helplees falle, allas,
> Out of his angle into the derkeste hous!

The difficulty here is not so much with the sense as with its application. We might patiently gloss each of the 'hard words' in turn and still be at a loss as to how to combine them into coherence. 'Tortuous', 'fall from an angle', 'darkest house' may all be explained fairly readily; the problem is to integrate them so that they will all lie together in the one sentence; and the danger is to suppose that the scheme one erects for the purpose of getting them to lie together then actually represents what Chaucer was 'really' saying. The very process of arriving at an integrated scheme is complex, and could easily leave one with the impression that Chaucer was being obscure.

It is the thrust of my argument, on the contrary, that he is merely being unspecific. To erect an astrological scheme that answered to Chaucer's constraints would be simply a methodological device—it would demonstrate that there was at least one possible configuration that answered. And that would be enough. We need only know that there is a possible answer; the passage does not require us to find the 'real' answer.

Indeed, in general terms the impression given by this passage is quite unambiguous: the ascendant is unfortunate (whereas any ascendant should be auspicious), and its lord, from having been in a strong position, in an 'angle' (ll. 17) is now weak ('helplees falle'), that weak position being in the 'derkeste hous'. This is certainly allusive, but the allusiveness is not at all inappropriate to Chaucer's purpose.

We still need to come to terms with the passage, however. First for the ascendant: this is described as being 'tortuous'. At the mundane level a tortuous sign is no more than one rising obliquely to the horizon. It is probable, then, that the word was chosen for its poetic resonance rather than for any specifically astrological application it might have. The tortuous signs are those lying (inclusively) between Capricorn and Gemini, the middle two (Pisces and Aries) being the most tortuous. Which, then, are the lords of the tortuous signs? They are:

| | |
|---|---|
| Saturn | Capricorn |
| Saturn | Aquarius |
| Jupiter | Pisces |
| Mars | Aries |
| Venus | Taurus |
| Mercury | Gemini |

We now face a decision. Mars has blighted the marriage, which suggests that this malign planet is still strong. The 'lord of the ascendant', however, is now helpless. Surely we must take this as implying that Mars cannot be lord of the ascendant.

A supposed syntactical connection between Mars and 'tortuous', however, has led many commentators to the view that Aries (Mars's mansion) must be the sign in the ascendant here—it is, after all, one of the two most tortuous signs. But there are other factors involved, and my emphasis all along is that they must all be taken into account.

At this point we recall, then, that the gist of Chaucer's lament is that at one time (when the lord of the ascendant was *not* fallen, and when the moon was *well* placed) the voyage could have been undertaken. No 'philosophre', though, was consulted to determine this moment. This being the case —it having been at one time advantageous for the voyage to begin—it must follow that the lord of the ascendant was then propitious. Which brings us back to Mars, and to the consideration that, even if in an angle, Mars would not have been propitious. In his *Treatise on the Astrolabe* Chaucer says very little about astrological doctrine; but fortunately for our present purposes, he does at least say this: 'Yit saien these astrologiens that the ascendent and eke the lord of the ascendent may be shapen for to be fortunat or infortunat, as thus:—A "fortunat ascendent" clepen they whan that no wicked planete, as Saturne or Mars . . . is in the hous of the ascendent . . .' (II. 4; ed. Robinson, p. 551). From this it follows that Chaucer would not have regarded the ascendant as propitious had Mars been in it. The logic of the scheme suggests that we look at the other most tortuous sign. This is Pisces, whose lord, Jupiter, would distinctly have been favourable. We may say, then, that it is Jupiter who has now fallen into 'the derkeste hous'. Astrological convention determines that this is the 12th house. The 1st is flanked by both the 12th and the 2nd houses. But it is the 12th into which a planet would pass when hurled 'from est til occident' by the course of daily rotation. Even an hour or so might have made the critical difference.

It is not only the lord of the ascendant, but also the moon (always vital in the matter of voyages) whose formerly favourable position has been let slip:

> O fieble moone, unhappy been thy paas!
> Thou knyttest thee ther thou art nat receyved;
> Ther thou were weel, fro thennes artow weyved.
>
> *paas*: degree

Chaucer continues to work in general terms: there is no need even for us to be familiar with the doctrine of 'reception' (II. 16. 1) to sense that the moon, too, is now powerless to achieve a happy outcome. The (unspecified) aspect she now undergoes is also ruinous. We do not need to know what it is —merely that it is damaging.

The remaining difficulty comes with the line: 'O Mars, o atazir, as in this cas!' (305). Not knowing what 'atazir' signified, we would be likely to suppose that Mars and atazir were here in apposition. Investigating its senses, however, will lead us to a different conclusion. Haly, for instance uses the term with two distinct applications. The first, and more complex, relates to the branch of astrology known as 'directions', the system that predicts an individual's future by the use of projections. The procedures are complicated enough, but the elements involved are firmly established by convention. The five 'hylegiacal places'—sun, moon, ascendant, 10th house, and *pars fortunae*—are moved on ('directed') from their actual position in a given figure to certain other positions, and these new relations are read doctrinally in just the same way as the original configuration. Haly indicates the sort of result to expect (my translation): 'when the sun is hyleg (astrologers) discover from directing it (*per eius athazir*) the individual's life and obstacles . . . and when the moon is hyleg from its direction they know the individual's life, courage, weakness . . .' (*De iudiciis astrorum*, IV. vii). It follows from the basic principles of this obscure art that, in this sense of the term, 'atazir' is a process, not a state, so that no planet can *be* atazir.

Taking the term in this sense, we could gloss Chaucer's line as follows: 'alas for Mars, alas for the atazir, as being in this condition!' The second, and less opaque, passage we have been considering here gives some colour to this interpretation. In it Chaucer implies that there is such a thing as making election for a voyage, and, further, that a 'root' of a birth may be known. This 'root' (radix) is precisely the initial horoscope which is used in making the progressions and predictions that atazir, or 'directions', involve.

There is, however, another sense of the word. Haly (VIII. xxix) also talks of the moon's *being* atazir if at certain specified distances from the sun. The pattern is as follows:

| | | |
|---|---|---|
| 0 = | 360 = | conjunction |
| +12 | 12° | |
| +33 | 45° | |
| +45 | 90° | |
| +45 | 135° | |
| +33 | 168° | |
| +12 | 180° | |
| 180 | | |
| +12 | 192° | |
| +33 | 225° | |
| +45 | 270° | |
| +45 | 315° | |
| +33 | 348° | |
| +12 | 360° | |
| 360 | | |

I take it, though, that the sequence: 'O Mars, o atazir . . . / O fieble moone' rather works against applying Haly's second sense, which would apply the word to the moon. The syntax works towards making the three elements interconnected in the unhappy circumstances, but each contributes separately to its unhappiness.

The key to reading this admittedly difficult passage lies in recognizing the fact that Chaucer is content to talk merely in generalizing terms; at this level of generality the passage is coherent and self-contained. Examined with patience, it is also intelligible.

### III. 8 Geoffrey Chaucer, *The Merchant's Tale*, 2132–3, 2219–24, and 1885–8 (ed. Robinson, pp. 124–5, 121):

> . . . er that dayes eighte
> Were passed, er the month of Juyn . . .
>
> .    .    .    .    .    .    .
>
> Bright was the day, and blew the firmament;
> Phebus hath of gold his stremes doun ysent,
> To gladen every flour with his warmnesse.
> He was that tyme in Geminis, as I gesse,
> But litel fro his declynacion
> Of Cancer, Jovis exaltacion.

Januarie, newly married to 'fresshe May', has been struck blind, and May has taken an impression of the key to Januarie's secret garden, in order to let Damyan into it. Before a week is out, Januarie, 'thurgh eggyng of his wyf' (2135), is eager one morning to go to the garden.

There is a typical obliqueness in the expression of the time when May implements her plan. North (pp. 274–80) interprets the Tale on the basis of taking the first two lines quoted above as indicating 8 June precisely. The repeated 'er', however, seems to me to mean 'before' in both cases—'before eight days were passed, before the month of June (began) . . .' And since the sun was in Gemini from 13 May to 12 June at this epoch, since also 'But litel fro . . . Cancer' is unspecific, there is no reason, on this evidence, why Chaucer should not be referring to a date near the end of May.

When Chaucer speaks of the sun's 'declynacion' of Cancer, he is expressing himself elliptically. He really means 'near its (maximum northern) declination, which it will have when entering Cancer'. The very compression suggests, however, that the audience is imagined to have the familiarity with the subject that will expand what is said into what is meant.

Chaucer also alludes to the astrological convention that Jupiter's exaltation (II. 14) occurs in Cancer (at Cancer 15°), but he alludes to the sign at large. Once again, then, we see the principle of interconnectedness in operation, a chain of constraints, each of which must be satisfied without invalidating any of the others. In general terms, Chaucer's point is simply that midsummer is not far off; and to have the major fortune's (Jupiter's) exaltation lying in the middle of the sign the sun is about to enter, adds to the general sense of cheerfulness.

The other astronomical reference in this Tale comes much earlier. May (the bride) stays in her chamber after the wedding, as delicate custom dictates:

> The moone, that at noon was thilke day
> That Januarie hath wedded fresshe May
> In two of Tawr, was into Cancre glyden;
> So longe hath Mayus in hir chambre abyden . . .
> (1885–8)

The length of May's retreat is expressed as a riddle, and even though it is quickly resolved (though not without a surprise in the answer), it is clear that the audience, as participants in the game, are expected to have at their command certain elementary facts. An answer cannot be attempted until one knows that Gemini interposes between Taurus and Cancer and that each of the signs has thirty degrees in it—the moon, in other words has travelled at least 59°. But at what rate? One must also know that the moon's mean motion is in the region of 13° a day. But before one has had chance to put thirteens into 59, Chaucer gives us an answer:

> The fourthe day compleet fro noon to noon,
> Whan that the heighe masse was ydoon,
> In halle sit this Januarie and May . . .
> (1893–5)

Four thirteens, however, are only 52; whereas the minimum distance of the moon's travel is implicitly 59°. Are we to conclude either that Chaucer bungled the figures, or that he anticipated that his audience would not have the adroitness to keep up? Either conclusion is possible; but a third has some attractiveness and saves the appearances. The adept, who for lack of evidence to the contrary, would assign 13° of motion to the moon on each of the intervening days, would also know, as a matter of course, that this was the *mean* between the occasions when she travels more slowly and those when she travels more rapidly. Faced with the intractable answer that May had spent *exactly* four days in retreat, and the express evidence that the moon had moved at least 59°, the adept would simply conclude that at this time she was 'swift of course'—itself an astrologically propitious condition. Even more propitiously, by the time May emerges, the moon is in her mansion. I do not see any evidence that Chaucer takes particular advantage of these considerations —any more than he later capitalizes on the sun's being close to Jove's exaltation. All three, none the less, are implicit; and a reader sensitive to them will register their contribution to a sense of well-being.

### III. 9 Geoffrey Chaucer, *The Nun's Priest's Tale*, 3187–99 (ed. Robinson, p. 203):

> Whan that the month in which the world bigan,
> That highte March, whan God first maked man,
> Was compleet, and passed were also,
> Syn March bigan, thritty dayes and two,
> Bifel that Chauntecleer in al his pryde,
> His sevene wyves walkynge by his syde,
> Caste up his eyen to the brighte sonne,
> That in the signe of Taurus hadde yronne
> Twenty degrees and oon, and somwhat moore,
> And knew by kynde, and by noon oother loore,
> That it was pryme, and crew with blisful stevene.
> 'The sonne', he seyde, 'is clomben up on hevene
> Fourty degrees and oon, and moore ywis'.

The date is expressed here so intricately and grandly that we must suppose that Chaucer is certainly playing games—but who with? All this fussiness reflects upon his precocious cockerel, and perhaps on the clerical narrator too; but how readily is the joke shared by the audience? Imagining it versed in some equivalent of the rhyme, 'thirty days hath September . . .', one may suppose it able to conclude that (1) March is over; (2) so also are 32 more days; (3) April consumes 30 of them; (4) it is therefore 3 May. On top of this, Chauntecleer observes that the sun is 21° into Taurus, knows by instinct that it is 'pryme', and comes to his conclusion that the sun's elevation is 41° (plus).

There is a reversal of procedures here. The Host, for instance, followed the normal practice of using the sun's position and shadow length to arrive at a time. Chauntecleer, on the contrary, knows it is 'pryme' and arrives at a solar elevation. We have already been told of his abilities (2853–8):

Wel sikerer was his crowyng in his logge
Than is a clokke or an abbey orlogge.
By nature he knew ech ascencioun
Of the equynoxial in thilke toun;
For whan degrees fiftene weren ascended,
Thanne crew he, that it myghte nat been amended.

It is only in the light of this earlier statement of his accomplishment that the later one makes sense: when he crows, on cue, the locals know another hour is up. How high the sun has risen is to that extent beside the point.

As a means to our verifying his reliability, on the other hand, Chauntecleer's conclusion is extremely useful. Is it the case, or not, that at 9 a.m. on 3 May in Chaucer's epoch, the sun would have risen 41° (+) above the horizon? Simple inspection of Nicholas's *Kalendarium* will tell us. The value he gives (ed. Eisner, p. 93) is 41° 17′.

North (pp. 418 ff.) has argued for 1392 as the year on which this Friday 3 May falls ('on a Friday fil al this meschaunce'; 3341). He also counts it among the ominous signs threatening Chauntecleer that the 8th hour of Friday belongs to Venus. This, however, is a confusion of clock and planetary hours (II. 33. 1). In fact 9 a.m. fell within the 4th planetary hour of day, and this hour belongs to Saturn.

The calculation involved here runs as follows: as Nicholas shows, the length of the artificial day on 3 May is 15 hrs. 17 mins. Half of this, subtracted from noon, gives 4 hrs. 21 mins. 30 secs. for the time of sunrise. Thrice add one twelfth of 15.17 hrs. to 4.21, and you will obtain 8.10; add it four times, and you will obtain 9.27.

In examining whether Saturn or any other planet has a covert significance in the action of the tale, we may readily draw up the framework of a horoscope. Whether or not we plot the positions of the planets in it will depend on how confident we are that we may also assign a year as well as a calendar date. For argument's sake, however, we may adopt North's date: 1392. How did the heavens look at the time North assigns? Tuckerman (I. 21. 2) allows us to determine the planetary positions, and Chaucer's method of establishing the houses is conveniently laid out for us in Nicholas's *Kalendarium*.

In his main table Nicholas gives the sun's noon position on 3 May as Taurus 21° 06′ (ed. Eisner, p. 89). In his table of houses, on the other hand, the ascension of Taurus 21 is given as 138° 32′ and the ascension of Taurus 22 as 139° 33′. In this instance 61′ of right ascension answer to 60′ of longitude. We may therefore add 6′ of right ascension to 138° 32′ to obtain a value that will answer to Taurus 21° 06′—138° 38′. We must now subtract an even 45° from this figure, in order to find the right ascension that answers to our even 3 hours before noon. This gives us 93° 38′, which is the degree of right ascension that lies on the meridian when Chauntecleer inspects the heavens with such knowingness. Seeking this value in the *oblique* ascension columns of Nicholas's tables, we find that 92° 50′ answers to Cancer 29, and that 94° 14′ answers to Cancer 30. And though we have so far taken account of fractions of a degree, from this point we need not be so particular, since Nicholas, like many an astrologer, works only to the nearest degree in tabulating the cusps. We may therefore place Cancer 29 in the 1st house, and read off the values for the remaining houses:

| | | | |
|---|---|---|---|
| 10 | Aries 4 | 4 | Libra 4 |
| 11 | Taurus 15 | 5 | Scorpio 15 |
| 12 | Gemini 22 | 6 | Sagittarius 22 |
| 1 | Cancer 29 | 7 | Capricorn 29 |
| 2 | Leo 20 | 8 | Aquarius 20 |
| 3 | Virgo 11 | 9 | Pisces 11 |

Next for the planets (from Tuckerman):

| Saturn | Virgo 28 | (3rd) |
|--------|----------|-------|
| Jupiter | Pisces 11 | (9th) |
| Mars | Aries 0 | (9th) |
| sun | Taurus 21 | (11th) |
| Venus | Aries 6 | (10th) |
| Mercury | Aries 27 | (10th) |
| moon | Virgo 27 | (3rd) |

There are two questions to be asked here: is the configuration sufficiently striking and sufficiently simple in schematic terms to be regarded (like the pattern in *The Knight's Tale*) as close to the surface of the poem; is it sufficiently striking and sufficiently appropriate to the action to be regarded (like the pattern in *The Complaint of Mars*) as active below the surface?

I would have no confidence in assenting to either choice— and here again, in my view, the poem exerts its own controls. In the unfolding of the narrative it is solely the sun and the ascensions that claim attention: Chauntecleer 'knew ech ascencioun' (2855), his wife bids him 'Ware the sonne in his ascencioun' (2956)—and he is warned of his fate by his dream rather than by any astrological portent. This is not to deny North's dating—merely to doubt whether, in this case, the assignable date had any formative influence on the narrative. And certainly the astrology does not seem to operate as a system of buried clues. There is nothing of the order of that hint in *The Wife of Bath's Prologue* (613). When she says 'Myn ascendent was Taur, and Mars therinne', we may be content merely to register that, appropriately enough, Mars played his part in her constitution. More alertly, though, we would recognize that if Taurus was her ascending sign, then Venus was Lady of her ascendant, and that Mars was in Venus's mansion—whether as agent or patient is a moot point.

**III. 10  Geoffrey Chaucer, Prologue to *The Parson's Tale*, 1–12 (ed. Robinson, p. 228):**

By that the Maunciple hadde his tale al ended,
The sonne fro the south lyne was descended
So lowe that he nas nat, to my sighte,
Degreës nyne and twenty as in highte.

Foure of the clokke it was tho, as I gesse,
For ellevene foot, or litel moore or lesse,
My shadwe was at thilke tyme, as there,
Of swiche feet as my lengthe parted were
In sixe feet equal of proporcioun.
Therwith the moones exaltacioun,
I meene Libra, alwey gan ascende,
As we were entryng at a thropes ende . . .

Chaucer here presents us with three items of information:
(1) the sun's altitude is less than 29° in the west; (2) it is
4 o'clock because an object six units in height is now casting
a shadow of approximately eleven units; and (3) Libra is
rising. We notice that he is constantly qualifying: the sun is
not quite 29° high, the time is 4 p.m. 'as I gesse', the shadow
is 11 feet 'or litel moore or lesse'. These qualifiers are perhaps
intended to suggest that there is no inappropriately pedantic
precision here, but they may also have another function. On
the face of it Chaucer seems to give us no warrant for supposing that he is equipped with tables or with some instrument.
Even so, he expects us to believe that he can judge, unaided,
that the sun is elevated, not a round 30° or so, but somewhat
less than 29°. Such precision is not possible without an
instrument. Are we then to modify our assumption, to conclude that merely by asserting the sun is 'not quite' *29°*
elevated, Chaucer expects us to imagine him armed with a
measuring device? Or did he derive his figures from a table
and surround them with qualifiers to make them look less
implausible in the open air?

As it happens Nicholas of Lynn again supplies us with
important documentary evidence. If we inspect his shadow
tables for April under 4 p.m., we find the following:

| April | | feet | parts |
|---|---|---|---|
| 13 | 27° 54′ | 11 | 20 |
| 14 | 28° 09′ | 11 | 13 |
| 15 | 28° 25′ | 11 | 06 |
| 16 | 28° 41′ | 10 | 59 |
| 17 | 28° 57′ | 10 | 51 |
| 18 | 29° 11′ | 10 | 45. |

These figures say that, for instance, at 4 p.m. on 16 April, in the latitude of Oxford, the sun will be elevated 28° 41′ above the horizon, and an object six units high will throw a shadow $10^{59}/_{60}$ units long, Chaucer's 'nat... Degreës nyne and twenty', together with his 'ellevene foot, or litel moore or lesse', would thus be valid for any date between the 14th and the 17th of April.

> It is worth noting the carefulness of Chaucer's phrasing here, which otherwise looks rather heavy-handed. The 'feet' he talks of are 'of swiche feet as my lengthe parted were / In sixe feet equal of proporcioun'. Had Chaucer been only 5′ tall, his 'feet' would have been units of 10″. Here, I believe, he may reflect what Nicholas's canon says on this subject. The user 'should take his own shadow according to six feet of the same, or the shadow of some other perpendicular object divided into six equal parts' (ed. Eisner, pp. 189, 191; my translation).

It seems evident enough, then, that Chaucer took his information from Nicholas or from a similar set of tables. He organizes it in the sequence (1) solar altitude, (2) time, (3) shadow length; though the sequence of *argument* appears to be (1) solar altitude, (2) shadow length, (3) *ergo*, time. This may have been cleverly done; it suggests a logical sequence and a continuity in argument, though in fact altitude and shadow length are simply functions of each other, neither of which will lead to a time of day without further information.

When he adverts to the ascendant, it is not as a means of further confirming the time, but a consequence of its being the time stated. It being 4 o'clock, on this day Libra 'alwey gan ascende'. Since our reference to Nicholas's tables did not narrow the calendar date beyond suggesting that any date between 14 April and 17 April would do, the further information relating to Libra might decide the issue. It could only do so, though, if the sign ascending changed during this period—if, for instance, Libra was not ascending on the 16th but was ascending on the 17th. If this is not the case, we must be content to remain in uncertainty.

Once again we may turn to Nicholas. What does one find, and how are his figures to be read or manipulated? The procedures may look complex at first sight, but they are orderly and reliable enough. Nicholas (ed. Eisner, p. 83) gives us the sun's noon position for each day in question. He also tabulates what the right ascension is (or, rather, that value with 90° systematically added to it) for each *even* degree of longitude (p. 165). We, in turn, know that four hours exactly have elapsed since noon, so that we will add 60° to the value of right ascension that answers most closely to our noon longitudinal value. Armed with this figure, we may then inspect the column which tabulates oblique ascension (pp. 169–70) and see what degree of the zodiac answers to it. As follows:

| date | noon sun | RA+90° | +60° | nearest OA | ascendant |
|------|----------|--------|------|------------|-----------|
| April | Taurus | | | | |
| 14 | 2° 50′ = 3° 00′ | 120° 46′ | 180° 46′ | 180° 00′ | Virgo 30 |
| 15 | 3° 48′ = 4° 00′ | 121° 44′ | 181° 44′ | 181° 25′ | Libra 1 |
| 16 | 4° 46′ = 5° 00′ | 122° 42′ | 182° 42′ | 182° 51′ | Libra 2 |
| 17 | 5° 44′ = 6° 00′ | 123° 40′ | 183° 40′ | 182° 51′ | Libra 2. |

Inspection of the ascendant column in this table shows us that Chaucer's assertion about Libra's ascension is consistent with the rest, but it does nothing to narrow the date—not that it needs to: consistency is enough.

It is interesting, none the less, that Chaucer presents himself, rather than one of his characters, making a set of calculations. They are redundant in the same way as the Host's (solar altitude and shadow length are *not* independent functions), and like the Host's, his calculations are readily verifiable in Nicholas's tables. Where is the audience in all this? It has been part of my objective to show that sometimes Chaucer plays a game that necessarily implies an ability in the audience to take part. (Calculating the length of May's retreat, for instance; knowing which half of the Ram's course is the one to take into account.) On the other hand, there are occasions (such as the clerk of Orleans's calculations, and the failure of Constance's father to make proper consultation) when the technicalities of the subject are so abtruse that one must conclude that, at best, only the general outline could be followed. I hope I have shown, however, that in the more difficult cases there is indeed a general outline, and that it can indeed be followed. Between the two extremes lies the splendid case of *The Complaint of Mars*, where an understanding of the mechanics of the general outline greatly enhances one's understanding of how the narrative works. What, then, of the Host and of Chaucer, dabbling in Nicholas's tables? Reluctantly I place them in a fourth category. To someone who understands what it is that the two of them purportedly perform on horseback on the way to Canterbury, the fact that the figures all sit there on the page in Nicholas— *and* that the figures are not reducible to wiseacre lore—make it difficult to conclude that the raw material of composition has been fully reworked. The best one can say, then, is that Chaucer may well have traded here on his audience's knowledge of the procedures he and the Host bring into play; and because they are complex, they were not, in these instances, expected to perform the calculations for themselves, or to keep up with the ones performed.

### III. 11 Geoffrey Chaucer, *The Squire's Tale*, 45-52 (ed. Robinson, p. 128):

> He leet the feeste of his nativitee
> Doon cryen thurghout Sarray his citee,
> The laste Idus of March, after the yeer.
> Phebus the sonne ful joly was and cleer;
> For he was neigh his exaltacioun
> In Martes face, and in his mansioun
> In Aries, the colerik hoote signe.
> Ful lusty was the weder and benigne . . .

The date, on a Roman calendar reckoning, is 'the last Ides of March', and on an astronomical reckoning it is the time when the sun is '. . . in his mansioun / In Aries'. If you do not know either where the sun's exaltation lies, or what the faces of Mars are, you are still able to use your knowledge of when the sun lies in Aries to deduce the season in general terms.

But guided only by grammar, syntax, and native wit, one would suppose that the sun's exaltation coincided with one of the faces of Mars—both lying within Aries: 'neigh his exaltacioun / In Martes face, and in his mansioun'. The fact is, however, that the sun's exaltation lies at Aries 19 (II. 14), whereas the 'face' bounded by Aries 11–20 is *not* that of Mars (who owns, instead, the first ten degrees of that sign). What do we conclude? One obvious possibility is that Chaucer has slipped up; another is that the lines have not been correctly punctuated, that they have been construed by scribes and editors who did not catch their drift. Let us try again:

> Phebus the sonne ful joly was and cleer;
> For he was (1) neigh his exaltacioun,
> (2) In Martes face, and (3) in his mansioun
> In Aries . . .

With this repunctuation the sun sits in Aries his mansion, near his exaltation, which lies just past the middle of the sign, and is still in Mars's face, i.e. the first 10 degrees of the sign. When Chaucer said that Libra was the moon's exaltation (Prologue to *The Parson's Tale*, 10–11), there was no escape —that is not the case. Here, however, an understanding of the elementary doctrines of the subject shows that our inherited text is at fault, not Chaucer.

The first piece of information we are given, however, is that the time is 'the laste Idus of March, after the yeer'. March having 31 days, its Nones fell on the 7th and its Ides on the 15th. What force, then, does 'after the yeer' have? Skeat, in his 'Glossarial Index', construed it as meaning 'according to the season of the year'. It is plain that he thought the phrase was governed by 'Idus', since the position of the Ides varies with the length of the month. This interpretation would hold good if it was a question here of picking one month from another. But that is not the issue. The king is wont 'fro yeer to yeer' to proclaim his birthday. Obviously the same date is involved on each occasion. It makes much more sense to take 'after the yeer' to mean 'after the (given) year had expired' since he last proclaimed his birthday. In any event, the date is 15 March, its Ides. This places the sun at Aries 3—a longitude, we notice, that *is* within Mars's face and the sun's mansion, and *does* place the sun near (16 days away from) his exaltation in Aries 19. Each item holds good, each is verifiable in its own right, and no one verification conflicts with another.

Here is what happens at the start of the following day:

Up riseth fresshe Canacee hireselve,
As rody and bright as dooth the yonge sonne,
That in the Ram is foure degrees up ronne——
Noon hyer was he whan she redy was——
And forth she walketh esily a pas . . .

(384–8)

Let us observe: from the deducible calendar date (15 March)
we have placed the sun in Aries 3. Now we have advanced to
the following day, to find that, indeed, the text tells us the
sun is 'up ronne' 4 degrees in the Ram. We recall that in *The
Franklin's Tale* the sun was bright as gold in Cancer (his
'hoote declynacion') and a duller coppery colour when in
Capricorn, these being the appearances he bore respectively
at midsummer and midwinter. Now, however, he is both
'rody' and 'bright'. He is ruddy in complexion because still
low on the horizon, but also bright because in the Spring sign.

Here, though, Chaucer may be working a switch, and to
see what is involved we must consider the manuscript tradition at this point. The sun, it seems, has 'up ronne' 4 degrees
in Aries, in the sense that this is its longitude. Canacee, however, is getting up at sunrise, or close to it. So that the consideration now shifts to how high the sun is elevated above
the horizon. Chaucer dovetails the two—the sun was *also*
no more than 4° degrees above the horizon when she rose.

This, at least, is what one would deduce from the received
text. Manly and Rickert, however, in their report on the
Chaucer manuscripts (VI. 543), indicate that forty-one MSS
read 'that in the Ram is *ten* degrees up ronne', or some close
variant of that. Only three MSS (Christchurch, Hengwrt, and
Physicians) read '. . . is 4 degrees'. Can sense be made of 'ten',
the majority reading, or are the editors who have accepted
four right in their judgement? Let us recover our ground,
then, and see whether the vote in favour of the minority
(three MSS only) is indeed acceptable. And here we will bear
in mind that even the standard printed text had not recognized
the relation between the sun's mansion, the sun's exaltation,
and Mars's face. We will be looking for strong argument based
on a firm understanding of astrological convention.

The expressed date (the Ides of March) is convertible into

our calendrical convention without ambiguity. The 15th of
March, in turn, may be converted into a solar longitude at
Chaucer's epoch: Aries 3. We are still on firm ground. Moreover, in speaking of the day before Canacee rises at dawn,
Chaucer has said only that it is the Ides, and that the sun is
in Aries. Without any inconsistency he may therefore say
that the sun (in Aries, no matter which degree) was only $10°$
above the horizon when Canacee herself arose from her bed.

Why do the MSS vary? One answer among many may be
that the scribes who wrote them knew perfectly well on what
calendar date in their own system the Roman Ides of March
fell, and also knew that the sun entered Aries on 12 March
at this epoch. They were thus able to make a mental note of
where the sun was. But shortly after, they found Canacee
rising at a time when the sun was supposedly *ten* degrees 'up
ronne'. What they did not see was that it could be 'up ronne'
in the sense of being elevated above the horizon, not in the
sense of being advanced in longitude. Looking at the text in
this light, of course they emended '10' to '4', since they
thought that otherwise there would be a week-long gap in the
chronology.

Let us recapitulate and consider merely the information
we are presented with, not the assumptions or deductions we
may make about it. The King proclaims his birthday. It is the
Ides of March, the sun is in (somewhere in) the first ten
degrees of Aries. On the next day Canacee rises when the
sun, still of course in Aries, is less than *10°* above the horizon.
Is there anything to choose between the two? Were the sun
about ten degrees above the horizon at this time of year it
would be more than an hour after sunrise. Canacee, however,
had told her 'maistresse' to get her up 'er that the sonne gan
up glyde' (373). In the event the reading 'four' is marginally
preferable, as meeting the further constraint that 'The vapour
which that fro the erthe glood / Made the sonne to seme rody
and brood' (393–4).

### III. 12  Geoffrey Chaucer, Prologue to *The Wife of Bath's Tale*, 697–705 (ed. Robinson, pp. 82–3):

> The children of Mercurie and of Venus
> Been in hir wirkyng ful contrarius;

Mercurie loveth wysdam and science,
And Venus loveth ryot and dispence.
And, for hire diverse disposicioun,
Ech falleth in otheres exaltacioun.
And thus, God woot, Mercurie is desolat
In Pisces, wher Venus is exaltat;
And Venus falleth ther Mercurie is reysed.

One would suppose, from this evidence, that the distribution of the planets' exaltations, which makes Venus and Mercury paired opposites, took account of their essential characteristics: Mercury loves learning, Venus loves riot, and 'for hire diverse disposicioun' they are placed in opposite signs. Ptolemy, however, indicates that the distribution had conventionally a seasonal base (II. 14). It is in the nature of astrological imagery, even so, that it is amenable to a great diversity of application. What Chaucer says, indeed, *sounds* like respectable astrological doctrine: it is exactly what we would expect to be the case. The only damper on it is the consideration that in many situations Mercury is thought merely to be neutral.

Different occasions, however, call for different emphases. At the end of *The Complaint of Mars*, for instance, it is Mercury who cheers and welcomes Venus after her flight from the sun.

*c.* 1420

III. 13  John Lydgate, Prologue to the *Troy Book*, 121–48: ,

And of the tyme to make mencioun,
Whan I be-gan of this translacioun,
It was the yere, sothely for to seyne,
Fourtene complete of his fadris regne,
125  The tyme of yere, schortly to conclude,
Whan twenty grees was Phebus altitude,
The hour whan he made his stedis drawe
His rosen chariot lowe under the wawe
.  .  .  .  .  .  .
And Lucyna, of colour pale and wan,

> Hir cold arysyng in Octobre gan to dyght,
> Tenchace the dirknesse of the frosty nyght,
> 135 In the myddes of the scorpion;
> And Esperus gan to wester doun,
> To haste hir cours ageyn the morwe graye;
> And Lucifer, the nyght to voyde a-waye,
> Is called than, messanger of day,
> Our emysperye to put out of affraye
> Wyth bright kalendis of Phebus upryst schene
>     .    .    .    .    .    .    .
> 145 Til after sone Appollo lyst nat tarie
> To take soiour in the Sagittarie.
> Whyche tyme I gan the prolog to beholde
> Of Troye Boke . . .

This passage appears to be highly circumstantial, suggesting
that a precise date may be recovered from it. It does have
some oddities, however. The first comes in line 124: 'His
fadris regne'. This is the reign of Henry IV, and the expression 'Fourtene complete' would normally have to be taken
to imply some time in the fifteenth year. Henry IV's reign,
however, did not enter a fifteenth year. The fourteenth began
on 30 September 1412, and he died on 20 March 1413. We
are forced to conclude, either that 'Fourtene' is an error for
'thirteen', or that 'complete' is being used in an awkward and
misleading sense—that it means, in effect, 'the completion
of . . .'. In either event, the year intended is 1412.

I see no warrant for Johnstone Parr's assertion that the 'fourteenth
"complete" year' of the reign was 'the king's fourteenth regnal year'
('Astronomical Dating for Some of Lydgate's Poems', *PMLA*, 67
(1952), 252).

In describing the time of year Lydgate says (125-6) that
the sun's 'altitude' was 20°, and later he moves the sun into
Sagittarius. The two pieces of information must be taken in
conjunction. The sun's altitude (that is, of course, at noon)
will be 20° twice in the year: once as it moves south to Capricorn, and again as it returns north towards the celestial
equator.

In the latitude of London (52°N) the celestial equator is
elevated 38° above the southern horizon. If, therefore the

sun's *altitude* is 20°, its declination must be (38 − 20 =) 18°
South. In Lydgate's day the sun (then in Scorpio) had a
declination of more than 17° and less than 19° between
1 November and 5 November. We must therefore look at the
remainder of the information if attempting to find a date.
The swift motion of the moon may well be of assistance here.

   Lydgate requires the moon to be in the middle of Scorpio.
This means that she will indeed be 'pale and wan', since the
sun is there too. Our tables tell us (see Tuckerman, p. 724)
that between 31 October and 5 November 1412 her longitude
at 4 p.m. moved from Virgo 28 to Sagittarius 4. She arrived
at Scorpio 15 late on 4 November.

   What then of Venus's position at this time? She is mentioned too, and must also be accounted for. She was at Sagittarius 12 on 4 November—i.e. behind the sun by some 21°,
as she is required to be by being described as Hesperus.

   Such is the general picture. But what are we to make of
the moon's October rising (133-4) and of the reference to
Venus as Lucifer (138-41)? In 1412 the moon was New on
6 October and Full on 20 October. Between this latter date
and 4 November, therefore, she was waning and rising progressively later—i.e. further on into the cold hours of early
morning. By the time she reached the middle of Scorpio,
however, she was rising only a quarter of an hour or so before
the sun. In this sense she could be said to be chasing off the
darkness, not so much by her own brightness as by herald-
ing dawn.

   The reference to Lucifer (138) is awkward if one supposes
that by it Lydgate imagines Venus as morning star to be
present in this sky, since she is already there as evening star.
It is worth noticing, however, that 'Is called than . . .' (139)
is the only verb in the passage that is in the present tense. It
may well mean not 'is then summoned', but 'is then called'
—when Venus voids the night away, she is then called
Lucifer. Indeed, there may be rather a subtle point in this
little digression on Venus as Lucifer. Though she was Hesperus on the evening of 4 November 1412, she was also
retrograde, in the process of moving ahead of the sun and
becoming Lucifer. The digression, though it is certainly not
deft, may be a reflection of her actual behaviour at the time.

*c.* 1424

**III. 14  James I, *The Kingis Quair*, 1–7 (ed. J. Norton-Smith, Oxford 1971, p. 1):**

> Heigh in the hevynnis figure circulere
> The rody sterres twynklyng as the fyre;
> And in Aquary, Citherea the clere,
> Rynsid hir tressis like the goldin wyre,
> That late tofore in fair and fresche atyre
> Through Capricorn heved hir hornis bright,
> North northward approchit the mydnyght . . .

This passage contains some problems to which there may be no answer. One involves the question of whether the text should read 'Citherea' or 'Cinthia'; the other involves the sense of the last line.

Some editors have argued that Citherea (Venus) will not do here, because Venus was not known to have 'hornis' (phases) until after the invention of the telescope. And even though Norton-Smith (p. 52) has pointed out that 'hornis' may be taken to refer to a mode of dressing the hair, half the appropriateness of this very pleasant image (rinse–Aquarius, horns–Capricorn) would still be lost, in my view, were it not applied to the sole planet then known to have horns.

None the less 'Citherea' is considered as a possible reading, and we should pause here to see whether there is an astronomical support for it.

The whole scene suggests an evening or night setting, rather than an early morning one. 'Late tofore', on the other hand, suggests that the planet is still near the boundary between Capricorn and Aquarius—i.e. that her longitude is about 300°. The poem has been dated, on external grounds, to late 1423/early 1424 (James married in February 1424). This constraint, combined with Venus's actual position, would narrow the date to some time between 27 November and 13 December 1423. Venus was then Hesperus, and close to her maximum elongation (I. 20. 4)—therefore visible for the longest period in the evening sky.

What of the moon, 'Cinthia', as an alternative? Here a different set of constraints emerges. Both 'fair and fresche atyre' and 'hornis' would now strongly suggest that the moon was new when in Capricorn. The question would then be whether there was a new moon within the longitude 270°–300° at the required time. There was one such—on 2 January 1424 (Goldstine, p. 203). The moon's longitude was then Capricorn 20.

In the event, therefore, both alternatives are equally possible on astronomical grounds. Nor is there a decisive element in the stanza's final line, which itself is by no means clear in its intention. What can be meant by 'North northward approchit the mydnyght'?

The syntactical choices open to us are (1) either the moon or Venus is approaching the midnight in a 'north northward' direction, or that (2) midnight is itself approaching in that direction. If 'midnight' meant the opposite of midday in this context, and if midday meant in effect the meridian, then James would mean that either the moon or Venus was approaching the mid-point of its invisibility. The thrust of the lines, however, strongly suggests that the planet is *visible*. The next alternative would be to take 'mydnyght' to mean 'the line of midnight', i.e. the meridian at 24.00 hrs. In this case, of course, the planet ought not to be Venus, since she would be too far away from the sun. But it could scarcely be the moon either. The strong implication that she had been new when in Capricorn would entail, in turn, that she was less than five days old if still in Aquarius. She would therefore be too close to the sun to be able to approach the meridian after dark.

What, then, is left? It may at first appear distinctly odd to speak of midnight as approaching 'north northward'. But I think we may take a hint here from Chaucer. In his *Treatise on the Astrolabe* (I. 17) he says: 'in this heved of Cancer is the grettist declinacioun northward of the sonne'. From this it will follow that Cancer is also the greatest declination northward of the sun's nadir—which, after all, is the point of the zodiac that will stand on the meridian at midnight. The Head of Cancer will approach the meridian at midnight at a time when the sun lies in the Head of Capricorn, i.e. at midwinter; which suits well enough with the present context. The situation James envisages, on this construction, is the steady climb northward of that part of the zodiac lying opposite the sun as the time of midnight approaches in mid-winter.

## 1450s

**III. 15 Anon., *The Floure and the Leafe*, 1-28 (ed. D. Pearsall, London and Edinburgh, 1962, p. 85):**

> When that Phebus his chaire of gold so hie
> Had whirled up the sterry sky aloft,
> And in the Boole was entred certainly;
> .    .    .    .    .    .
> ... up I rose, three houres after twelfe,
> About the springing of the day,
> And on I put my geare and mine array,
> And to a pleasaunt grove I gan passe,
> Long or the bright sonne up risen was ...

The sun's 'whirling up the sky' could at first suggest diurnal motion. It could be said to 'whirl' (in the sense of speeding along) in so far as it will rise more quickly when in the oblique signs than when in the direct ones (II. 16. 2(e) ). Taurus, moreover, is a sign of oblique (i.e. of rapid) ascension. The continuation, however, makes it plain that it is the sun's annual, not his diurnal, course that is in question; it becomes plain that the sun is not in fact imagined to be visible—the poet rises a little before dawn.

The elevation implied by 'up', therefore, must be referred to the sun's travel north of ('above') the celestial equator. This consideration, in turn, raises the question whether 'whirled up' still has a distinct astronomical appropriateness. Sense may be made of the phrase if one refers it to the daily rate of increase in the sun's declination.

Giving some force to 'entred certainly', we may place the sun at or near Taurus 5. At this period (c.1450s) that would make the date 17 April. The poet rises at three in the morning, at which time dawn is beginning to break ('About the springing of the day'). The convention was that dawn began at the time the sun arrived within 18° of the horizon. In the latitudes of southern England, with the sun at Taurus 5, this would be at about 2.20 a.m., actual sunrise coming at about 4.40 a.m. In this respect, then, there is no confusion—rather, a quite proper distinction—between the poet's rising 'About the springing of the day' and simultaneously 'Long or the . . . sonne up risen was'. The poem's introduction seems to have been carefully and competently worked.

## 1470s

### III. 16 Hary's *Wallace*, Bk. IX, lines 125–46 (cf. M. P. McDiarmid (ed.), Edinburgh and London, 1968, I. 231–2):

In Aperill, the one and twenty day,
The hie calend, thus Cancer, as we say,
The lusty tym off Mayus fresche cummyng
Celestiall gret blythnes in to bryng;
Pryncypaill moneth forsuth it may be seyn,
130　The hewynly hewis apon the tendyr greyn.
Quhen old Saturn his cloudy cours had gon,
The quhilk had beyn bath best and byrdis bon;
Zepherus ek with his suet vapour,
He comfort has, be wyrking off natour,
All fructuous thing in-till the erd adoun
At rewllyt is wndyr the hie Regioun:
Sobyr Luna in flowyng off the se,
Quhen brycht Phebus is in his chemage hie.
The Bulys cours so takin had his place;
140　And Iupiter was in the Crabbis face;
Quhen Aryet the hot syng coloryk,
In-to the Ram quilk had his Rowmys Ryk,
He chosyn had his place and his mansuun
In Capricorn, the sygn off the lioun.
Gentill Iupiter with his myld ordinance
Bath Erb and tre reuertis in plesance . . .
　　*bon*: bane

Both the narrative sequence and the syntax of this passage are difficult to untangle: I have therefore punctuated it more heavily than McDiarmid, in order to make clearer my interpretation of it.

There is an appearance of considerable muddle in Hary's temporal description. Let us resort, then, to the least imprecise item—the calendar date. It is 21 April, and May is hastening on. But what of 'calend' and 'Cancer'? 21 April is in fact XI Kal. May: eleven days before the kalends of May, while 'Cancer' (if meaning the summer solstice) is even further off. In short, 'we' do *not* say that the sun's being in Taurus is the 'Cancer' of anything.

Hary now (131) associates the passing of winter with the ending of Saturn's 'cloudy cours', which is appropriate enough, not least because he has as his mansions two of the three winter signs: Capricorn and Aquarius. Hary then passes to the balmy winds of springtime—but the moon, the tides, and the sun in his 'chemage' then suddenly obtrude themselves. The relationship and sequence is obscure here, and continues to be so. Lines 138-9 must contain some corruption, but their general drift—that the sun is in Taurus—does at least suit the declared calendar date. At Hary's epoch the sun was at or close to Taurus 10 on 21 April.

Plodding on, we find Jupiter supposedly 'in the Crabbis face'. Now, the faces of Cancer (II. 16) are owned by Venus, Mercury, and the moon. It may be, then, that Hary has confused astrological 'face' with astronomical 'head' and means merely that Jupiter was at the beginning of Cancer.

Alternatively, there is the heterodox astrological tradition known by the name of 'Arcandam', by which the 12 signs of the zodiac were divided into 29 sections, each sign having a 'head' and a 'tail' and five of them having a 'belly' in addition. Hary might conceivably be alluding to Cancer's 'head' in this sense.

Arcandam (*The Most Excellent Profitable, and Pleasant Book of the famous Doctor and expert Astrologian Arcandam*) gained great popularity in England from 1562 onwards, after its translation from the French by William Wade. Its Arab origins, however, are plain from the names used for the various parts. The Crab's Head, for instance, is 'Albacra'.

McDiarmid (II. 240) claims that 'in the first "face" . . . of Cancer which he now rules, the beneficient Jupiter is "exalted" '. The first face of Cancer, however, belongs to Venus, and Jupiter's exaltation falls within the second face. It is difficult not to agree with those who believe Blind Hary's astrology lives up to his name.

No attempt at generous construction will succeed with what follows. Capricorn is of course not the 'sygn off the lioun', and to say that 'Aries, whose house ('Rowmys') is in the Ram, had chosen his place in Capricorn' would be mere raving. Is there some simple emendation that restores the text to sense, as is the case with Fletcher's *The Bloody Brother* at several points? One possibility offers itself; but, as we shall see, it does not take us far enough. 'Ares' (without the 'i') is the Greek name for Mars, who is indeed a choleric planet and whose mansion is indeed in the Ram. Supposing some confusion between these similar words, one could try to argue, then, that Hary might have been saying, trying to say, that 'the choleric Mars, whose mansion is in Aries, was situated in Capricorn'. But even this attempt to smooth the path would not accommodate Capricorn described as Leo; and I have little confidence in the wisdom of trying to torture Hary into sense.

There is one further point of interest in these lines. My own view of the question of poetic 'borrowing' is that the most extreme scepticism is the only safe course. Hary, though, describes 'Aryet' as 'the hot syng coloryk', whereas for Chaucer in *The Squire's Tale* (line 51) Aries is 'the colerik hoote signe'. How is one to proceed? I take this view. The choleric, as one of the four humours, distinguishes itself from the other three by being hot and dry. To describe Aries as both 'choleric' and 'hot' therefore carries an element of partial tautology in it, whereas to describe it as 'choleric; hot and dry', would provide a gloss for 'choleric'. The question, then, involves not only the verbal similarity between Chaucer and Hary, but also what we may describe as a shared oddity. On these grounds I would be prepared to hazard that Hary picked up (and ill digested) a phrase from Chaucer in the course of this confused passage.

## 1495

### III. 17 John Skelton, *The Garland of Laurel*, 1–7

Arectyng my syght towarde the zodyake,
The sygnes xii for to beholde a farre,
When Mars retrogradant reuersyd his bak,
Lorde of the yere in his orbicular,

> Put vp his sworde, for he cowde make no warre,
> And whan Lucina plenarly did shyne,
> Scorpione ascendynge degrees twyse nyne . . .

This (with the main verb still to be reached) is the abrupt end of the astronomical information in the poem, except for a much later mention of Janus 'Makynge his almanak for the new yere' (line 1516).

This passage suggests that there are three constraints to be met if it is to yield an astronomical date.

(a) Mars must be retrograde;
(b) the moon must be full (or near full);
(c) Scorpio 18° must be rising.

In themselves these are not very severe restrictions, in the sense that we may expect them to be met at not very large intervals. Skelton, however, has not given us a solar position or a calendar date, with the consequence that we have no further criterion to judge between those years in which the three constraints are met.

In these circumstances it is only when we make the further assumption that the moon is—or that both the moon and Mars are—at Scorpio 18°, that we can proceed further, and there will be those who feel that the syntax of the verse does not encourage the assumption.

Let us deal with the two cases in turn, none the less.

First: The moon at Scorpio 18° (Mars elsewhere).

We may limit our search for a date to a period that lies within the bounds defined by the biographical evidence. Skelton's first compositions were written in the early 1480s and this poem was published in October 1523.

To determine whether the moon was close to full and near Scorpio 18, with Mars retrograde and visible (though, for the moment, at an unspecified longitude) is a simple matter, when once one has determined what 'close to' will mean. If we allow one day's latitude in determining the precise time of fullness, for instance, then the full moon may fall anywhere within Scorpio. (If the moon was at Scorpio 15 one day after being full, it would have been full at about Scorpio 2.)

There are 47 Full Moons between 1480 and 1523 that will qualify, but on only four occasions was Mars then retrograde:

| moon full in Scorpio: | Mars then retrograde: |
|---|---|
| 24 April 1480 | Sagittarius 15 |
| 9 May 1495 | Scorpio 15 |
| 15 April 1508 | Virgo 12 |
| 25 April 1510 | Libra 25 |

A choice among these dates would have to be made on other than astronomical grounds.

Second: Both the moon and Mars at Scorpio 18. From the above table it can be seen that only 9 May 1495 will qualify if we also limit Mars's longitude to the middle of Scorpio. A date would thus be defined uniquely within the period, and it would be of considerable assistance, if we were able to say with any confidence what is meant by Mars's being 'Lorde of the yere'. The rules for determining this honour are, in my experience, so complex and so various, however, that one could not be at all certain of being able to duplicate the procedure Skelton had in mind.

In conclusion, then, we must be content to say that while the date suggested by Gingerich and Tucker is attractive, it is achieved only at the cost of narrowing down the frame of reference perhaps more narrowly than it should be.

See the interesting article by Owen Gingerich and Melvin J. Tucker, 'The Astronomical Dating of Skelton's *Garland of Laurel*', *Huntington Library Quarterly*, XXXII, 3 (May 1969), 207-20.

## Sixteenth Century

### 1528

III. 18 Sir David Lindsay, Prologue to *The Dreme*, 57-9 (in *Works*, ed. Douglas Hamer, Vol. I, Edinburgh and London, 1931, p. 6):

> In to the Calendis of Ianuarie,
> Quhen fresche Phebus, be mouying circulair,
> Frome Capricorn wes enterit in Aquarie . . .

*The Dreme* has been dated to 1528 (ed. Hamer, II. 1), and at this epoch the sun was entering Aquarius on 11 January (Tuckerman, p. 782). Hamer (III. 13) was mistaken in saying that Lindsay's calendar was 'fourteen or fifteen days behind'. The interval is roughly eleven days. By the 'Calendis of Ianuarie' Lindsay (unless sadly mistaken) meant, simply, 'the early days of January'.

The body of the poem contains some lengthy passages expounding medieval cosmology (see, e.g. 382-511, and 636-58). They are not of sufficient interest or complexity to warrant our attention here.

## 1529

III. 19 Sir David Lindsay, *Complaint*, 1-13 (ed. Hamer, I. 40):

> Schir, I beseik thyne Excellence,
> Heir my complaynt with pacience.
> My dolent hart dois me constrane
> Off my infortune to complane,
> Quhowbeit I stand in gret dowtance
> Quhome I sall wyte of my myschance:
> Quhidder Saturnis creueltie,
> Ryngand in my Natyuitie,
> Be bad aspect, quhilk wyrkis vengeance,
> Or vtheris heuinlye influence;
> Or geue I be predestinate
> In Courte to be Infortunate,
> Quhilk hes so lang in seruyce bene . . .

While casting round for the cause of his disfavour at James V's court Lindsay gives only token regard to the possibility of malign planetary influence at his birth: 'Quhidder Saturnis creueltie, / Ryngand' (reigning), though ambiguous, does not seem to amount to an assertion that Saturn did in fact control his nativity. Rather, it suggests that Lindsay feels so poorly about his state of affairs that, were the stars to blame, it would prove to be the most malign of them that had ruled *his* fortunes.

In any event, Lindsay is not here presenting us with a

cryptic birth date. Hamer (III. 49) thought that it would follow from Saturn's controlling his nativity that Lindsay was born 'between December 22 and February 19, for Saturn reigns in Capricorn and Aquarius'. This, though, is twice in error. It is, of course, the sun's position, not that of any planet, that determines calendar date; and in any case, at this epoch the sun was in Capricorn and Aquarius between 14 December and 9 February. Lindsay's invocation of astrology here is merely token. The politics of court, not heavenly machinations, are the cause of his plight.

## 1530

**III. 20 Sir David Lindsay, *Testament of the Papyngo*, 113–35 (ed. Hamer, I. 59–60):**

That day Saturne nor Mars durst not appeir,
Nor Eole of his coue he durst nocht steir.
115 That daye perforce behuffit to be fair,
Be Influence and cours celestiall;
No planete presit for to perturbe the air,
For Mercurious, be mouyng naturall,
Exaultit wes, in to the throne tryumphall
120 Off his mantioun, vnto the fyftene gre,
In his awin souerane signe of virginee.

That day did Phebus plesandlie depart
Frome Geminie, and enterit in Cancer;
That daye Cupido did extend his dart;
125 Uenus, that daye, coniunit with Iupiter;
That daye Neptunus hid hym lyke one sker;
That daye dame Nature, with gret besynes,
Fortherit Flora to keyth hir craftynes;

And retrograde wes Mars in Capricorne,
130 And Synthea in Sagitter assesit;
That daye dame Ceres, goddes of the corne,
Full Ioyfullie Iohane Upponland applesit;
The bad espect of Saturne wes appesit,
That daye, be Iono, of Iupiter the Ioye,
135 Perturband spretis causyng to hauld coye.

Lindsay's description is of an ideal situation, not an actual one, and we can quickly establish its degree of formality. The sun, we note, is precisely at the first point of Cancer, precisely at the midsummer mark (123). And what of the other planets?

| | |
|---|---|
| Mercury | in Virgo 15 (its exaltation) |
| Venus | in conjunction with Jupiter |
| Mars | in Capricorn and retrograde |
| moon | in Sagittarius |
| Saturn | nullified. |

This disposition is achieved at some cost: Mercury is 75° away from the sun—53° more than the maximum possible (I. 20. 4). We notice, too, the presence of a number of non-planetary deities—Juno, Ceres, and Neptune. Indeed, of the twelve Olympians only Pallas, Vulcan, and Vesta are absent. There may, then, be some reminiscence here of the Manilian alternative to Ptolemy (II. 16. 4); but if so, it is not strong. The Manilian system, for instance, makes Mercury's 'souerane signe' Cancer, whereas Lindsay has placed Mercury firmly in its Ptolemaic mansion. In fact, where the matching of planet and sign is concerned Lindsay's indebtedness to either system is not strong. Of the remaining planetary deities, Venus and Jupiter are joined together, the sign not being specified: the point, instead, is that the two benign planets combine their influence. The two malign ones, on the other hand, are invisible ('durst not appeir'); and Mars is further incapacitated by being retrograde. What, though, of his being in Capricorn? That sign contains his exaltation, and Lindsay has already made something of the power flowing to Mercury from his being in his. It would seem that he has slipped up here.

Six of the seven planets, then, are in situations that have some astrological bearing, one obvious enough for a reader moderately versed in the subject to catch the drift. But what of the moon, 'in Sagitter assesit' (130)? She has no essential dignity here, other than a 'face' (II. 16) in the second ten degrees. We may conclude that 'Sagitter' was chosen rather for its alliteration with 'assesit' than for any other reason.

The picture Lindsay presents is ebullient and partly reliant for its effect on one's general grasp of the basic elements of astrology. There is, however, some suggestion of a subtler touch in the prominence given to Mercury in the scheme and in the importance of the popinjay to the poem. One among the host of attributes and appurtenances given to the planets is their rule over birds. William Lilly, for example, assigns planetary rulers to forty-four different species, several of them having more than one. The sole appearance that the parrot and the popinjay make—those garrulous animals— is under Mercury (p. 79).

## 1530s

III. 21 John Bellenden, 'The Benner of Peetie' (Piety), in *The Bannatyne Manuscript*, ed. W. Tod Ritchie, Vol. II (Edinburgh and London, 1928), p. 3:

> st. 1 Quhen goldin phebus movit fra the ram
> In to the bull to mak his mansioun
> And hornit dean in the virgin cam
> W^t visage paill in hir assentioun
> Approcheand to hir oppositioun . . .

> st. 2 The sesoun quhen the greit Octauian
> Baith Erd and seis had had in govirnance . . .

> st. 3 The samyne tyme quhen god omnipotent
> Beheld of man the greit callamitie
> And thocht the tyme wes than Expedient
> Man to redeme fra thrald captiuitie . . .

The poem's heading says that it concerns itself with 'the incarnatioun of our saluiour chryist'. Its narrative, however, concerns the debate of the Daughters of God which leads up to the Annunciation. Now, the feast of the Annunciation (falling on 25 March) is associated traditionally with the vernal equinox, just as the Nativity itself is associated with the winter solstice. One would have every reason to expect, therefore, that the time in the solar year with which the poem opens would see the sun moving into the Ram, not out of it. It is obvious, though, that the opening has been carefully organized: stanza 1 begins with the time in the solar year; stanza 2 gives the time in history; and stanza 3 gives God's time. Can we explain Bellenden's locating the sun in Taurus in calendrical terms, or do we conclude that it was placed there for other reasons—reasons in conjunction with which the calendar date must be considered irrelevant?

In this connection we may turn to a pair of lines from Virgil's *Georgics* (I. 217–18):

> *Candidus auratis aperit cum cornibus annum*
> *Taurus . . .*

'the white bull with its gilded horns opens the year'. Taken out of context—and ill understood, these lines could be supposed to imply that Virgil thought the Bull 'opened the year', in the sense that we would say the Ram opens it.

R. H. Allen (*Star Names, Their Lore and Meaning*, repr. New York, 1963, p. 378) and W. M. O'Neill (*Time and the Calendars*, Sydney, 1975, p. 20) both present Virgil as supposing as much. They fail to take account of the fact that Virgil has only just written (line 208) '*Libra die somnique pares ubi fecerit horas*', which clearly places the autumn equinox in Libra, and therefore the spring equinox in Aries. By 'aperit', therefore, Virgil means 'opens up' (sc. the agricultural year).

It is possible, then, that Bellenden had some recollection of the Virgilian tag in mind, though the possibility is no more than remote. More plausibly one would argue that the astronomical reference at the opening of the poem works merely at the level of poetic appropriateness—that for once it does not carry implications of a calendrical date at all. The associations are between Christ, the sun, and Taurus; and Mary, the moon, and Virgo (that being the sign into which Bellenden says the moon had moved).

Another work that employs the zodiacal signs independently of the calendrical dates we are accustomed to associate with them is *The Pilgrimage of the Soul* (edited and published by William Caxton in 1483). This work is organized partly on the principle of correlating the events of Christ's life with the signs of the zodiac—an indication in itself of how variously the workings of the heavens could be related to the affairs of the world. There we read: 'Also soone as Cryste the sonne of ryghtwysnes was born of his moder, he mette with the signe of Taurus; Herodes, the cruell horned boole . . .'. This same work also makes the 'Sonne' dwell in the sign of Virgo 'fully nyne monethes', where (clearly) poetical aptness parts company with astronomical reality.

There is one further point to be considered here: if Bellenden is working purely at the level of poetic association, is he also able to control his imagery, to make it work rationally? The sun, we are told, has moved into Taurus; the moon, on the other hand, is in Virgo. She has a 'visage paill' (4), and is approaching 'hir oppositioun'. This, like any other astronomical allusion with any degree of specificity, may be subjected to orderly analysis. The sun is at longitude 30°, or so; the moon is at longitude 150°, or so. So far from being 'pale' she is in fact, on the terms Bellenden himself specifies, something like ten days past new and still waxing!

III. 22 John Bellenden, 'The Proheme of the Croniculs', 1-13, in *The Bannatyne Manuscript*, ed. W. Tod Ritchie, II. 9:

> Quhen siluer diane full of bemis bricht
> fra dirk eclips wes past this vther nicht
> And in the crab hir propir mansioun gane.
> Artophilax contending at his micht
> In the grit Eist to set his visage richt.
> I mene the ledar of the charle wane
> Aboif our heid wes the vrsis twane.
> Quhen sterris small obscuris in oure sicht.
> And Lucifer left twinkland him allane.
>
> The frosty nicht w^t hir prolixit houris
> hir mantill quhyt spred on the tendir flouris.
> Quhen ardent labour hes addressit me
> Translait the story of oure progenitouris.
>   *grit Eist*: due East

Were we to take this passage on trust, we would say it describes an actual occasion, one on which the poet considered the project he had in hand. So Lydgate, and Skelton, as we have seen; and so Douglas, as we will find. What of Bellenden? He provides us with other information that must be assimilated before an answer can be given. In his Envoy to the translation of Hector Boece's *Scotorum Historiae* (Paris, 1527), to which this passage is a prologue, Bellenden tells us that he has been at work for a year:

> Quhill goldin Titan with his birnand chare
> Past all the signis in the Zodiak
>
> .    .    .    .    .    .    .    .
>
> And Phebus turnit vnder Capricorne,
> The samyn greis quhare I first began . . .
> ('The Translator sayis to his buke as followis')

Bellenden also dates an Epistle addressed to James V 'at Edinburgh, the last day of Septembre', 1531.

> See *The Chronicles of Scotland* . . . *Translated into Scots by John Bellenden*, ed. E. C. Batho and H. W. Husbands, Vol. II (Edinburgh and London, 1941), p. 437.

Each of these components, then, must be taken into account.

(1) The translation took a year, in which time the sun moved from Capricorn to Capricorn.

(2) Its Epistle is dated 30 September 1531.

(3) At the time of starting on the work an 'eclips' of the moon occurred, and the moon was then in (or close to) Cancer.

(4) Boötes was then rising at evening.

(5) Venus as Lucifer was alone in the sky towards dawn.

We may observe here that the 'Proheme' is purportedly both documentary and occasional. While, then, the poet must of course be allowed to invent whatever fictions he pleases, it would still be rather odd, in these circumstances, for him to invent an eclipse.

A point of departure is offered by the express statement of the Envoy that the sun was in Capricorn when Bellenden began, and by the apparent confirmation of the Proheme that an eclipsed (opposing) moon was lying in Cancer ('in the crab hir propir mansioun gane'). The two documents appear to confirm one another.

Before we consider the eclipse more closely, we may consider 'Artophilax' (Boötes) and Lucifer. None of the stars in Boötes (including its primary star, Arcturus) rises due east, and yet Bellenden says that 'Artophilax' *was* attempting to set his face 'in the grit Eist' (5). How, then, do we accommodate the fact that in the latitude of Scotland Arcturus rises some 40° *north* of east? The answer is simple: we were wrong to assume that 'set his visage' meant 'rise'. Instead Bellenden means what he says—'Boötes was coming to a point where (having risen some time earlier) he did lie directly above the east point of the horizon.'

There is more, and it also ties in coherently. Bellenden also says that the two Bears were 'Aboif oure heid'. At his latitude they are always overhead, in the sense that they never set. If the phrase has any sharpness, then, it must mean that the Great Bear was at its upper transit of the meridian, and so 'overhead' in a strict sense. And indeed this is the case. Place Boötes such that it lies directly above the eastern horizon, and at the same time Ursa major will be bisected almost exactly by the meridian.

We notice, next, that it appears to be close to dawn: Lucifer (Venus as morning star) is 'left twinkland him allane'. Now we can attempt to verify Bellenden's date in general terms. At his epoch the sun entered Capricorn on or about 12 December. At this time Boötes and the Bears would be where Bellenden says they were at about 4.30 a.m.

In these general terms, then, the passage seems to square with itself readily enough. Now, however, we are obliged to meet a very particular constraint. Was there a lunar eclipse at the time? Reference to Oppolzer shows that between April 1526 (the month by which Boece dated his address to James V, on completion of the original *Chronicles* which Bellenden was translating) and December 1531 (the date of Bellenden's own Epistle to James) there were ten lunar eclipses; but only one, that of 18 December 1526, will come anywhere near satisfying the constraints (taking place at night, at a longitude close to 90°).

Can anything be done to accommodate this alarmingly early date? I do see one possibility. Later in the poem (lines 71–2) Bellenden sees 'ane crownit king appeir / With tender downis rysand on his beird'. It is patent that this is intended to place James himself in the poem. But the image of James as pubescent at nineteen (as he was in 1530) is hardly credible.

It would tally much better, however, with his being about fourteen and a half, as he was in December 1526. It seems that we must be content to regard the Proheme either as an early piece rather badly patched up for a later occasion, or as indeed written for its purported occasion and containing not only a curiously juvenile James, but a major astronomical event that did not in fact take place.

## 1550s

III. 23  Gavin Douglas, *Virgil's Aeneid*, Prologue to Bk. VIII
(ed. D. Coldwell, Edinburgh and London, 1957, p. 121):

                    . . . to reid I began
The roytast ane ragment with mony rat rane,
Of all the mowys in this mold sen God merkyt man—
The moving of the mapamond, and how the moyn schane,
The Pleuch, and the polys, the planettis began,
The son, the Sevyn Starnys, and the Charl Wayn,
The Elwand, the elementis, and Arthurus Hufe,
The Horn and the Hand Staf,
Prater Iohne and Port Iaf . . .

This passage is deliberately confused and nonsensical ('the roytast ane ragment'). But in the confusion there must be some control. How would Douglas's audience see that it was a crazy assortment unless they had at least some comprehension of its contents?

In the jumbled list seven constellations can be identified— neither Prester John nor Port Jaffa (*pace* Coldwell) being among them. We may be confident, too, that 'the Horn' is not Monoceros (the Unicorn), as some have suggested, since that constellation was not invented (by Petrus Plancius) until a century after Douglas was writing.

The seven constellations are:

| | |
|---|---|
| the Pleuch (plough) | Ursa major |
| the Sevyn Starnys | Ursa major (or the Pleiades) |
| the Charl Wayn | Ursa major (certainly) |
| the Elwand | Orion's belt |
| Arthurus Hufe (house) | Arcturus (in Boötes) |

the Horn                Ursa minor
the Hand Staf       Orion's sword.

To identify the constellations in this way shows us how the jumbled list should be read. They are all well known, so that the confusion lies in the randomness in the order of their being named and in the way the names fall over one another —Ursa major is named by three different means and in a manner which spuriously suggests the names are three different entities. Construing Douglas's tactic in this way, one would prefer to take 'the Sevyn Starnys' as yet another variant for Ursa major rather than as a reference to the Pleiades.

In his translation of *Aeneid*, Bk. III Douglas has to accommodate the following, a scene at some time before midnight:

> *Arcturum pluviasque Hyadas geminosque Triones,*
> *Armatumque auro . . . Oriona.*
> (515–16)
> ('Arcturus, the rainy Hyades, and the twin Bears;
> and Orion in golden armour'.)

Virgil himself alludes to the best known of the constellations. How does Douglas render the lines?

> Arthuris Huyf, and Hyades betakynnand rayn,
> Syne Watlyng Streit, the Horn and the Charle Wayn,
> The fers Orion with hys goldyn glave.
> (III. viii. 21–3; ed. Coldwell, II (1957), 136)
> *Syne*: then             *glave*: sword

In making three lines of two, Douglas introduces 'Watlyng Streit' and expands the two Bears into 'the Horn' (Ursa minor) and 'Charle Wayn' (Ursa major). We may be sure of Watling street—it is the Milky Way, as is plain from Chaucer's *House of Fame*, 936–9:

> . . . the Galaxie,
> Which men clepeth the Milky Wey,
> For hit is whyt (and somme, parfey,
> Kallen hyt Watlynge Strete) . . .

The identity of 'the Horn' is also clear, as may be seen from Richard Eden's translation of Martin Cortes's *Arte of Navigation* (1561). There instructions are given for finding the elevation of the pole by means of Polaris: 'The North Starre: which is a Starre in the extremitie or ende of the tayle of the lesse Beare, being a constellation commonly called the Horne' (fol. lxxiv).

**III. 24  Gavin Douglas, *Virgil's Aeneid*, Prologue to Bk. XII (ed. Coldwell, IV (1960), 67-8):**

> Dyonea, nycht hyrd and wach of day,
> The starnys chasyt of the hevyn away,
> Dame Cynthia down rollyng in the see,
> And Venus lost the bewte of hir e,
> Fleand eschamyt within Cylenyus cave;
> Mars onbydrew, for all his grundyn glave,
> Nor frawart Saturn from hys mortall speir
> Durst langar in the firmament appeir,
> Bot stall abak yond in hys regioun far
> Behynd the circulat warld of Iupiter
>
> .     .     .     .     .     .     .
>
> Quhill schortly, with the blesand torch of day,
> Abilyeit in hys lemand fresch array,
> Furth of hys palyce ryall ischit Phebus . . .
>                    *onbydrew*: retreated

Later in this Prologue (line 268) we learn that the date is 'The nynt morow of fresch temperit May'. Douglas then also takes his time from the sun:

> . . . by hys hew, but orleger or dyall,
> I knew it was past four howris of day.
>                              (278-9)

Since the sun is 'newly aryssyn' (line 277), it is clear in the context that the 'four howris' are time after midnight, not time after sunrise.

In some occasional lines, 'The tyme, space and dait of the translatioun' (ed. Coldwell, IV. 194), Douglas indicates that the work, completed on 22 July 1513, has occupied him for 'auchteyn moneth space'. By this reckoning, the 9 May of the Prologue to Bk. XII will be that of 1513 and the 9 December of the Prologue to Bk. VII will be that of 1512.

Coldwell (I. 204) claimed that Douglas was writing on Christmas Eve. But the sun entered Capricorn on 12 December at this epoch, and Douglas expressly says that Phebus 'So neir approchit . . . his wyntir stage' (solstice) that 'Reddy he was to entyr the third morn / In clowdy skyis vndre Capricorn' (Prol. VII. 6–8). This makes it clear that the winter solstice is still three days away—i.e. it is 9 December.

There is always the possibility that Douglas's description might reflect actuality, but in the event it costs little effort to establish that it does not:

| Douglas: | Tuckerman: |
|---|---|
| Venus is Lucifer | sun 57°, Venus 102° (Hesperus) |
| the moon is ahead of the sun | moon 112° (behind). |

What, then, *is* the principle of organization? It is noticeable that only Jupiter and Mercury are not mentioned directly, but that even so, the position of Venus is related to 'Cylenyus' (Mercury) and Saturn is said to be hiding behind Jupiter's sphere. Indeed, effectively speaking, all the planets are made invisible at sunrise, the objective being to clear the sky in preparation for the arrival of the sun, who is given rapturous celebration in the remainder of the Prologue.

Douglas's allusions are straightforward enough, except in the case of Venus. The scene opens with her, as daughter of Dione, extinguishing the stars. This makes her 'Lucifer' and places her ahead of the sun. Then comes the moon, which is setting. Thereafter Venus is mentioned again, in terms that can be made consistent with the rest only if 'Fleand eschamyt . . .' is taken to refer, not to Venus's sinking below the horizon (which would not take place for another 12 hours or so), but to her disappearance in the gathering light of the sun.

In *The Complaint of Mars* Chaucer has Venus fly to 'Cilenios tour' and to a 'cave' within that tower. In that context it is clear that the 'cave' is the 2nd ('pitted') degree of Gemini. It may well be, then, that Douglas's reference to 'Cylenyus cave' is a conflation of Chaucer's expression. And even if it were not, the reader would be likely to construe the phrase as intending either Gemini or Virgo (Mercury's two mansions), depending on which of the two the sun's position made it possible for her to occupy. The early May date, however, locates the sun at the end of Taurus, whereas Venus's disappearance in the gathering light of dawn places her *ahead* of the sun. In the event, then, neither sign is accessible to her.

Since, however, she is the only planet above the horizon when the sun appears, she must be given somewhere to retreat —and here, it would seem, Douglas borrows a hiding place from Chaucer, without troubling himself with the mechanics of the situation.

## III. 25 Gavin Douglas, *Virgil's Aeneid*, Prologue to Bk. XIII (ed. Coldwell, IV (1960), 141-2):

Towart the evyn, amyd the symmyris heit,
Quhen in the Crab Appollo held hys sete,
Duryng the ioyus moneth tyme of June,
As gone neir was the day and supper doyn,
5 I walkyt furth abowt the feildis tyte . . .
. . . . . . . .

The son enfyrit haill, as to my sight,
Quhirlit about hys ball with bemys brycht,
15 Declynand fast towart the north in deid,
. . . . . . . .

And Esperus in the west with bemys brycht
20 Vpspryngis, as forrydar of the nycht.
. . . . . . . .

65 I walk onon, and in a sege down sat,
Now musyng apon this and now on that.
I se the poill, and eik the Vrsis brycht,
And hornyt Lucyn castand bot dym lycht,
Becauss the symmyr skyis schayn sa cleir;
70 Goldyn Venus, the mastres of the yeir,
And gentill Ioue, with hir participate,
Thar bewtuus bemys sched in blyth estait:
That schortly, thar as I was lenyt doun,
For nychtis silens, and this byrdis sovn,
75 On sleip I slaid . . .
. . . I for feir awoik
155 And blent abowt to the north est weill far,
Saw gentill Iubar schynand, the day star,
And Chiron, clepit the syng of Sagittary,
That walkis the symmyrris nycht, to bed gan cary.
Yondyr dovn dwynys the evyn sky away,
160 And vpspryngis the brycht dawyng of day

Intill ane other place nocht far in sundir
That tobehald was plesans, and half wondir.
Furth quynchyng gan the starris, on be on,
That now is left bot Lucifer allon.

The June date of this passage (line 3) is consistent with the May date of the Prologue to Bk. XII and the late-July date given for the completion of the translation (ed. Coldwell, IV. 194).

Since Venus unambiguously makes a double appearance in this protracted scene (19, 156), we are not likely to have much confidence in being able to assign an astronomical date to it. (The sun entered Cancer on or about June 12 at Douglas's epoch and was therefore still in that sign at the end of the month. During this time in 1513, Venus, as Hesperus, was well behind the sun, passing from Leo 14 to Leo 26.)

We may picture Douglas as strolling out at about 8 p.m. Sunset would be at about 8.30, but the sky would remain light for a long while. The sun would be close to its most northerly point of setting (cf. line 15: 'Declynand fast towart the north'), and Venus would shortly 'vpspryng' not, of course, in the sense that she rose above the horizon, but in the sense that she appeared in the west as the light gradually faded. Ursa major would be in the western quarter of its circle above the horizon and Ursa minor in the south quarter of its circle (line 67: 'I se . . . the Vrsis'). (Douglas has the moon and Jupiter also supposedly visible, though neither was in fact.)

Now the poet falls asleep, and when he wakes Lucifer— Venus miraculously now ahead of the sun—has appeared in the north-east (as she would indeed have done, had she been ahead of the sun). On the other horizon Sagittarius is setting (as it would have done completely about an hour before sunrise).

Here Douglas is rather particular: the sun, he says, rises 'intill ane other place nocht far in sundir' (line 161). This is true, in the sense that the sun's declination and its point of rising will change each day; but at this time of year—the solstice—the rate of change is in fact at its slowest.

Douglas makes Venus and Jupiter joint Lords of the Year

—unless one takes 'participate' to refer to Jupiter's supposed proximity or aspect with Venus. As indicated in the discussion of Skelton's *Garland of Laurel*, however, the rules governing the choice of Lord of the Year are in my view too various and too complex to allow one to impose them on doubtful passages.

Douglas's picture has charm and a good deal of apparent circumstantiality, but no basis in the supposed astronomical date. Not, of course, that there is the slightest obligation that it should. But it is a naturalistic description; it bears no signs of having been conceived in the schematic terms that make for astrological significance.

## 1589

### III. 26  Robert Greene, *The Scottish History of James the Fourth*, I. i. 205-7 (ed. N. Sanders, London, 1979, p. 23):

> . . . Saturn combust,
> With direful looks at your nativity,
> Beheld fair Venus in her silver orb.
>
> (I. i. 205-7)

This passage looks simple enough; but on analysis it raises some fascinating questions.

That Saturn, whose 'looks' are by nature direful, was in some aspect to Venus ('beheld'), is enough in itself to convey the essential message of these lines. Our question, though, is whether they have any greater astrological complexity and, indeed, whether they even make proper astrological sense.

On first analysis, one would be tempted to say that they do not. If Saturn is 'combust', then by definition he is less than 8½° away from the sun (II. 25). Venus, on the other hand, cannot move more than 47° away from the sun (I. 20. 4). The smallest of the recognized aspects is 60°, and Saturn and Venus cannot be physically more than 55½° apart on the present configuration.

However, it would be legitimate to allow the 'orbs' of the two planets to be taken into account. Saturn's is 10° and Venus's is 8°: half the sum of these two figures is 9°, so that Saturn and Venus would be in partile sestile aspect as soon as they were 51° apart, which is within our margin. I do not suggest, here, that Greene's readers would, or could, have taken this into account on the run: I merely point out that what he says is astrologically possible. There is a consequence, however. Since the only aspects which can properly be entertained are conjunction (which seems unlikely) and sestile, it will follow that the 'lookes' were 'direful' not in the sense that the aspect was malign, but from the very fact that they were Saturn's. The importance of stressing this factor becomes clear when one examines the interpretation of the passage that has previously been given. It is one that the layman would be likely to take on trust and —worse still—it has the appearance of being bolstered by contemporary evidence.

In *Tamburlaine's Malady* (pp. 50 ff.), Johnstone Parr assumed that the aspect Greene talks of must itself have been malign and therefore was either square (90°) or opposition (180°)—either of which puts Saturn and Venus an impossibly great distance apart when the other constraints are considered. Some colour was given to the interpretation by a quotation from Claude Dariot, which so happens to make it appear that at least one Renaissance author countenanced the idea that Venus could attain the excessive distance from the sun (and therefore from Saturn combust with the sun) that Parr requires.

As we shall see, however, the impression given is not Dariot's fault, nor even the fault of his first English translator, but that of 'G. C. Gentl.', who had a hand in the edition from which Parr quotes. This is the 1598 edition of *A Briefe and most easie Introduction to the Astrological Judgement of the Starres*, tr. Fabian Wither. The point is impossible to summarize, so I shall try for conciseness instead. Dariot's concern is with predicting the likelihood of marriage: 'If the lord of the ascendant or the *Moone* bee in the seventh house, and the *Sunne* do behold or apply unto Venus, it signifieth that the marriage shall come to passe, but with much labour and difficultie . . . But if the lord of the seventh house be placed in the first, . . . or that *Venus* doth behold by a trine or sextile aspect the *Sunne*, the querent shall easily obtaine his wife.' We observe two things here: first that the pattern and the consequences of it as expressed in the first half are formally reversed in the second half ('the lord of the ascendant' / 'the lord of the seventh'); and, second, that it appears that Venus may be allowed to behold the sun 'by a trine or sextile'. This alarming impression, however, is the work of 'G.C.', as is made plain if one consults the earlier edition of Dariot, that of 1583. It then becomes plain that 'G.C.' has been tinkering with the prose, in an attempt to make the passage easier to understand. In order to recognize what has happened one needs to consider the earlier version entire:

> If the lorde of the ascendent or the Moone be in the seuenth house, and the Planet from whome the Moone is seperate [i.e. separating], doth beholde or applye vnto the Planet whereunto the Moone doth apply, or the Sunne doe beholde or apply vnto Uenus, it signifieth that the mariage . . . [etc.]. But if the Lord of the seuenth house be placed in the firste . . . or that the Planet vnto whom the Moone doth apply, doth beholde the planet from whom she is separate [i.e. separating], by a trine or sextill aspect, or doth applye vnto him by like aspect, or that Uenus doeth the like vnto the Sunne, the querent . . . [etc.]
>
> (1583, sig. K1$^{r-v}$)

One can see that converses apply in both versions, but 'G.C.' has tried to simplify, and in the course of doing so has modified 'doeth the like unto the Sunne'. In the context, however, and in the light of astrological doctrine, it is plain that 'doeth the like' answers to the earlier phrase 'doe beholde or apply unto': in the first half the sun is 'applying'; in the second half Venus is 'applying'.

> The apparatus of 'application' (II. 20) indicates that in the first case Venus will be ahead of the sun and retrograde; in the second case Venus will be behind the sun but moving towards conjunction.

In other words, the trine and sestile aspects which 'G.C.' transfers to Venus are mentioned merely in relation to the (unspecified) planets with whom the moon is engaged: if she (for example) is applying to Mars and separating from Jupiter, and *they* are in trine or sestile with each other, then the marriage will go smoothly. Dariot did *not* ignorantly suppose Venus could be in trine to the sun—or in sestile, for that matter.

> The maximum elongation of Venus from the sun—47°—plus half

the sum of their orbs (8° and 17° respectively) still amounts only to 59½°.

So far we have rationalized the passage along the conventional lines that come most readily to mind. There is, however, one further possibility that should be investigated. It involves the principle of 'antiscions' (II. 13. 2). According to this convention, 'Saturn . . . Beheld faire Venus' would mean 'Saturn cast his antiscion to Venus'.

Saturn and Venus (as we have seen) could not, in the circumstances described, by physically more than 55½° apart. If we take half this amount, we obtain 27° 45′; and by the law of antiscions we could place Saturn, for instance, at Gemini 2° 15′ (27° 45′ distant from the first point of Cancer), and he would then cast his antiscion to Venus at Cancer 27° 45′. This is at least a possibility—a legitimate way of squaring Greene's lines with astrological doctrine. It has the advantage, too, of being schematically more simple. There is no necessity to supply figures or hypothetical locations, except as a means of clarifying for ourselves what might be at issue. The schematically more complex (but astrologically more accessible) explanation, on the other hand, does have this to commend it: it does not defy elementary astrological doctrine (in this case based on astronomical reality) and it may suggest that by describing Venus as being 'in her silver orb' Greene was not merely employing a poetic filler, but alluding to the particular element in astrological doctrine that in fact allows what he says to make sense.

## 1590

**III. 27  Edmund Spenser, *The Faerie Queene*, I. iii. 16 (ed. J. C. Smith and E. de Selincourt, London, 1912, p. 15):**

> Now when *Aldeboran* was mounted hie
> Aboue the shynie *Cassiopeias* chaire,
> And all in deadly sleepe did drowned lie,
> One knocked at the dore . . .

This is how Spenser marks the return home of Kirkrapine (plunderer of churches) after a night's employment. How are

we to read it? Spenser's mode of expression assumes a familiarity with Aldebaran (alpha Tauri, the Eye of the Bull), and
with the 'W' of Cassiopeia, and implies that we will accept,
even if we cannot picture, a situation in which Aldebaran will
lie poised *above* Cassiopeia. The thrust of the lines is not to
define a time of night, it is merely to present us with a stellar
configuration consistent with that time. We know that every-
one is asleep—it is the dead hour of night for most. Una's
condition, however, is different. She

> . . . euermore does steepe
> Her tender brest in bitter teares all night,
> All night she thinks too long, and often lookes for light.
>
> (I. iii. 15)

The repetition of 'all night' itself suggests the slow passing of
the time, and her looking for light (sunrise) in turn suggests
that dawn is not all that far away. If Kirkrapine may also be
supposed to have tempered greed by prudence, then he may
be imagined as returning home an hour or so (let us say)
before dawn.

The state of the heavens, then, is merely a concomitant
of this situation—it is not employed as a means of defining
it. Even so, we should examine what Spenser says, to see
whether it will in fact stand up. To do this we must fix upon
a time of year by means of satisfying two constraints: (1)
Aldebaran must be mounted high, at a time (2) when the sun
is an hour or so from rising. Inspection of a globe or an
astrolabe will show that the conditions are met by the sun's
being very nearly at the beginning of Libra, the autumn
equinox.

So far we have taken 'mounted hie / Aboue' on trust. It
may be, too, that our tacit reasoning has been quite complex.
We might be saying to ourselves, 'I would not guarantee to
identify Cassiopeia or alpha Tauri, but I recognize it as reasonable of Spenser to assume many of his readers could; and I
would expect that the sky described would be readily imagined
by someone who did know his way around it.' There may
even seem to be something perverse or pedantic in the proposition that we should *not* take Spenser on trust. But observe!

At his latitude Cassiopeia's minimum altitude above the horizon is about 15°. She lies within that disk of stars that never sets, but she does sink quite low. One might think that it would be easy enough, therefore, to find Aldebaran high above her. However, when Cassiopeia *is* at her minimum altitude, Aldebaran has been set for two hours. On the other hand, when Aldebaran reaches its greatest altitude (the extreme case of its being 'mounted hie'), it will be lying on the meridian, will be elevated some 55° above the horizon, and will then have Cassiopeia lying off to the west but some 65° above the horizon. In other words, Aldebaran can *never* mount above Cassiopeia with respect to the horizon. Has Spenser slipped up, or is there another way in which the situation should be construed?

All stars have a moment of 'culmination', a moment when they stand at their highest above the horizon. Since this coincides, by definition, with their lying on the meridian, there is a sense in which, of two bodies, the one that lies nearer to the meridian may be regarded as being the 'higher', irrespective of their positions relative to the horizon. If, then, Aldebaran is imagined in fact to be lying on the meridian, a line running north–south through the zenith will pass through that star. This provides one co-ordinate. If the other co-ordinate, the plane of the southern horizon, is now raised so that it too passes through the star, then to run one's eye across to Cassiopeia in the west may well produce the sensation that one is moving 'down' to it, despite its in fact being further above the horizon.

Such an explanation might well appear cumbersome to one unpractised at star-gazing, but that reaction would be a symptom of one's unfamiliarity with the procedures, rather than a mark of their complicatedness. We should also reflect that the alternative is to suppose that in the elementary matter of Cassiopeia's W, Spenser did not know what he was talking about. In short, my point is this: we need not only to be able to identify the constellations Spenser speaks of, but also to be able mentally to orientate ourselves correctly when looking at them.

### III. 28 Edmund Spenser, *The Faerie Queene*, I. ii. 1 (ed. Smith and De Selincourt, p. 9):

By this the Northerne wagoner had set
His seuenfold teme behind the stedfast starre,
That was in Ocean waues yet neuer wet,
But firme is fixt, and sendeth light from farre
To all, that in the wide deepe wandring arre:
And chearefull Chaunticlere with his note shrill
Had warned once, that *Phœbus* fiery carre
In hast was climbing vp the Easterne hill,
Full enuious that night so long his roome did fill.

At its most banal level this stanza says no more than that dawn was approaching. The elaboration, though—given the simplicity of the essential information conveyed—draws one's attention. It is obvious that recognition of the 'Northerne wagoner' (Ursa major) and of 'the stedfast starre' (Polaris in Ursa minor) is assumed—if they could not be recognized, what could?

That Polaris was 'in Ocean waues yet neuer wet' may draw upon, and modify, a repeated line in Homer, which says that the Great Bear 'alone' is not bathed in the ocean (*Iliad*, XVIII. 489, *Odyssey*, V. 275). Homer was so well known in antiquity that, in defending this expression, Aristotle (*Poetics*, 1461[a] 20-1) used just two words from this line to call it to mind: 'alone not-sharing'. Aristotle was defending Homer against the pedants who had objected that other constellations besides Ursa major never set. Aristotle quite fairly replied that Homer merely used the best-known constellation in the group to do duty for them all. Spenser's phrase, then, may be a reminiscence of Homer, transferred from Ursa major to Ursa minor. But it contains an addition. Spenser says that the Pole Star was 'yet' never wet and 'firme is fixt'. How closely is this to be read? If 'yet' does mean 'so far', 'to date' (and why should we doubt it?), does Spenser wish to imply that one day Polaris *will* set? To consider the phrase so narrowly might seem unwarrantable, were it not for a passage in the Proem to Book V. There Spenser bemoans the progressive running down of the cosmos. What has happened, for instance, to the sun?

. . . since the terme of fourteene hundred yeres,
That learned *Ptolomæe* his hight did take,
He is declyned from that marke of theirs,
Nigh thirtie minutes to the Southerne lake;
That makes me feare in time he will vs quite forsake.

(V, Proem 7)

In one sense, of course, Spenser's apprehension here is opportunistic. The variation in the obliquity of the ecliptic was recognized to be cyclic—there was no genuine fear that the sun's declination would actually decrease to a point where eventually the sun would abandon the northern hemisphere. But in the mood of the poem at this point it suits Spenser to indulge this gloomy, if whimsical, question. It is one that the Mutability Cantos eventually resolve.

Read in the light of this passage from Book V, Spenser's contention that Polaris has not, *so far*, taken a bath may indeed carry more implication than would at first meet the eye.

To return to the scene depicted: Ursa major has 'set His . . . teme' 'behind' Polaris. On what orientation? We know (cf. Bellenden, 'Proheme') that the Great Bear in fact never does 'set' in the sense of sinking below the horizon. Being visible throughout the year, though, it can be seen to cross the meridian at two points: it has both a 'superior' and an 'inferior' culmination. Clearly, then, by 'had set his teme' Spenser means 'had placed' his team; and 'behind' Polaris means 'beyond', in the sense that if the eye of an observer facing north travels along the meridian starting from the zenith, it will move first past Polaris (marking the North Pole) and only then encounter Ursa major, positioned at the low point of its orbit.

So much for the orientation. What we now realize is that Ursa major will adopt this position once in *any* period of twenty-four hours. This is why the cockerel has a part to play. The crowing of the cock was once a way of dividing the night into its phases, the last of its crowings being the signal that dawn was coming. And here Chaunticlere has crowed 'once'. Spenser offers a further constraint, however, one which indicates that 'once' does not mean 'for the first time', since the sun is in haste to rise. The inference is plain: Ursa major is at its low point, *and* dawn is approaching. Satisfy these two constraints on a celestial globe set at Spenser's latitude, and you will find that the sun lies in Cancer. This, in other words, is a midsummer dating, though it has cost us some effort to see what store of knowledge Spenser draws upon in presenting the approach of dawn so grandly. There is one other point to be considered here. We have concluded that Spenser's description is consistent—and consistent only—with a midsummer date. But is that the thrust of the lines? Surely it is not. He was not cryptically inviting us to work out the season of the year; he was assuming a season (even if the assumption is a buried one) and describing a time that accorded with it. What we have had to do, however, is to work in reverse—to say that the situation described will hold good only if the season is midsummer.

**III. 29  Edmund Spenser, *The Faerie Queene*, II. ii. 46 (ed. Smith and De Selincourt, p. 80):**

> Night was far spent, and now in *Ocean* deepe
> *Orion*, flying fast from hissing snake,
> His flaming head did hasten for to steepe . . .

Here we may again reverse the direction of the implied argument: Spenser says that at this (unspecified) time of year Orion was setting when the night was well advanced. We may proceed, on the contrary, by asking, if Orion *is* setting late at night, what time of year will it be?

First, we must attempt to determine whether 'far spent' can be narrowed down. There is some assistance provided by the fact that Guyon has been three months away from the Faerie Queene's court and that he was entrusted with his task at a 'yearely solemne feast', held on 'The day that first doth lead the yeare around' (II. ii. 42). There are, at first sight, three possibilities here: the day that 'leads' the year could be New Year's Day, or the Vernal Equinox, or Elizabeth's Accession Day (17 November), in which case the year would be regnal. The Vernal Equinox, however, can be discounted at once, since the three-month interval since Guyon's departure from the court would bring the calendar to mid-June and place the sun in Cancer. Orion would then be setting just *before* the sun, at about 4.45 p.m.

Three months from New Year's Day, on the other hand, would bring the date to the beginning of April, placing the sun near the middle of Aries. At this time, though, Orion would be setting before 10 p.m. The last alternative is the best: three months from the Queen's Accession Day would bring the date to mid-February, would place the sun near the beginning of Pisces, and (more in accordance with 'far spent') Orion would be setting at about 1.30 a.m.

What is the 'hissing snake' from which Orion flees? Three of the four notes in the Spenser Variorum, ad loc., invoke Scorpio and the myth that, after he had stung Orion to death, both were translated to the heavens. In token of their enmity, one was made to rise as the other set. There are precedents for regarding the scorpion as a snake, as also for regarding the snake as an insect. Thomas Hood (*The Use of the Celestial Globe in plano*, also 1590) refers, for instance, to an interpretation of Scorpio's mythology that sees it as 'the Scorpion or Serpent' that caused Pharaoh to release the children of Israel. There is evidence, then, that Spenser could have intended Scorpio when he alluded to a 'hissing snake'.

But there are other considerations, ones relating to celestial cartography. Almost 180° separate Orion and Scorpio, and rather more than half of that interval is occupied by a very snaky object—the (single-headed) Hydra. The conventional representation of Hydra, deriving ultimately from Ptolemy's Catalogue, placed Orion with his back to the viewer, or else half turned to the West, while to the East, and bearing down upon him, was Hydra's head, poised to strike.

See, for instance, Dürer's influential planisphere of 1515, or the planisphere in Hood's *Use of the Celestial Globe*.

At least in graphic terms, then, and according to the convention that was becoming firmly established in Spenser's lifetime, 'flying fast' (with its sense of urgency and its possible hint of the closeness of the pursuit) makes a great deal more sense if applied to Hydra.

### III. 30   Edmund Spenser, *The Faerie Queene*, III. i. 57 (ed. Smith and De Selincourt, p. 146):

> By this th'eternall lampes, wherewith high *Ioue*
> Doth light the lower world, were halfe yspent,
> And the moist daughters of huge *Atlas* stroue
> Into the *Ocean* deepe to driue their weary droue.

We are alerted, by now, to the fact that a stellar rising or setting is useless in itself as a time reference: it must be accompanied by a second component, operating as a co-ordinate.

Spenser could have contented himself here by saying, straight out, that the Hyades (in Taurus) were setting. He chose, however, to dignify them into 'the moist daughters of huge *Atlas*'. By doing so, he calls upon us to distinguish between them and another seven of Atlas's daughters who also inhabit Taurus—the Pleiades. Here lies the force of 'moist'. The Hyades, when they came to be setting at dawn, signified the onset of rain; whereas the Pleiades, when rising with the sun, indicated the time at which taking to the sea (Gr. *plein*, to sail) would again be safe.

The Hyades are setting, we are told here, at midnight. From this it follows that the sun will be close to Aries—we are in a Spring setting. Or rather, it is a configuration consistent with Spring. In these instances (as I have been indicating) I do not consider that Spenser necessarily intends us to deduce a season: it is rather that the configuration he portrays is consistent with the season he has in mind.

### 1594

### III. 31   Edmund Spenser, *Epithalamion*

Since this poem, in which Spenser celebrates the day of his own marriage, has twenty-four stanzas, it would be surprising indeed if we could *not* link the poem's narrative structure in some way with a time scheme. One's initial assumption might well be that one stanza represents one clock hour, and the task would then merely be to find how the clock hours and the stanzas fit together.

On the other hand, we may also wish to examine whether or not there is a form of correspondence between the 'unequal' hours (II. 33. 1) of 11 June 1594 and the structure of the poem.

In the event, there does prove to be a correlation between Spenser's planetary allusions and the actual rising and setting of the sun, Venus, and the moon on the day in question. To establish what it is, we need first to tabulate the unequal hours in terms of clock time (in order to give ourselves a bearing). Since the day of the wedding is the summer solstice, the longest day of the year ('This day the sunne is in his chiefest hight'; st. 15), the unequal hours of day and night will be at their maximum inequality: the 'hours' of day will each have 1 hr. 22 mins. in them, and the hours of night will each have only 38 mins. in them.

These figures are derived from Mathematical Formulas 3, using a latitude of 52°.

Reference to Tuckerman (p. 815) allows us to determine that on 11 June 1594 the sun was at Cancer 1; Venus at Cancer 10 with 1° of northern latitude; and that the moon moved from Leo 10 at rising to Leo 16 at setting, with 4° of northern latitude. Now we can tabulate:

| stanza | unequal hour | clock time | event |
|---|---|---|---|
| 5 | 1st of day | 3.48 | sunrise |
| 6 | 2nd | 5.10 | Venus (elevated 5°) |
| | 3rd | 6.32 | |
| | 4th | 7.54 | |
| 9 | 5th | 9.16 | moon (elevated 20°) |
| | 6th | 10.38 | |
| | 7th | 12.00 | |
| | 8th | 1.22 | |
| | 9th | 2.44 | |
| | 10th | 4.06 | |
| | 11th | 5.28 | |
| 16 | 12th | 6.50 | Venus (elevated 15°) |
| 17 | 1st of night | 8.12 | sunset |
| | 2nd | 8.50 | |
| | 3rd | 9.28 | |
| | 4th | 10.06 | |
| 21 | 5th | 10.44 | moon (elevated 2°) |
| | 6th | 11.22 | |
| | 7th | 12.00 | |

It will be clear that as soon as one makes a match between
stanza 5 and sunrise ('Phœbus gins to shew his glorious hed')
one is constraining the poem to make its other astronomical
references on cue, as it were. If, for instance, the moon had
in fact set by the clock time that matches with, say, stanza 18,
then our scheme would collapse. Let us see, then, what the
poem itself presents.

In stanza 6 we find the following:

> My loue is now awake out of her dreame,
> And her fayre eyes like stars that dimmed were
> With darksome cloud, now shew theyr goodly beams
> More bright than Hesperus his head doth rere.
>
> (93-6)

—Hesperus, we notice, not Lucifer; Venus behind, not ahead
of the sun, and rearing her head some 5° above the horizon at
the time which answers to the beginning of stanza 6.

The next allusion comes in stanza 9, where the bride
emerges:

> Loe where she comes along with portly pace
> Lyke Phœbe from her chamber of the East . . .

By this time the moon was indeed some 20° above the eastern
horizon—coming from her chamber of the east, as required.

With the marriage ceremony completed, Spenser bemoans
the fact that his marriage falls on the longest day and the
shortest night of the year. Eventually, though, night does
begin to fall. Stanza 16, on our scheme, matches with the last
planetary hour of day. In it Spenser invokes the sun and the
'euening star', firstly, the sun:

> Hast thee O fayrest Planet to thy home
> Within the Western fome:
> Thy tyred steedes long since haue need of rest.
> Long though it be, at last I see it gloome,
> And the bright euening star with golden creast
> Appeare out of the East.
> Fayre childe of beauty, glorious lampe of loue
>
> .    .    .    .    .    .    .
>
> How chearefully thou lookest from aboue . . .
>
> (282-91)

On our scheme Venus is elevated some 15° above the horizon —but of course she lies in the west, not the east. But the 'euening star', of course, *cannot* 'appeare' out of the east, either in the sense of rising in that quarter, or in the sense of beginning to be seen there in the fading light of the sun. The reference here to the 'East', then, is not merely a setback to our scheme, but an astronomical impossibility on any terms. There is little doubt that 'East' is an error; and there is no difficulty in emending. 'East' has already been rhymed with 'best' in stanza 9 and is supposedly rhymed with 'creast' here; so that 'West', as a substitute, would in no way interfere with the rhyme scheme.

One might argue, further, that whoever was responsible for 'Appeare out of the East' might ignorantly have taken 'Appeare' to mean 'rise' and so deployed what they thought was the appropriate horizon. On the other hand, it may simply be one of those reversal errors (left for right) to which we are all prone.

Taking 'East' to be an error for 'West', therefore, we may say that with the onset of dusk ('I see it gloome') Spenser sees Venus as Hesperus in the *western* sky. Then, after the due interval, in stanza 21 Spenser sees the chaste Cinthia:

Who is the same, which at my window peepes?
.    .    .    .    .    .    .
Is it not Cinthia, she that neuer sleepes,
But walkes about high heauen al the night?
(372-5)

Here our scheme matches with the poem only by the narrowest of margins. The clock time answering to the beginning of stanza 21 is 10.44 p.m., and by this time the moon needs her 4° of northern latitude, and her progression on to Leo 16, in order still to lie above the horizon. Had no account of her latitude been taken, she would have been thought to have set. As it is, Tuckerman's tables show us that the moon was indeed so low in the sky as to be able to peep in at the window.

The congruence between the actual situation on the day celebrated and the events of the poem when the time-scheme of unequal hours is imposed upon them is remarkable. It must surely be beyond the realms of mere coincidence that the match is so good. After all, we began merely by taking the plain indication of stanza 5 that the sun then rose. By using the common convention of unequal hours and by deriving from Tuckerman the positions of the planets on the day named, we conclude by finding Cinthia, in what we might describe as the poem's real time, placed where the poet may directly invoke her blessing on his marriage.

### III. 32  Edmund Spenser, *Epithalamion*, st. 15:

> This day the sunne is in his chiefest hight,
> With Barnaby the bright,
> From whence declining daily by degrees,
> He somewhat loseth of his heat and light,
> When once the Crab behind his back he sees.

These lines mark the point of the solar year opposite to that in Chaucer's *Franklin's Tale* ('But now in Capricorn adoun he lighte'). The sun is here in his 'chiefest hight'—at its maximum altitude above the southern horizon. This occurs at noon on mid-summer's day (I. 12. 2). Its declination thereafter steadily decreases through the signs Cancer, Leo, and Virgo, until it reaches 0° upon its arrival in Libra at the autumn equinox.

The phrase 'declining daily by degrees' could suggest to the layman that the sun's decrease was at the rate of one degree per day when the Crab was behind its back. This is never the case, however. The daily rate of decrease in declination is in the order of $12''$ at the beginning of Cancer and $11' 14''$ at the end of it—at no time, either in this quadrant or any of the other three, does it even approach $1°$ per day. 'By degrees' here means no more than 'gradually', or, perhaps, 'by gradual increase'.

## 1596

### III. 33  Edmund Spenser, *Prothalamion*

Alastair Fowler has explored one way in which the mythological allusions of the *Prothalamion* may be given astronomical extension, such that a pairing of the zodiacal signs by opposites (Aries with Libra, etc.) may be used to image the 'Bauldricke of the Heauens' mentioned in the poem's final stanza.

*Conceitful Thought: The Interpretation of English Renaissance Poems*, Edinburgh, 1975, pp. 59–86.

Fowler's system is ingenious: each of the images capable of astronomical extension fits his pattern with some degree of immediacy. For instance, Spenser's reference to 'faire *Venus* . . . With her heart-quelling Sonne' in stanza 6 answers, on Fowler's scheme, to the sign of Pisces, one of whose alternative names was 'Venus et Cupido'. There is a limitation, however. By its very nature (since it groups the zodiacal signs by pairs) the scheme will move through an entire cycle within six stanzas, whereas the poem has ten stanzas. Is there, then, a way of conceiving the poem's structure such that only ten signs have been matched when the poem has run its course of ten stanzas? I believe there is.

Its conclusion presents the two prospective grooms advancing to meet the two prospective brides (whose stellar counterpart is Ariadne's bridal crown). They are then likened to 'the twins of *Ioue* . . . Which decke the Bauldricke of the Heauens bright'—the comparison with Gemini is explicit. What follows? If a match is made between the rising of Virgo/Libra and of Corona borealis and stanza 1, the progression of the scheme will itself (having regard to Spenser's latitude) determine that Gemini/Cancer will rise to match with stanza 10. And if this is how the heavens are disposed at the poem's conclusion, then the constellation Gemini (answering to the grooms) will lie poised above the eastern horizon some 50° *east* of north; while the constellation Corona will simultaneously lie poised above the western horizon some 50° *west* of north. There will be a precise symmetry in the disposition of the heavens that answers splendidly to the pageantry of the poem's conclusion.

The intermediate allusions, such as that to '*Ioue* himselfe when he a Swan would be' (a reference extendable to the constellation of the Swan—Cygnus—and so to Leda), will match equally with mine or with Fowler's scheme. The allusion to Jove as swan, for instance, occurs in stanza 3, and the scheme I am advocating causes Scorpio/Sagittarius to rise. When it does, at Spenser's latitude the constellation Cygnus also rises.

> By Scorpio/Sagittarius, etc., I mean the latter part of the first sign and the initial part of the second. I do not mean both signs entire, which would give me too much leeway.

Any construction of the poem that attempts to place a schematized pattern upon it should, of course, give its account of why there are just 180 lines—half a circle of lines. My answer would be that at its conclusion, when the 180 lines are completed, it is the semicircle of the heavens lying above the horizon that draws the eye. The poem begins with Virgo/Libra rising and ends with Pisces/Aries rising (its 180° opposite). After this revolution through half a circle the poem comes to its point of rest, placing the appropriate constellations in equipoise above their earthly counterparts.

## Seventeenth and Eighteenth Centuries

### 1606 (acted)

**III. 34  William Shakespeare, *Macbeth*, I. ii. 25-8 (ed. Kenneth Muir, London, 1964, p. 7):**

> CAPT.:  As whence the sun 'gins his reflection,
>         Shipwracking storms and direful thunders break,
>         So from that spring, whence comfort seem'd to come,
>         Discomfort swells . . .

These two pairs of lines have a see-saw rhetorical balance. Their function, by expressing essentially the same sentiment twice, is to mark a pause in the Captain's account of the battle from whose flurry the play takes its narrative origin. In broad and unrefined paraphrase, the Captain is merely saying that 'just when you expect good news, what you get is bad news' (though, in a further twist, he immediately reverses his emphasis). If, however, we attempt to read the first pair of lines closely, what do we make of them? (We are entitled to use the leisure we have as readers which the audience does not.)

The main problem is to determine the point of the compass intended by '*whence* the sun . . .'. We cannot expect the second line of the pair to give us an answer, however, since weather lore will have an adage for every conceivable occasion. What, then, of the first line in itself? We need to determine a direction from which it can be said with some persuasiveness that the sun ' 'gins his reflection'.

If we consult the editions, we find two schools of thought: one takes 'reflection' to mean 'shining', and points to the East. But what merit is there in using 'reflection' in connection with the *source* of light? Those who have seen this interpretation as a contradiction in terms have argued, instead, that the sun 'reflexes' as it approaches the vernal equinox. This interpretation, however, fails to recognize that the sun does not then turn round (re-flex) when it crosses the celestial equator—it merely continues its northerly progress. Had the Captain meant that the sun 'begins to return his beams' (i.e. to the northern hemisphere), this interpretation would have held good. But he means, instead, that the sun 'begins his turning-round'.

The sun satisfies this condition when it turns back from the Tropic of Capricorn at the winter solstice. In other words, what the Captain may be taken to be saying is that just when the sun, having reached its furthest point of travel away from the northern hemisphere, is turning round to come back and so promises a seasonal up-turn—what you get, instead, is a down-turn in the weather.

The myth of equinoctial gales (storms around the time of the vernal equinox) and the seductiveness of reading 'spring' in line 27 as a pun (a shift from Spring as season to spring as water) have prevented editors from seeing the plain sense of ' 'gins his reflection'. Their interpretation makes Shakespeare blind to etymology ('re-flex') and ignorant of the sun's annual course.

## *c*. 1 6 1 4 (a c t e d)

**III. 35** John Webster, *The Duchess of Malfi*, II. iii. 72–80
(ed. F. L. Lucas, London, 1958, p. 69):

BOSOLA. What's here? a childes Nativitie calculated! [*Reads*] *The Dutchesse was deliver'd of a Sonne, 'tweene the houres twelve, and one, in the night*: Anno Dom: 1504. (*that's this yeere*) decimo nono Decembris, (*that's this night*) taken according to the Meridian of Malfy (*that's our Dutchesse: happy discovery!*). *The Lord of the first house, being combust in the ascendant, signifies short life: and* Mars *being in a human signe, joyn'd to the taile of the Dragon, in the eight house, doth threaten a violent death*; Caetera non scrutantur.

Although this passage is very precise about the date, time, and latitude of the nativity (19 December 1504, lat. Amalfi, *c*. 12.30 a.m.), it both names and locates only one planet—Mars in the eighth. We have no cause, in these circumstances, to suppose that an actual configuration provided Webster with his information.

Bosola finds that the figure is '*taken according to the Meridian of Malfy*', and one might at first suppose Webster has here confused 'latitude' (on a north–south axis) with 'meridian' (on an east–west axis). It is probable, however, that he is using 'meridian' in its looser sense (*OED*, *sb.* 5) of 'locality or situation'.

The conditions relating to the (unspecified) Lord of the Ascendant are that it should be

(a) combust
(b) actually in the ascendant
(c) at some time between midnight and 1 a.m.

Now, 'combustion' involves a planet in being less than 8½° away from the sun (II. 25). From this it follows that the sun, in turn, must also be not far from the ascendant, since the planet in combustion is here said to be physically in the 1st house. But . . . the time of year is December, and the time of day close to midnight. How then can the sun possibly be close to rising? It cannot, and the passage contradicts itself at a rather elementary level.

Johnstone Parr (*Tamburlaine's Malady*, pp. 94 ff.) has misled a number of the play's editors on this point.

How, then, is the passage to be read? The answer must be that Webster knew enough of his subject to be able to provide his audience merely with the appropriate signals. He is trading on their knowledge that the ascendant is the most powerful point in the horoscope; that to be 'combust' bodes no good; that Mars is necessarily malevolent; that conjunction with the Dragon's Tail also bodes no good; and that the eighth house is a bad house, one of the two worst.

I take it that these details would be apprehended intuitively and that the unfolding of the horoscope moves so rapidly that its inconsistency would be likely to escape notice. Webster is playing with the resonances of the terminology.

In bare essence the message is admirably succint: the Lord of the First is combust and signifies short life; Mars threatens a violent death. If you also happen to know that the Dragon's Tail functions as an infortune and that the 8th house is the house of Death, you will receive Webster's message all the more clearly.

## *c*. 1 6 1 6 ( a c t e d )

III. 36 John Fletcher, *The Bloody Brother* [*Rollo, Duke of Normandy*], IV. ii (cf. J. D. Jump (ed.), London, 1948, pp. 58–9):

```
        NORB.          . . . what's here?
160     The geniture nocturnall longitude
        At twenty one degrees the latitude
        At forty nine and ten minutes, how are the Cardines?
        FISK. Libra in twenty foure, forty foure minutes,
        And Capricorne.
        NORB.              I see it, see the Planets
165     Where, how they are dispos'd; the Sunne and Mercury,
        Mars with the Dragons taile, in the third house,
        And pars fortunæ in the Imo cœli.
        Then Iupiter in the twelfe, the Cacodæmon.
        BUB. And Venus in the second, inferna porta.
170     NORB. I see it, peace; then Saturne in the fift,
        Luna ith' seaventh, and much of Scorpio,
        [That's] Mars his gaudium, rising in the ascendant,
        [And joyn'd] with Libra too, the house of Venus,
        And [in Imo] Cœli, Mars his exaltation[;]
```

175    Ith' seaventh house, *Aries* [,] being his naturall house,
       And where he is now seated: [all] these shew him
       To be the *Almuten*.
       RUS.          Yes he's Lord of the geniture,
       Whether you examine it by *Ptolomies* way,
       Or *Masahales*, *Saell*, or *Alkindus*.
180    FISK. No other Planet hath so many dignities
       Either by himselfe, or in regard o'th *Cuspes*.
       NORB. Why hold your tongue then, if you know it; *Venus*
       The Lady of the *Horoscope*, being *Libra*,
       The other part *Mars* rules: so that the geniture
185    Being nocturnall, *Luna* is the highest,
       None else being in sufficient dignitie,
       She being in *Aries* in the seaventh house
       Where *Sol* exalted is the *Alchocodon*.
       BUB. Yes for you see he hath his termine
190    In the degrees where she is and enjoyes
       By that six dignities.
       FISK.                 Which are clearly more
       Then any else that view her i' the scheme.
       NORB. Why I saw this, and could ha told you too
       That he beholds her with a trine aspect
195    Here out of *Sagitary*, almost partile
       And how that *Mars* out of the selfe same house,
       (But another signe) here by a platique aspect
       Looks at the hilege with a quartile [,] ruling
       The house where the sunne is; all this could I
200    Have told you, but that you will out-run me, and more,
       That this same quartile aspect to the Lady of life,
       Here in the seaventh promises some danger,
       *Cauda Draconis* being so neere *Mars*,
       And *Caput Algoll* in the house of death.
205    LAT. How Sir? I pray you cleere that.
       NORB.                 What is the question first?
       RUS. Of the Dukes life, what dangers threaten him?
       NORB. Apparent and those suddaine: when the *Hyleg*,
       Or *Alchocodon* by direction come
       To a quartile opposition of the place
210    Where *Mars* is in the geniture (which is now
       At hand) or else oppose to *Mars* himselfe, expect it.
       LAT. But they may be prevented.
       NOR.                 Wisdome only,
       That rules the starres may doe it, for *Mars* being
       Lord of the geniture in *Capricorne*,

215    Is (if you mark it) now a Sextile here
With *Venus* Lady of the Horoscope,
So she being in her *exilium*, which is *Scorpio*
And *Mars* his *gaudium*; is o're rul'd by him,
And cleere debillitated, five degrees
220    Beneath her ordinary power, so
That at the most she can but mittigate.

This is much the most complex passage with which we have to deal. At first sight it seems scarcely penetrable. When one gains some familiarity with it, however, one's perspective changes considerably. I would go so far as to say that with appropriate stage business and a deal of gesticulation, an audience could be lulled into following the scene in some

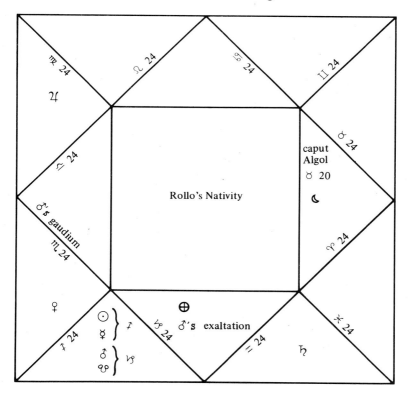

FIG. 11

detail. As we shall see, the author provides considerable assistance to his audience, his scheme is largely recoverable (see Fig. 11), and the general outline of the analysis follows exactly the procedures an astrologer would adopt.

Given the complexities of the scene, I shall divide my analysis into three sections: first, an editorial commentary on the entire passage; second, a discussion of the lines I consider to be corrupt; and third, a general view of how the scene proceeds. (Some readers may care to begin with section 3.)

## 1. *Editorial*

160–1 longitude . . . latitude] Normally a horoscope would express longitude by giving the name of the place. The co-ordinates here point to Caen.

162 *Cardines*] Primary houses (II. 17). The continuation ('*Libra* . . . And *Capricorne*) indicates that Fletcher is using the equal house system of division (II. 3. 1).

166–7 Dragons taile . . . *pars fortunæ*] See II. 11. 1. The two are very commonly grouped together.

168–9 *Cacodæmon* . . . *inferna porta*] Alternative names for the houses specified. They are correctly applied, but may be taken as atmospheric descriptions in this context.

172 *gaudium*] Preferred mansion—here Scorpio (see further in section 2).

173 house] Here, mansion (II. 13).

174 exaltation] Mars's exaltation is Capricorn 28, and the cusp of the 4th house is defined (by implication—line 163) as Capricorn 24.

175 naturall house] The context shows that 'mansion' is meant.

177 *Almuten* . . . Lord of the geniture] The author obligingly glosses his hard word.

181 in regard o'th *Cuspes*] By examining which signs define the various houses, Fisk purports to have determined that Mars is senior Dispositor (II. 17. 3).

183 Lady of the *Horoscope*] Venus is so by virtue of its being Libra that ascends.

183 being *Libra*] The subject of 'being' is properly '*Horoscope*'. Jump followed Dyce in emending to 'being in *Libra*'.

Clearly both of them thought that Venus was in that sign, but line 217 makes it plain that she is in Scorpio.

184-5 *Mars* rules . . . *Luna* is the highest] Norbrett is plainly at odds with himself. The objective here is to blind with science, and the fact that the horoscope is nocturnal gives colour to the moon's being promoted. She is *not* 'the highest', however, since the rest of the scene validates the fact that '*Mars* rules'.

187 *Alchocodon*] 'Giver of Years' (II. 31).

189 hath his termine] The sun, like the moon, does not have any 'terms' (II. 16); and in any case the standard practice is to allot one point only for a term. Although this nonsense is given to one of the minor villains, it is implicitly endorsed by the major one, Norbrett (line 193).

194-8 trine . . . partile . . . platique] See II. 13. 1 and II. 18. 3.

198 hilege] See II. 30. Line 201 obligingly makes it clear that the moon is considered to be 'hyleg' in this figure ('Lady of life').

203 *Cauda Draconis* being so neere *Mars*] Validated by line 166.

204 *Caput Algoll*] The star Algol in Caput Medusae (part of the constellation Perseus). It is a malign star, often considered along with the planets in evaluating a horoscope. On the implied scheme, the 8th house is defined by Taurus 24, whereas the longitude of Algol at this period was Taurus 20. On this account it lies within five degrees of the cusp of the 8th, and astrological convention would therefore consider it as though it was actually in that house (II. 4. 2).

208 direction] An entire subsidiary branch of astrology (II. 35).

209 quartile opposition] Either a contradiction in terms, and so an absurdity, or else a way of indicating that the square aspect (as well as opposition proper) was malign.

210-11 which is now At hand] A good instance of how economically the information in the scene is manipulated. Here it is said that the hyleg will soon come to a square aspect with Mars; earlier (lines 196-8) the converse was employed—that Mars was almost in square with the hyleg.

211 or else oppose to *Mars* himselfe] The implication, in the context, is that a distinction can be made between being

in 'quartile opposition' to where Mars is in the scheme and being opposed to '*Mars* himselfe'. I see no way of distinguishing between the two—this is word-spinning.

213-16 *Mars* . . . in *Capricorne* Is . . . Sextile . . . With *Venus*] Confirmation of the fact that Venus is *not* in Libra, but (as line 217 makes plain) in Scorpio.

217 *exilium*] Detriment (II. 13).

219 five degrees] Clearly not of arc, but of power in an astrological sense. Though earlier (lines 189-91) Bubo erroneously allowed six points to a planet for being in a 'term', here Norbrett correctly allows five minus points for its being in an *exilium*.

## 2. *Emendations*

The reader will readily imagine that a passage of this complexity will be likely to contain corruptions. (The play was first printed fifteen years after Fletcher's death.) A proper understanding of what is involved allows us, however, to make certain changes whose validity relies upon the internal evidence of the text.

(a) The received text of lines 171-2 reads as follows:

> *Luna* ith' seaventh, and much of *Scorpio*,
> Then *Mars* his *gaudium* rising in the ascendant.

If allowed to stand, this text would plainly imply that 'much of *Scorpio*' was in the 7th house, with the moon. But consider: we can firmly deduce (lines 162-3) that Libra lies in the ascendant—Scorpio, the next sign on, therefore cannot possibly be half a circle away. Furthermore, the convention is that Mars's *gaudium* is Scorpio—and we can establish that the author knows as much, when he says (lines 217-18) that Scorpio is the *exilium* of Venus and the *gaudium* of Mars. It is plain, then, that the text should be emended. Ideally, it would read as follows:

> *Luna* ith' seaventh, and much of *Scorpio*
> —That's *Mars* his *gaudium* —rising in the ascendant,
> And joyn'd with *Libra* too . . .

To clinch the matter: since the cusp of the 1st is defined by Libra 24 (line 163), it will be inevitable that 'much of *Scorpio*' must also lie in the 1st, there being only six degrees of Libra remaining. The point is obvious, when once the terms of reference are understood.

(b) The immediate sequel is also patently nonsensical to anyone who understands the terminology. The received text reads as follows:

> And *Imum Cœli, Mars* his exaltation
> Ith' seaventh house . . .
>
> (174-5)

Now, 'imum coeli' is the common name for the 4th house, just as 'medium coeli' is the common name for its opposite, the 10th. Furthermore, an exaltation is a particular degree of the zodiac (never a house)—in Mars's case it is Capricorn 28. Finally, the 7th house is (after all) the 7th house. We are faced with a choice here—either to accept rubbish and conclude that the author did not know his subject (despite his getting so much of the rest of it right), or to pay attention to the conventions of the subject, emend the text, and conclude that the author is not responsible for the blunders of the printer and their perpetuation by his editors.

Let us gloss what the received text says: 'the fourth house, [which is] Mars's exaltation, is [in] the seventh house'— obvious rubbish. And not only that. The scene itself declares differently. We have known from the beginning that the 4th house is defined by Capricorn 24. The conventions of astrology make Mars's exaltation fall in the 28th degree of Capricorn—ergo the first of these lines is trying to say 'In the 4th house (imum coeli) lies Mars's exaltation'. The continuation then turns its attention to the 7th house: 'Ith' seaventh house, *Aries* . . .'. And we *know* the 7th house should indeed be occupied by Aries, since at the beginning we are told the 1st is occupied by Libra. The text does not only hold together, but also allows us to identify its corruptions.

(c) The received text declares as follows:

> *Mars* . . .
> Looks at the hilege, with a quartile ruling
> The house where the sunne is . . .
>
> (196, 198-9)

We can do better than this. If we pay attention to the doctrines of astrology, we will learn that aspects, including quartile aspects, cannot rule houses. Only planets can do so, usually by virtue of having one of the signs that are their mansions lying on the cusp of the given house. We also know (from the reverse situation of the hyleg being close to a quartile with Mars—lines 207-11) that Mars does indeed 'look at the hilege with a quartile'. We may also deduce that Mars 'rules' the house where the sun is. How? Look at what we are told: the sun, Mercury, Mars, and the Dragon's Tail are all in the 3rd house (lines 165-6); Mars and the sun, however, though in the same house, are in different signs (lines 196-7); the sun is in Sagittarius (line 195); ergo Mars must be in the next sign on—Capricorn. What we now need to determine is why it should be that Mars rules the 3rd house, where the sun is. We do not have far to look. Not only does Mars rule the entire horoscope—he is '*Almuten*' (line 177)—but he is also said to be the most powerful planet 'in regard o'th *Cuspes*' (line 181). We can take it on trust, then, that if Mars rules because of his power over the cusps of the houses, it will follow—in a somewhat banal fashion—that he rules the 3rd house just as much as any other. At first sight the scene appears hopelessly obscure: upon investigation it transpires that the author gets the best mileage he can out of only a few astrological considerations. In any case, it is clear where the punctuation should be placed in the line. We know that Mars is looking at the hyleg with a quartile, and we can readily accept that he rules the house in which the sun lies, even though Sagittarius is not in fact one of his mansions.

### 3. *Outline*

The way in which the rogues go to work is, in astrological terms, respectable. They bicker with each other and they make doctrinal pronouncements that are patently false (giving the sun 'terms', for instance), but the main outline is none the less orthodox, and there can be no question that the author had a considerable understanding of the technicalities.

Would we wish to argue, however, that the author thought his audience could keep up? If we did, we would conclude that their competence was far in advance of ours. After much deliberation, I conclude, regretfully, that the question cannot be answered. Webster made dark-sounding reference to combustion and short life—even an ignorant audience would know how to respond. Fletcher, on the other hand, makes his villains bicker among themselves (providing entertainment at that level), and in the end the narrative of the play is not advanced in the slightest by the astrological altercations: after all their spectacular rubbish, when faced with the question of saying how Rollo will fare, their spokesman Norbrett replies 'The starres tells not us.'

One's conclusion would be that the author (like Chaucer in the case of *The Franklin's Tale*) has hedged his bets. Those who did not know enough astrology to follow the scene would not lose track of the play's development (which the scene does not influence), but would enjoy watching the rogues exercise their craft.

In astrological terms, even so, the rogues'/the author's display is impressive. They define the place for which the horoscope is drawn up, they define where the planets lie, and then they analyse—they find which planet is Lord of the Ascendant, which is Hyleg, what the aspects are, and what the 'directions' imply. All of this is routine procedure. Since the number of points at which the text exhibits consistency makes it plain that the author knew what he was doing, we may forgive him the doctrinal nonsense he puts into his characters' mouths.

1632 (acted)

III. 37 **Philip Massinger, *The City Madam*, II. ii. 59–69 (in *The Plays and Poems*, ed. P. Edwards and C. Gibson, Oxford, 1976, IV. 44–5):**

STARGAZE. *Venus* in the West-angle, the house of marriage the |
    seventh house, in Trine of *Mars*, in Conjunction of *Luna*, and
    *Mars* | Almuthen, or Lord of the Horoscope.
PLENTY. Hoy day!
LADIE. The Angels language, I am ravish'd! forward.
STARGAZE. *Mars* as I said Lord of the Horoscope, or geniture, | in

mutual reception of each other, shee in her Exaltation, and he ⌐ in
his Triplicitie trine, and face, assure a fortunate combination to |
*Hymen*, excellent prosperous and happie.
LADIE. Kneel, and give thanks. [*The Women kneel.*]
LACIE. For what we understand not.
| PLENTY. And have as little faith in't.

Stargaze is an instrument of Lady Frugal's designs, her objective being that the women, when Hymen has filled his
office, should wear the trousers. He is treated by her as a sort
of guru (saying what she wants to hear), but is regarded by
Lacie as a jargon-monger ('For what we understand not') and
by Plenty as a fraud ('And have as little faith in't').

The scene is spirited, the attitudes diverse; but it is plain
that the astrologer—as all his kind—is bogus. What, then is
he given to say? Does it make sense in astrological terms?

Let us examine. The first thing to note is that Venus is said
to be in the 'West-angle, the house of marriage the seventh
house'. Even the rank amateur would know that the 7th
house is defined by the western horizon; and if he knew his
houses, he would know that the seventh controls marriage.
Stargaze's beginning, then, is auspicious. (The hard word
'Almuthen' is also glossed.) Indeed, the seven ingredients in
Stargaze's opening speech could be reduced to four: Venus is
in the house of marriage (the 7th; in the west); she is also in
conjunction with the moon; in trine with Mars; and Mars is
almuten (lord of the horoscope). Clearly Massinger knows his
business; but he expands the bare data (rather to make the
most mileage of it, one would suspect, than to provide oblig-
ing glosses)—and immediately lands Stargaze in trouble.
Those in the audience who have no astrology will of course
be prompted by the reactions of Lacie and Plenty; those who
do have some, will react in the same vein but also ask how it
can be, if it is Mars who is Lord of the horoscope, that the
'fortunate combination' will be of the kind that Lady Frugal
has in mind?

There is more: Venus is said to be 'in Trine' with Mars, and
this is a favourable (in this context one might say a harmonious) aspect, and therefore one which also goes against
Lady Frugal's wishes. An astrologer would shake his head,
even if Lady Frugal does find the analysis ravishing.

After her command to continue, Stargaze peers again at his piece of paper and finds more on the subject of Mars and Venus. Of Mars he says that he is in his 'Triplicitie trine, and face', and this presents a problem. The essential dignity known as a 'term' conventionally lies between 'triplicity' and 'face', which rather suggests that 'trine' is a scribal error for that word. But on the other hand, 'Triplicity trine'—'a grouping of three that is threefold'—has a charlatan ring about it that rather suits the occasion. It would be a pity, then, to emend Stargaze's verbal inanity merely in the interests of tidiness.

Stargaze has not done yet: he entered with two schemes. The second of them runs as follows:

STARGAZE. . . . *Saturn* out of all dignities in his detriment and fall, combust: and *Venus* in the South-angle elevated above him, Ladie of both their Nativities; in her essential, and accidental dignities; occidental from the Sun, oriental from the Angle of the East, in Cazimi of the Sun, in her joy, and free from the malevolent beams of infortunes; in a sign commanding, and *Mars* in a constellation obeying, she fortunate, and he dejected, the disposers of marriage in the Radix of the native in feminine figures, argue foretel, and declare rule, preheminence and absolute soveraignty in women.

(II. ii. 76–85)

Given Stargaze's (as distinct from Massinger's) performance in his first speech, where he gives too much power to Mars to serve Lady Frugal's purposes, we will be on the alert here for further signs of his undermining himself. And we may wish to suppose, too, that these signs will be designed for detection. We may expect that Stargaze could not carry on for long without coming rather obviously to grief.

In fact he does so immediately: Saturn cannot simultaneously be both in his detriment (Cancer or Leo) and in his fall (Aries); and, furthermore, if Venus is 'in Cazimi' (7' away from the sun) and Saturn is also combust (8½° away from the sun), Venus's 'elevation' over him will be considerably more marginal than Stargaze's tone implies. And even if we do note that Venus, by being 'in her joy' (gaudium), will have to lie in Taurus, and that Taurus does happen to be one of the 'commanding' signs (II. 16. 2(d)), this small indication of internal consistency is nothing like enough to rescue Lady Frugal's idol.

The essence of Massinger's presentation can easily be grasped by a person with no understanding whatever of the technicalities. His creator causes Stargaze to operate at the level that was to content Beckett in *Murphy*: the language *sounds* right, and that is enough. To come to such a conclusion, however, does not preclude the author from some degree of expertise. Massinger knew more than enough to make his character plausible, and there are some hints that he anticipated his audience would be competent to do more than simply take their hint from Lacie and Plenty. I would argue that an author who can talk of commanding signs, disposers of the radix, almuten, combustion, etc., without making an utter fool of himself, is likely to know that a planet cannot occupy its detriment and its fall simultaneously. From which argument it would follow that his making one of his characters assert as much was designed as an in-joke— one which would be pointless if not picked up.

In any event, Massinger's is a highly entertaining display, akin to Dryden's in *An Evening's Love*, though well below Fletcher's in *The Bloody Brother* as regards its technical difficulty. I take it that his audience was not necessarily intended to keep up, but that he wrote in a vein that would entertain the competent amateur. As for the others, their attitude is governed not by an ability to read the absurdities, but by the stance of Stargaze's victims and by his own sheer volubility— such a torrent must be nonsensical. Massinger has it both ways.

1663 (acted)

III. 38 John Wilson, *The Cheats* (in J. Maidment and W. H. Logan, eds., *Dramatists of the Restoration*, Vol. XI: *The Dramatic Works of John Wilson*, Edinburgh and London, 1874):

*Enter* MOPUS, *solus, with a book, etc.*

MOPUS. Saturn and Jupiter come to a trine in Taurus and Capricorn. Huh! We shall have strangers come to town, and their wives ne'er miss 'em in the country. Next month they all meet

in the house of Mercury, he being lord thereof and significator
5    of speech: it may intend advocates, cryers of courts, splitters
of causes, oyster wives and broom-men—Hold!—Saturn—
(nothing but this malevolent planet) in the sign Virgo, in conjunction with Venus in her detriment. Beware, women, of
green gowns; great men, of stone and cholic; and costermongers,
10    of rotten pippins. Again, *pars torturæ* [sic], coupled with the
*Catabibason*—that is to say, the Dragon's Tail—huh, huh—
children shall be subject to convulsion fits, young wenches to
the falling evil, and old women to cough out their teeth . . .
But all this is no money. Many an honest man has but one
15    house, and maintains his family very well; but, such an unlucky
rogue, the whole twelve will hardly pay my rent.

(I. iii, pp. 23–4)

The stage direction indicates that Mopus is talking to himself. Here, then, is an instance where there is no 'fall guy':
the absurd conclusions Mopus draws from the chart he
is inspecting are, for the moment, a reflection on himself (demonstrations of why his rent is a problem), rather
than ways of duping a client. That they are absurd is a
matter the audience may take on trust, without having
any inkling about the astrology on which they are supposedly based.

What, though, of that section of the audience that might
hear what Mopus was saying? They would register, to begin
with, that he places Saturn in Taurus and Jupiter in Capricorn (lines 1–2), asserting that this is a trine aspect: it is. But
both planets are so slow-moving that they could not conceivably both be present in either of the houses of Mercury
(Gemini or Virgo) 'next month'. Mopus goes on to maintain
a partial consistency when the house of Mercury in question
proves to be Virgo, but immediately spoils it by making that
sign the detriment of Venus—it is the other one of her two
debilitating signs—her fall (II. 14). So far, then, Mopus's
performance is distinctly uneven. (It is likely, though, that
the printer is at fault in the case of '*Torturæ*'—a plausible
misreading of '*Fortunæ*'.)

The evidence of this passage would suggest that Wilson, like Massinger, was content to play rather idly with
the subject, but that he had a less secure grasp of its

terminology. Later in the scene, however, he becomes remarkably specific:

> SCRUPLE. I have heard, sir, you are a man of art; and therefore I
> would fain know what you conceive of this notable conjunction
> of Satan and Jupiter in October next, which the learned believe
> to be the forerunner of doomsday, if not the thing itself.
> 5 MOPUS. Saturn and Jupiter, you mean, in Sagitary?
> SCRUPLE. The same. What may it portend? Good or evil?
> MOPUS. Much good, no doubt! . . . And here we are to observe,
> which of the two planets, Saturn and Jupiter,—this the very
> best, that the very worst,—is strongest at the time of his con-
> 10 junction; for according to his nature will the effects follow.
> SCRUPLE. In truth, learnedly. Pray, sir, on!
> MOPUS. The last conjunction of these two planets happened—
> SCRUPLE. Pray, sir, no chance or happening. Was, I pray!
> MOPUS. Then, was in February 1643, in 25 degrees of Pisces—
> 15 a sign of the wat'ry triplicite, not known in nature before,
> which produced those monstrous actions not heard of in the
> world before. And now, forasmuch as their conjunction is in
> Sagitary, the day-house and triplicite of Jupiter, we may con-
> clude it is the more considerable, in regard they have wholly
> 20 left the aquatic trigon, and will for many years make their con-
> junction in the fiery tranquillity . . .

Unfortunately, 'tranquillity' could well be a scribal error for 'triplicity' (after the manner of 'torturae' for 'fortunae'): otherwise, one could say—if any confidence could be placed in 'tranquillity'—that Wilson was making an in-joke here. Malapropisms, after all, are pointless unless the audience hears the word intended but mistaken.

But even if we cannot be sure of his playing to a knowing audience at this level, we can recognize that in this interchange Wilson becomes remarkably specific—and accurate. The play was first performed in May 1663, which locates the conjunction of 'October next'; and there was indeed a conjunction of Saturn and Jupiter to match Mopus's assertion. It occurred in early October at longitude 255°—i.e. in Sagittarius, as required (see Stahlman and Gingerich, p. 509). And the previous conjunction did indeed begin on 16 February 1643 at 355°—i.e. in Pisces 25, as claimed. Furthermore Pisces is indeed in the 'wat'ry triplicite' (line 15), and Sagittarius is indeed one of the mansions of Jupiter and in his triplicity (line 18).

Conjunctions of the major infortune and the major fortune were regarded as momentous by astrologers, and great attention was paid to them. Their pattern was as follows (conjunctions that fall in the fiery triplicity—line 21—are here marked in italics):

| | | | |
|---|---|---|---|
| 1544 | Sagittarius | | |
| 1563 | | | Cancer |
| 1583 | | Pisces | |
| 1603 | Sagittarius | | |
| 1623 | | | Leo |
| 1643 | | Pisces | |
| 1663 | *Sagittarius* | | |
| 1683 | | | *Leo* |
| 1702 | | *Aries* | |
| 1722 | *Sagittarius* | | |
| 1742 | | | *Leo* |
| 1762 | | *Aries* | |
| 1782 | Sagittarius | | |
| 1802 | | | Virgo |
| 1822 | | Aries | |
| 1842 | Capricorn | | |

It seems clear that, for whatever motive, Wilson consulted some astrological document (probably a treatise on the conjunctions) in writing this scene. However, he does cause Mopus to say that the previous conjunction, that of 1643, was 'not known in nature before', which the very nature of the phenomenon denies.

There is more in the same vein:

> SCRUPLE. But pray, sir, what effect do you conceive this conjuncjunction may have upon the whore of Babylon?
> MOPUS. Why, truly, that is somewhat uncertain; in regard it will
> depend so much upon that great eclipse of Sol in Cancer in the
> 5    house of the moon, the 22d day of June 1666, and will appear
> almost total at Rome.
>
> (p. 58)

The date given here is Old Style (I. 24), and corresponds to 2 July 1666 New Style. On that day there was indeed a solar eclipse (see Oppolzer, p. 274), whose track passed directly over Southern Italy (Oppolzer, chart 137). The sun was in Cancer (the moon's mansion) at the time, as Mopus claims.

> SCRUPLE. . . . now I find you so near the Flood, give me the exact time . . ., and I'll say you're a scholar.
> MOPUS. For the time, it was, according to our computation, the 5th day of June, in the 1656th year of the world, one month
> 5 and seventeen days, nor more nor less; and by all good tokens, upon a Friday—*Sol* in *Gemini*. The Dominical letter that year D—fifteen minutes precisely after sun-setting.
> SCRUPLE. I see you're very exact.
> MOPUS. Alas! we must be so; half a minute's loss so many years
> 10 ago had been the Lord knows what by this time.

(pp. 58–9)

Wilson's year for the Flood coincides with Archbishop Ussher's; but on the other hand, Ussher dated Creation to 23 October in Julian Year 710 (in his 'Epistle to the Readers', *Annals of the World*, London, 1658, sig. A5$^r$). An interval of 'one month and seventeen days' would therefore bring us to 10 December, not 5 June. But presumably the audience is so badly lost by this time that any calendar interval would do.

At this time the sun was certainly not in Gemini. The year propounded is 2348 BC, and the sun was at Taurus 24 on 5 June in that year (Stahlman and Gingerich, p. 21). Indeed, it may seem at first to be absurd to pursue Mopus with this degree of perseverance, but the Julian Day (I. 26. 3) of 1 January that year was 863817—i.e. a Thursday, and consequently the Dominical Letter was indeed D (line 7). The Julian Day number of 5 June 2348 BC, on the other hand, was 863972—which makes it a Friday, as Mopus requires! Wilson may have been lucky, or he may have been relying on a persevering chronologist.

Late in the play (V. i) Mopus finds himself having to define the character of Afterwit:

> He receives his knowledge from Mercury in Virgo. His complete-ness of body from Caput Draconis in Gemini. Saturn and Venus, in Libra, direct him to the light of nature. Fortuna major and Populus, figures of geomancy, give him health, and Puella be-
> 5 friends him. Mars, in Cancer, is his enemy; Jupiter, in Capricorn, somewhat uncertain; and two ideas of geomancy conspire against

him. But he shall receive treasures from the sun and jewels from
the moon; and his guardian angel shall defend him, and make the
spiteful dragon bite his tail in Sagitarius, because he cannot be
10  reveng'd of him.

(p. 85)

First for Mercury in Virgo: he is guardian of scholars (of
eloquence, wits) and here well dignified because in his mansion. These traditional connections lend support to Mopus
—the scheme, if elementary, is astrologically respectable, at
least to begin with.

To locate the Dragon's Head in Gemini (line 2) is also
orthodox: it receives its exaltation in Gemini 3 (II. 14).
Saturn and Venus in Libra continues the vein: Saturn in his
exaltation and Venus in one of her mansions: the consequence,
however, is another matter: 'direct him to the light of nature'
may verge on blasphemy, since 'light of nature' was a phrase
used to describe man's capacity to apprehend divine truths
without revelation (*OED*, 'light', *sb.* 6b). The phrase, though,
had a decidedly Puritan currency (the *OED* cites Prynne and
Bunyan) and Wilson's motive is satirical here.

Perhaps recognizing that his astrology is run-of-the-mill,
Wilson now causes Mopus to add a little geomancy. He names
three of the sixteen recognized 'lots', and his reference to
'guardian angel' may also be geomantic: John Case's book on
the subject, for instance, is entitled *The Angelical Guide*
(1697). The doctrines and apparatus of geomancy make
astrology look like simplicity itself, even though it does
redeploy many of its terms. Its conventions include making
a connection between Fortuna major and the sun in Aquarius,
between Populus and a full moon in Capricorn, and between
Puella and Venus direct (in motion) in Libra. I see no hint
in the text, though, that Wilson took advantage of these
associations, unlike the more accessible ones relating to
Mercury, etc.

That Mars, in Cancer, is Afterwit's enemy is not altogether
banal—but it is not particularly apposite either. Mars would
be an enemy regardless; but it so happens that Mars's 'fall'
occurs in Cancer, so his power is to that extent weakened.
Finally, the 'spiteful dragon' explains itself at one level; but it

is also true that since Afterwit has 'Caput Draconis in Gemini', the Tail will necessarily lie in Sagittarius (six signs away), as Mopus asserts.

Our objective, in addition to coming to an understanding of the plain sense of the texts we examine, is also to form some estimate of the level at which they are pitched. From the sort of thing the author says (once we understand it), what can we conclude about the degree of knowledge it implies in the audience?

In Wilson's case we are faced with a strange mixture. The fine detail concerning the conjunctions of Saturn and Jupiter, and the verifiable accuracy of the details concerning the solar eclipse of 1666 have to be taken together with the vague (but not ignorant) allusions to geomancy and the chronology of the world. On balance, one would conclude that Wilson did not demand from his audience the degree of expertise that, say, Chaucer relied on. And the appeal is different. Chaucer may seem to invite us to derive some amusement from the Host and Chaunticleer, but I see no grounds for regarding the Clerk of Orleans in the same light. Massinger's Stargaze, Wilson's Mopus, and Congreve's Foresight, on the other hand, are essentially targets. They, and their profession, invite a response of amused contempt, the contempt being at least in part self-defensive—*we* are not going to be duped. Our difficulty is to get inside this defence mechanism: as a mechanism it works without discrimination—the bath-water (the astrologer fall guy) and the baby (astrology) are both ejected.

Astrology, however, is so complex, and its technicalities so closely interconnected with each other, that it is easy to tell whether or not an author understands the subject. Wilson gives us sufficient evidence, in the end, to conclude that he did understand: his assertions (where they may be related to the basic conventions) have a sufficient tendency to hold good. Mopus's absurd conclusions (especially the wonderful argument that if we did not get the time of the Flood right we would have lost 'the Lord knows what' by now) are sufficiently entertaining in themselves, just as the bickering of the rogues was in *The Bloody Brother*. But being in the know is decidedly an optional extra.

1668 (acted)

III. 39 John Dryden, *An Evening's Love: or, The Mock Astrologer*, in *The Works of John Dryden*, Vol. X (University of California Press, 1970).

DON ALONZO. What Judgment may a man reasonably form from the trine Aspect of the two Infortunes in Angular houses?

(II. i. 394-5)

In assessing this poser, which the pedant Don Alonzo puts upon the unfortunate Bellamy (who thought the guise of astrologer would secure him in his attempt to get at Don Alonzo's daughter), we may take into account the fact that three decades after the appearance of this play Dryden was casting horoscopes for his own private purposes. A letter of his survives, written in 1697, in which he predicts the (good) health of one of his sons; he is sure of his diagnosis, he says, because he has performed the astrological calculation himself. His attitude is instructive: he is confident of the prediction, it would seem, because *he* has performed the calculations: the implication is that he believes in astrology, but prefers to trust to his own abilities.

*The Letters of John Dryden*, ed. Charles E. Ward (1942; repr. New York, 1965), pp. 93-4.

How does an author with an enduring interest in the subject present an astrologer to the theatrical public of 1668? Don Alonzo's question (pedant though he is) is one that he confesses 'almost gravels' him. We have seen other authors whose manner of operation allows them to have it both ways: reference to 'direful Saturn' (Greene), 'Saturn combust' (Webster), or 'spiteful dragon' (Wilson) will convey a distinct impression, even to one who knows nothing of the subject; but to those who do know, there is the added interest of seeing the technicalities deftly handled. Can we say the same of Dryden? What do we make of a 'trine Aspect of the two Infortunes in Angular houses'?

First for the basics: the trine aspect is one of the two aspects that is benign; there are, indeed, only two 'Infortunes' —Saturn and Mars; and the 'Angular houses' are the main houses—1, 4, 7, and 10. We can now begin to examine the thrust of the pedantic question. Saturn and Mars are bad; the trine aspect is good; to be placed in any angular house is a position of power. Question: put the bad planets into good aspect and powerful houses—and what happens? Is it the malignity of the planets or the beneficence of the aspect that is accentuated by the powerfulness of the houses?

> The California Dryden (X. 472) is mistaken in supposing that the signs of the zodiac are involved here. Aries, Cancer, Libra, and Capricorn are admittedly 'cardinal' signs; but Don Alonzo is asking about 'Angular houses'.

This question might well have 'gravelled' Don Alonzo, since it was one that the writers of the astrological handbooks did not resolve. It would be valid to say in reply, 'it all depends'. The theoretical answer, if there was one, would in fact be of little practical use to the astrologer, since the constraints of each particular horoscope would override it. Just as supposedly meaningful paragraphs about having Saturn in Cancer in your horoscope would take account only of one factor in a dozen or more that should be considered (where, for intance are all the other planets located?), by the same token only a rash or an ignorant astrologer would give a straight answer here.

Dryden also uses astrological atmospherics:

> WILDBLOOD. I am half afraid I your *Spanish* Planet, and my *English* one have been acquainted, I and have found out some by-room or other in the 12 houses: I I wish they have been honorable.
> JACINTA. The best way for both were to take up in time . . .
>
> (II. i. 116-20)

This is lewd by-play. There was (of course) an astrological allocation of countries to planets, but it is doubtful whether Dryden calls on his audience to recognize it. Similarly, in astrological terms the 'by-room' in which the 'Spanish' planet encountered the 'English' one could be either a 'term' or a 'face' within the '12 houses'. It seems obvious, though, that Dryden is not working at this level: it is rather the lewd (and plausible) implication of 'acquainted . . . by-room . . . in the 12 houses' that is operative. This is evidenced by Jacinta's response: to 'take up in time' may equally mean 'reform in due course' (*OED*, s.v. 'take', 90 n.), or 'stop before it's too late' (ibid.). The hint of *coitus interruptus* suggests that the 'planets' are here astrological (and thoroughly libertine) equivalents of guardian angels.

Don Alonzo tackles Bellamy again:

DON ALONZO. What think you, | Sir, of the taking *Hyleg?* or of the best way of rectification for a | Nativity? have you been conversant in the *Centiloquium* of | *Trismegistus?* what think you of *Mars* in the tenth when 'tis | his own House, or of *Jupiter* configurated with malevolent | Planets?

(II. i. 408-13)

Bellamy is not even a quack: he is an utter imposter—any question at all would stop him in his tracks. Dryden, though, puts four posers in Don Alonzo's mouth: 'taking hyleg', we know, is a sophisticated matter, and 'rectification' is also a distinctly advanced process; whereas asking the poor fellow whether he knows his Hermes Trismegistus is merely to test whether he knows the literature of his pretended subject. The fourth question is of a different kind, being a technical conundrum similar to the first one he posed.

It invites Bellamy's opinion on the status of '*Mars* in the tenth when 'tis his own House'. Here we should take some time to consider. Bellamy, it is patent, will not have the first idea; the audience may or may not have an answer.

First, then, we should decide upon a sense (if one can be found) for '*Mars* in the tenth *when* [my italics] 'tis his own house'. This question is ambiguous to anyone who understands its terms, and the ambiguity must first be declared. Don Alonzo is asking one or other of two questions. Either, what is the power of Mars when it is in the 10th house (the second most powerful house) and when its cusp is defined by one of his signs; or, what is the power of Mars when it is in the 10th, considering that the 10th belongs to him?

To pursue the matter so closely may seem tedious. The audience, after all, has only a second or two in which to assimilate what is going on. But on the other hand, we have reason to believe that Dryden knew his astrology. From this it ought to follow that even if he wished to guy Don Alonzo, the pedantic rubbish he fed him would none the less have, in astrological terms, a 'rational' base. Perseveringly, then, we pursue the terms of Don Alonzo's poser.

The California Dryden (X. 472) notes that 'Mars . . . is always harmful, though least so in the sixth house'—which ill-digested fact fails to satisfy the issue. What particular relation, if any, does Mars have to the 10th house? If we consider the special properties of the houses (II. 17. 1), we find that the 10th controls trade and honours, so no obvious relation to Mars is apparent. Simply to make the 10th do duty as an angle, on the other hand, would be feeble and obscure. What alternative is there? If we invoke the convention of 'Consignificators' (II. 17. 3), we find that there is an established association, one that has status as common astrological doctrine, and so may be taken as a possible expansion of Don Alonzo's puzzle.

When the zodiacal signs are paired with the astrological houses and then distributed among the planets, the 10th house and Capricorn fall to Mars. It may, then, be in this sense that Dryden intends 'when 'tis his own House'. The force of the question, in other words, may be to invite speculation on a particular configuration in which Mars is 'bodily' in a house that convention assigns to him in any case. As with his then imagining Jupiter in conjunction with the Infortunes, though, no meaningful answer can be given to the question, since its terms are too generalized. From another point of view we can also say that it is enough for Dryden's purposes if the language sounds right. Quite undeservingly Bellamy can legitimately reply that Don Alonzo's are 'School-boyes' questions.

Bellamy is subjected to yet another moment of inquisition:

DON ALONZO. Well, then, we'll but cast an eye together, upon my |
    eldest Daughters Nativity.
| BELLAMY. Nativity!—
| DON ALONZO. I know what you would say now, that there wants
    the | Table of Direction for the five Hylegiacalls; the Ascendant, |
    *Medium Cœli,* Sun, Moon, and *Sors:* but we'll take it as it is.
(III. i. 283–8)

Dryden again invokes a highly technical branch of astrology (taking directions, II. 35), but he obliges his audience by naming the five main ingredients in this 'art'. The California Dryden (X. 475) claims that 'to erect a nativity according to the five hylegiacals . . . was considered an alternative to judging the lord of the nativity according to the moon (see Partridge, pp. 83–84; Lilly, *Christian Astrology*, pp. 525–531, 656–657)'. But both authors in fact reject the idea of taking the hyleg to be Lord of the Geniture, in favour of choosing the planet with most dignity in the figure. This, of course, is outside Don Alonzo's (or Dryden's) range. And in fact Don Alonzo is not talking about finding the Lord of the Geniture at all, nor about erecting a nativity. He is analysing the nativity at large—even though the tricky business of analysing its 'directions' must be forgone.

Dryden handles the terminology with the same deftness as his predecessors. No great learning is required to follow the jargon: Dryden allows his audience to be buffeted, as Bellamy is, by the pedant's enthusiasms. But at the same time they can relish Bellamy's discomfiture at meeting a bumbling 'expert' in his own pretended field.

## 1695

**III. 40 William Congreve, *Love for Love*:**
   (1) ed. Emmett L. Avery (London, 1966)
   (2) ed. A. Norman Jeffares (London, 1967)
   (3) ed. Herbert Davis, in *Complete Plays* (Chicago, 1967)
   (4) ed. M. M. Kelsall (London, 1969)
   (5) ed. A Norman Jeffares, in *Restoration Comedy*, Vol. III
      (London, 1974).

At the risk of appearing not to have a good word to say, I feel none the less obliged here to canvass what modern editors of the play have observed in connection with its astrological component. All too often a likely-looking phrase has been found in a dictionary or a handbook and attached to the play with too little regard for the context.

Congreve's astrological allusions are employed primarily for the purposes of creating obscene innuendo; and when they do have some technical component, they serve their purpose merely by sounding right.

The astrologer is Foresight, and he speaks after this manner:

. . I have travelled . . . in the celestial spheres, know the signs and the planets, and their houses; can judge of motions direct and retrograde, of sextiles, quadrates, trines and oppositions, fiery trigons and aquatical trigons; know whether life shall be long or short, happy or unhappy, whether diseases are curable or incurable, if journeys shall be prosperous, undertakings successful, or goods stolen recovered, I know—

(ed. Kelsall, II. v. 185–92)

(note: *direct and retrograde*: I. 23
   *sextiles . . . oppositions*: II. 13. 1
   *trigons*: II. 15)

The order in which this list of Foresight's accomplishments unfolds makes it sound precisely like the contents page of a Renaissance handbook: its function is to show the nature of his foolish genius and there are no astrological in-jokes. What happens subsequently, instead, is that Foresight's interlocutors (particularly his niece Angelica) take up the ridiculous or lewd implications of the language:

FORESIGHT. . . . there's but one Virgin among the twelve signs, spitfire, | but one Virgin.
ANGELICA. Nor there had not been that one, if she had had to do with | anything but astrologers, uncle. That makes my aunt go | abroad.

(ed. Kelsall, II. iii. 125–9)

There is much advantage in this approach to the subject: the language of astrology tends to adapt itself very readily to metaphoric extension, particularly in its dire or foreboding elements, which are especially vulnerable to facetious application. By this means the language can be employed to effect upon an audience that has no more than a glimmer of understanding at the technical level.

There are a few passages in the play, however, that deserve close attention, since they achieve some level of technicality.

FORESIGHT. . . . 'Tis now three o'clock, a very | good hour for business; Mercury governs this hour.

(ed. Kelsall, II. ii. 35–6)

We are no wiser for being told (by Jeffares, 1967, p. 113) that Mercury is 'the smallest of the major planets'; the point of Foresight's remark relies, instead, on the traditional association of Mercury with business (and thieving). This association, patent to the point of banality, is sophisticated by Foresight when he claims that 'three o'clock' in the afternoon is

Mercury's hour: here he misapplies the doctrine of planetary hours, which do not go directly by clock time (II. 33. 1).

ANGELICA. . . . [I'll] leave you to erect a scheme and find who's in | conjunction with your wife. Why don't you keep her at | home, if you're jealous when she's abroad? You know my | aunt is a little retrograde (as you call it) in her nature. Uncle, | I'm afraid you are not lord of the ascendant, ha, ha, ha!

(ed. Kelsall, II. iii. 60-4)

In commenting on 'lord of the ascendant' Congreve's editors have served his readers ill. Avery (p. 39) makes reference to 'the easternmost star [*sic*] in the sign of the zodiac under which a person was born' as though this were lord of the ascendant. In this he is followed by Kelsall (p. 36) and Jeffares (1974, III. 268). Jeffares's original note, however, gives another, and equally misleading, view, referring to the planet in the house of the ascendant as though that were its lord (1967, p. 113).

The lord of the ascendant, however, is determined simply by discovering which zodiacal sign is rising; the planet whose mansion that sign is, then automatically becomes lord of the ascendant. More importantly, though, Angelica's jibe has little or nothing to do with astrology. In the context 'lord of the ascendant' may be glossed as 'master of the thing that is rising'—a lewdness compounded by the fact that 'retrograde' means (moving) 'backwards'.

FORESIGHT. I will have patience, since it is the will of the stars I | should be | thus tormented. This is the effect of the malicious con- | junc | tions and oppositions in the third house of my nativity; | there the curse of kindred was foretold . . .

(ed. Kelsall, II. iii. 112-14)

Lilly will tell us that indeed the 3rd house is concerned with 'Brothers, Sisters, Cozens or Kindred' (p. 52). The notion, though, of 'oppositions' (180-degree separations) taking place within a single house is hard to swallow. What are we to say? Congreve has been getting it right—the 3rd house does apply to kindred; and later he correctly identifies the 6th house with sickness. The evidence, then, suggests that, knowing this much, he would also know how the aspects work. On the strength of this inference we may argue that by 'conjunctions and oppositions in the third house' Congreve (though we will not give Foresight the benefit of this doubt) intends us to understand 'conjunctions in and oppositions to the 3rd house'.

FORESIGHT [*to Angelica*]. Does I my wife complain? Come, I know women tell one another. I She is young and sanguine, has a wanton hazel eye, and was I born under Gemini, which may incline her to society ...

(ed. Kelsall, II. iii. 132–5)

It can hardly be a coincidence that Lilly, for instance, includes among the characteristics of a Gemini 'a good piercing hazel eye, and wanton ... of excellent understanding, and judicious in worldly affairs' (p. 94). I take it, though, that Congreve has mediated this 'fact', such that the choice of Gemini might equally appear to be governed by the consideration that it is the only sign made up of two human bodies.

FORESIGHT [*to Nurse*]. ... d'ye hear—bring me, let me see— I within a quarter of twelve—hem—he—hem!—just upon I the turning of the tide, bring me the urinal; and I hope | neither the lord of my ascendant nor the moon will be I combust; and then I may do well.
I SCANDAL. I hope so. Leave that to me; I will erect a scheme; and I I hope I shall find both Sol and Venus in the sixth house.

(ed. Kelsall, III. xiii. 566–72)

Congreve's choice of house is again well informed: the 6th house is indeed the one that governs sickness (II. 17. 1).

Unaccountably Davis (p. 271) maintains it is 'a good sign, free from sickness', while Kelsall confuses sign and house, supposing that it is hoped Sol and Venus will be in Virgo.

Stargaze's anxiety about the position of the lord of the ascendant and of the moon has the appearance of being met by Scandal's pious wish that the sun and Venus will be in the 6th. Someone with a smattering of astrology, however, would see immediately that 'within a quarter of twelve', would place 'Sol' close to the 10th house at midday and close to the 4th house at midnight—in neither case could the 6th house be occupied by the sun. There is also a wonderful inconsequentiality between Foresight's testy desire and Scandal's supposed remedy for it.

Congreve shows himself at ease with the jargon, employing it in very much the manner that suited Dryden. The distinct similarity between Foresight's diagnosis of his wife's character and Lilly's version of a Gemini also suggests that he had at least dipped into the literature, even if only for the purpose of using its absurdities to his advantage.

### c.1725

**III. 41 William Hogarth, Illustration to Samuel Butler's
*Hudibras*, Part II, canto III: 'Hudibras beats Sidrophel
and his Man Whacum'.**

The caption to the illustration claims that the larger of the two astrological schemes (speaking of Hudibras):

> *Discovers how in fight you met
> At Kingston with a May-pole Idol.
> And that y'were bang'd both back & side well;
> And though you overcame the Bear,
> The Dogs beat You at Brentford Fair . . .*

Hogarth would have needed to be expert indeed to give appropriate astrological representation to these lines—and had he possessed the facility, it is doubtful whether he would have carried his contemporaries with him. As it is, then, we can think of him as at liberty to devise whatever scribbles he pleases. Since the scheme is obligingly oriented towards us, and since it forms a central detail (being at once the link and the barrier between the chief combatants) we may inspect it with some attention.

It is soon obvious that, despite its prominent position, the main diagram is random and fragmentary. The central square carries the symbols for quartile aspect, opposition, and conjunction, but without any indication of which planets are involved. Houses 2, 8, 9, and 11 also carry symbols, but they are in considerable disarray. In the 2nd house the message is that Saturn is in opposition to Mars—information that properly belongs to the central square. The 8th house carries the symbol for Sagittarius, the 9th the symbol for Scorpio (the proper order of signs is reversed); and the 11th carries the symbols (left to right) for Capricorn, Gemini, Leo, and Taurus—four signs in one house and in an utterly scrambled order.

The details of the second and smaller scheme are less easy to decipher. The orientation of the symbol for Saturn, however, suggests that the figure is indeed turned towards Sidrophel (as one would expect it to be). Its primary, and perhaps its only, message is that Saturn is in opposition to Venus. This I take to be a gloomy comment on the occasion of Hudibras's visit to Sidrophel: to find a way of winning over a wealthy widow. The appropriateness to the occasion of this detail suggests that Hogarth was not working in entire ignorance—a supposition confirmed, to some extent, by the inscriptions on the horizon table of the celestial globe in the left foreground. We can set it down to artistic licence that the segment of the zodiacal circle which is visible shows eight of the twelve signs in a sweep of less than 180°. But at least the eight symbols are correctly drawn, and they are in their proper order, both as to sequence and as to direction.

We may doubt whether Hogarth anticipated that he would ever have his illustration subjected to such a solemn analysis; but in our defence we may argue that at one stage in its composition he himself had to ponder on what devices he would use. He drew the basic shape of the horoscopes precisely in accordance with convention, and he plotted a series of symbols which also conform to their traditional shape. He also seems to have conveyed a nicely barbed message in the smaller of the diagrams. These considerations, and a recognition of Hogarth's famous attention to fine detail, may lead us to conclude that he scrambled the main figure as a means of commenting on Sidrophel's proficiency.

*c.* 1760

### III. 42  Laurence Sterne, *Tristram Shandy*, Vol. IV: 'Slawkenbergius's Tale' (ed. J. A. Work, pp. 260-2):

It happened . . . that the two universities of *Strasburg*—the *Lutheran*, founded in the year 1538 by *Jacobus Sturmius*, counsellor of the senate, —and the *Popish*, founded by *Leopold*, arch-duke of *Austria*, were . . .

William Hogarth, 'Hudibras beats Sidrophel and his man Whacum'

employing the whole depth of their knowledge . . . in determining the point of *Martin Luther*'s damnation.

The *Popish* doctors had undertaken to demonstrate *a priori*; that from the necessary influence of the planets on the twenty-second day of *October* 1483—when the moon was in the twelfth house—*Jupiter*, *Mars*, and *Venus* in the third, the *Sun, Saturn*, and *Mercury* all got together in the fourth—that he must in course, and unavoidably be a damn'd man—and that his doctrines, by a direct corollary, must be damn'd doctrines too.

By inspection into his horoscope, where five planets were in coition all at once with scorpio (in reading this my father would always shake his head) in the ninth house which the *Arabians* allotted to religion—it appeared that *Martin Luther* did not care one stiver about the matter— and that from the horoscope directed to the conjunction of *Mars*—they made it plain likewise he must die cursing and blaspheming . . .

The little objection of the *Lutheran* doctors to this, was, that it must certainly be the soul of another man, born *Oct.* 22, 83, . . . inasmuch as it appeared from the register of *Islaben* in the county of *Mansfelt*, that *Luther* was not born in the year 1483, but in 84; and not on the 22d day of *October*, but on the 10th of *November*, the eve of *Martinmas*-day, from whence he had the name of *Martin*.

Most of this highly circumstantial account—though of course with Shandeian twists—comes from the article on Luther in Bayle's *Dictionnaire*. It is instructive to see how Sterne selected and moulded his material. The rhetorical balance of his account—the papists with one position, the Lutherans with another—simplifies and in fact distorts the issues of the original squabble, as is evident at one point in Stern's account itself.

The polarity of the argument appears to be:

> Popish camp 22 October 1483
> Lutheran camp 10 November 1484.

In accordance with these lines of battle, one might have expected to find that 'the moon . . . in the twelfth', etc., represented the Popish construction, whereas the 'five planets . . . in coition' would then serve as the Lutheran riposte. It does not, though—it serves supposedly to confirm that Luther would die blaspheming. The Lutherans are not given any con- figuration from which to argue their case—the Islaben register does that duty instead.

Since the papists have seemingly only one date, how can they be served by two horoscopes? And where does the second, and more spectacular one come from? Here we may adduce Aby Warburg's essay, 'Heidnisch-antike Wessagung in Wort und Bild zu Luthers Zeiten' (1920; in *Gesammelte Schriften*, 1969, pp. 483 ff.). This essay shows that the placing of the five planets in Scorpio (so disturbing to 'my father') was the work of Lucas Gauricus. It represents the position of the heavens on 22 October 1484, one year later than the date Sterne adduces.

The horoscope for 22 October 1483, on the other hand, was the work of Jerome Cardan (as Bayle reports), and it was adopted, as Bayle says *'par malignité'*, by Florimond de Réymond in his attack on Luther. Both versions were Catholic assaults, but curiously, a number of people in the Lutheran camp—Melanchthon, Erasmus Reinhold, Carion, and Pfeyl (see Warburg, Tables LXX, LXXI, LXXII, and p. 502)— took up Gauricus's date (22 October 1484, as opposed to 10 November 1484), merely altering the time of day (on supposedly biographical considerations) and thereby clearing the spectacular cluster of five planets out of the house of religion to more neutral ground.

What of the technicalities that Sterne chooses to preserve? There is no connection made, for instance, between the configuration and the conclusion in the first horoscope—what if the moon *is* in the 12th? We may suppose that the hiatus between supposed cause and dire effect (Luther's damnation) is to be taken on trust. The connection of the 9th house with religion, however, is made explicit, while the five planets all in Scorpio—dire-sounding enough—are greeted by a sorry shake of the head. The rest is 'atmospheric'. The principles of 'direction' may not be understood; but since it is *Mars* to whom the direction is made and since Luther dies cursing and blaspheming (Gauricus's very words, reproduced by Bayle), then the situation is plain enough.

Sterne, then, is working at a considerable distance, both in time and in sympathy, from the Renaissance astrology that had been brought into the service of religious politics.

The association was not token at the time, however. Gauricus was in earnest; was expert in astrology; and also a churchman (he became Bishop of Civitate). Looking past both Sterne and Bayle for a moment, we may use our own expertise and the surviving documents to see whether or not the direction of the horoscope to Mars in Gauricus's version of Luther's nativity did indeed have Gauricus's desired result. In his figure (Warburg, Table LXXI) the ascendant is defined by Capricorn 21, whose oblique ascension is given as 322° 24'. The position of Mars, on the other hand, is Aries 29° 47'. From this we can calculate that the interval between their oblique ascensions is 50° 50'.

Mathematical Formulas 9 comes into play here.

Gauricus used the directed conjunction of the ascendant with Mars to proclaim for Luther a death such as Dr Faustus died. And he used the apparatus of astrology to say when it would take place. Fifty degrees converts to fifty years, and 50' converts to 300 days. Luther, then, according to one dire and fervent Catholic prediction, would depart this life on 18 August 1535.

For myself, I am pleased to say that Luther gave the Bishop of Civitate the lie by some eleven years.

# Appendix: Mathematical Formulas

The examination of a text that contains an astronomical or an astrological component may sometimes call for the verification of the values it presents or implies. In what follows I present some of the formulas that are required in such cases. I have used a continuous example for Formulas 1–8.

A word of warning: minor differences from the values presented in my example should not be regarded as cause for alarm. They will (if minor) be the result of differences in rounding, as between four-figure and seven-figure tables, for instance.

Symbols:

| | |
|---|---|
| terrestrial latitude | P(hi) |
| celestial longitude | L(ambda) |
| obliquity of the ecliptic | E(psilon) |
| right ascension | RA |
| oblique ascension | OA |
| declination | D(elta) |
| semi-diurnal arc | H(alf)D(ay) |
| circle of position | CP |
| azimuth | AZ |
| altitude | AL |

1. To find the right ascension of the meridian ($RA_{10}$).

(The purpose here will often be to convert a celestial longitude to a right ascension, in order to make a calculation, and then to convert back to a new celestial longitude.)

Formula: $\tan RA_{10} = \tan L_{10} \cos E$

Example: to find $RA_{10}$ when $L_{10}$ is Pisces 5:

$$\tan RA_{10} = \tan 335^\circ \cos 23.525^\circ$$
$$= -0.4275$$
$$RA_{10} = 336.8508^\circ$$

This calculation relates to bodies located on the ecliptic; their celestial latitude is therefore 0°, and disregarded.

2. To find the declination of the sun (D).

Formula: *either*, sin D = sin E sin L
  *or*,    cos D = (cos L cos RA) + (sin L sin RA cos E)

Example: to find D when L = Pisces 5:

$$\cos D = (\cos 335° \cos 336.85°)$$
$$+ (\sin 335° \sin 336.85° \cos 23.525°)$$
$$= 0.9857$$
$$D = -9.7115°$$

Declinations are positive between Aries and Virgo, negative between Libra and Pisces.

3. To find the semidiurnal arc (HD).

Formula: cos HD = −tan P tan D.

Example: to find HD when L = Pisces 5:

$$\cos HD = -\tan 53° \tan -9.7115°$$
$$= 0.2271$$
$$= 76.8731°.$$

Convert degrees to time: = 5 hrs 7 mins 29 secs.

In other words, at the given terrestrial latitude, the day will be 10 hrs 15 mins long when the sun is at Pisces 5.

4. To find the duration of dawn (d):

Formula: $d = y - HD$, where $\cos y = \dfrac{\cos 108° - \sin P \sin D}{\cos P \cos D}$

Dawn is conventionally taken to begin when the sun comes to be 18° below the horizon: 90° + 18° = 108°.

Example: to find d when L = Pisces 5:

$$\cos y = \frac{\cos 108° - \sin 53° \sin -9.7115°}{\cos 53° \cos -9.7115°}$$
$$= -0.2938$$
$$y = 107.0874°$$

$$y - HD = 107.0874° - 76.8731°$$
$$= 30.2143°.$$

Convert degrees to time: = 2 hrs 0 mins 52 secs.

5. To find the oblique ascension of the horizon ($OA_h$).

Formula: $OA_h = RA_h + (90 - HD)$

Example: to find $OA_h$ when $L_h$ = Pisces 5:
$$OA_h = 336.8508° + (90° - 76.8731°)$$
$$= 349.9777°$$

OA is less than RA between Aries and Virgo, greater between Libra and Pisces.

6. To find the astrological houses.

I describe two methods: the first is the one in common use in the middle ages, the second the one in common use in the Renaissance.

6.1  The Right Ascension Method (Alchabitius):

| | |
|---|---|
| let | $(RA_1 - RA_{10})/3$ be $x$; |
| then | $RA_{10} + x = RA_{11}$ |
| | $RA_{10} + 2x = RA_{12}$ |
| and | $RA_{11} + 120° = RA_3$ |
| | $RA_{12} + 60° = RA_2$ |

Convert RA to longitudes by adapting Formula 1

Example: to find the cusps of the houses when $L_{10}$ is Pisces 5:
1. If $L_{10}$ is $335°$, $RA_{10}$ is $336.8508°$ (Formula 1).
2. $L_1$ is then found by the following:

$$\cot L_1 = \tan(-RA_{10}) \cos E - \frac{\sin E \tan P}{\cos RA_{10}}$$

$$L_1 = 100.4289°.$$

3. Hence, $RA_1 = 101.3508°$ (Formula 1).
4. $(RA_1 - RA_{10})/3 = 41.50°$.
5. Therefore:

| | | | |
|---|---|---|---|
| $RA_{10} = 336.8508°$ | and | $L_{10} = 335°$ | (Pisces 5) |
| $RA_{11} = 18.3508°$ | | $L_{11} = 19.8886°$ | (Aries 20) |
| $RA_{12} = 59.8508°$ | | $L_{12} = 61.9623°$ | (Gemini 2) |
| $RA_1 = 101.3508°$ | | $L_1 = 100.4289°$ | (Cancer 10) |
| $RA_2 = 119.8508°$ | | $L_2 = 117.7527°$ | (Cancer 28) |
| $RA_3 = 138.3508°$ | | $L_3 = 135.8725°$ | (Leo 16) |

The values for houses 4-9 are found by the rule of opposites—same degree, opposite sign. The 4th house, for instance, will be defined in this example by Virgo 5.

6.2 The Equatorial Method (Regiomontanus):

$$\cot L = \cos E \cot (RA_{10} + CP) - \frac{\sin E \tan P \sin CP}{\sin (RA_{10} + CP)},$$

where CP = the given circle of position

$$
\begin{aligned}
CP &= 30° & \text{for} & \quad 11\text{th} \\
&= 60° & & \quad 12\text{th} \\
&= 120° & & \quad 2\text{nd} \\
&= 150° & & \quad 3\text{rd.}
\end{aligned}
$$

Example: to find the cusps of the houses when $L_{10}$ is Pisces 5:

1. If $L_{10}$ is $335°$, $RA_{10}$ will be $336.8508°$

$$
\begin{aligned}
\text{therefore} \quad RA_{10} + CP &= 6.8508° & \text{for} & \quad 11\text{th} \\
&= 36.8508° & & \quad 12\text{th} \\
&= 96.8508° & & \quad 2\text{nd} \\
&= 126.8508° & & \quad 3\text{rd.}
\end{aligned}
$$

2. Then, for the 11th house:

$$\cot L_{11} = \cos 23.525° \cot 6.8508° - \frac{\sin 23.525° \tan 53° \sin 30°}{\sin 6.8508°}$$

$$
\begin{aligned}
&= 10.4698° \\
&= \text{Aries 10.}
\end{aligned}
$$

3. Similarly,

$$
\begin{aligned}
12 &= 65° \, 22' = \text{Gemini 5} \\
1 &= 100° \, 25' = \text{Cancer 10} \\
2 &= 119° \, 47' = \text{Cancer 30/Leo 0} \\
3 &= 135° \, 31' = \text{Leo 16}
\end{aligned}
$$

7. To find a body's azmith (AZ) on rising (r) or setting (s).

Formulas: $\cos AZ_r = \dfrac{\sin D}{\cos P}$; $AZ_s = 360° - AZ_r$.

Example: with the sun at Pisces 5:

$$
\begin{aligned}
\cos AZ_r &= \frac{\sin -9.7115°}{\cos 53°} \\
&= -0.2083 \\
AZ_r &= 106.2779°
\end{aligned}
$$

This distance is measured from north through east.

8. To find a body's altitude (AL) and azimuth (AZ).

Formulas:

(1) $\sin AL = \sin D \sin P + \cos D \cos P \cos HA$

where HA is the distance of the body from the meridian as measured along the celestial equator;

$$\text{(2)} \qquad \cos AZ = \frac{\sin D - \sin P \sin AL}{\cos P \cos AL}$$

Example: to find AL and AZ at 10 a.m., when sun at Pisces 5:
(1) if   time = 10.00 hrs, HA will be $30°$; then,
$$\sin AL = \sin -9.7115° \sin 53° + \cos -9.7115° \cos 53° \cos 30°$$
$$= 0.3789$$
$$AL = 22.2716°$$

$$\text{(2)} \quad \cos AZ = \frac{\sin -9.7115° - \sin 53° \sin 22.2716°}{\cos 53° \cos 22.2716°}$$

$$= -0.8464$$
$$AZ = 147.8208°$$

9. To find the oblique ascensions/descensions of the Significator and the Promittor.

In a given horoscope the following values are known or may be found:

P    latitude
E    obliquity of the ecliptic
DH distance at the horizon between the equator and the ecliptic
DE distance along the ecliptic from the horizon to a given body.

Then

$$\text{(1)} \quad \sin Z = \frac{\cos P}{\sin E} \sin DH, \text{ where } DH = 90 - AZ_r \text{ (Formula 7)}$$

$$\text{(2)} \quad \tan \frac{R}{2} = \frac{\cos \dfrac{Z - DH}{2}}{\cos \dfrac{Z + DH}{2}} \cot \frac{P + E + 90}{2}$$

(3)  $\cos Y = (\cos DH \sin DE \cos R) - (\sin DH \cos DE)$

$$\text{(4)} \quad \sin K = \frac{\cos DH}{\sin Y} \sin R$$

(5)  $\cos S = (\cos K \cos E) - (\sin K \sin E \cos (DE - Z))$

(6)  Finally, the complement of S may be substituted for P(hi) in Formula 3, whereupon Formula 5 will give the oblique ascension/

descension of the Significator. The *same* value is retained for finding the acension/descension of the Promittor.

Example: to find the oblique descensions of the moon (Significator) and of the 8th house (Promittor) in Burton's horoscope:

$$P = 52° 20' \text{ (given)}$$
$$E = 23° 31' 30'' \text{ (by calculation)}$$
$$DH = 18° 19' \text{ (by Formula 7)}$$
$$DE = 13° 29' \text{ (by inspection)}$$

Then

(1) $\dfrac{\cos 52.333°}{\sin 23.525°} \sin 18.316° = 0.481 \text{ (sin Z)}$

$$Z = 28.766°$$

(2) $\dfrac{\cos 5.222°}{\cos 23.541°} \cot 82.929° = 0.134 \text{ (tan R/2)}$

$$R = 15.346°$$

(3) $(\cos 18.316° \sin 13.483° \cos 15.346°)$
$$- (\sin 18.316° \cos 13.483°)$$
$$= -0.092 \text{ (cos Y)}$$
$$Y = 95.292°$$

(4) $\dfrac{\cos 18.316°}{\sin 95.292°} \sin 15.346° = 0.252 \text{ (sin K)}$

$$K = 14.615°$$

(5) $(\cos 14.615° \cos 23.525°)$
$$- (\sin 14.615° \sin 23.525° \cos -15.283°)$$
$$= 0.790 \text{ (cos S)}$$
$$S = 37.809°.$$

Then, with the moon at 222.25°, D = −15.567° (Formula 2).

$\cos HD = -\tan (90 - S) \tan D$
$HD = 68.958°$
$OD = RA - (90° - HD)$, and $RA = 219.788°$ (cf. Formula 2).
Therefore $OD = 198.747°$.

Similarly with the 8th house at 250.833°, D = −22.149°

$\cos HD = -\tan (90 - S) \tan D$, as before.
$HD = 58.358°$ and $RA = 249.238°$
$OD = 217.596°$.

The difference (the 'arc of direction') is 18.849° = 18° 51'.

# Index of Terms and Subjects